T5-DHI-465

The *SageWoman* *Cauldron*

A Collection from Our First Five Years

Edited by Lunaea Weatherstone

Mayflower Bookshop
Astrology - Metaphysics
2645 12 Mile, Berkley, Mi 48072
(313) 547-8227

SageWoman Magazine 1993
Point Arena, California 95468

The SageWoman Cauldron: A Collection from Our First Five Years

Published by SageWoman Magazine
P.O. Box 641, Point Arena, CA 95468
707•882•2052

First published in 1993

Copyright © SageWoman Magazine 1993
All Rights Reserved

ISBN 0-9630-360-1-7

Cover artwork by Joann Powell Colbert.
Book design and production by Lunaea Weatherstone.
Section title art by Cris Palomino.

Printed in the United States of America
Set in Times New Roman, SansSerif and SlenderGold

No portion of this book may be reproduced by any means
whatsoever without written permission of the publisher.
Excepted are short passages quoted for the purpose of reviewing.

Table of Contents

Introduction 5

Part 1: Empowerment

A Maiden, Two Mothers and a Crone: *Interviews with the Goddess* 9
Love and the Altar Space: *Loving the Goddess, loving yourself* 18
Making Medicine Shields: *Magickal crafts* 21
The Earth is My Mother 24
Ovulation Magick: *Celebrating your egg-time* 25
The Moon Lodge: *A place of woman power* 26
Birth Empowerment: *Birthing from Goddess wisdom* 28
Birth from the Sea: *A healing and renewing rite* 31
I am a Gift I Give Myself: *A self-esteem ritual* 32
The Age of Kali 34
Making Empowerment Necklaces: *Magickal crafts* 35
Epitaph 38
Once in a Blue Moon: *Wishes come true* 39
She Changes Everything She Touches: *Body change as ritual magic* 41
A Red Tape Ritual: *Working through obstacles* 44
A Magic Mirror: *Creating your own Tarot images* 45
Madonna Mia 46
Earthworks: *Pentacles in the Tarot* 47
The Cowry Wish Charm 50
The Moon in Me: *Life in the moonlight* 51
Looking Within: *Transforming yourself, transforming your life* 52
The Belly Dancer 54
Self-Blessing Belly Dance: *A sensuous solo ritual* 55
Old Year, New Year: *Egyptian new year magick* 56
The Right to Choose: *An empowerment ritual* 60

Part 2: Community

The Lessons of Power: *Daughters of the Goddess work together* 63
Avalon 67
Circles of Self-Love: *Group support for opening your heart* 68
Invocations for Winter Solstice 69
In Praise of Santa Lucia: *Lady of light* 70
Spell to Send Away Mal Occhio 72
Spring Planting Rite: *Honoring the Earth Mother in community ritual* 73
Prayer of Thanksgiving 74

A Birthday Ritual: *Celebrating the gaining of wisdom*............................75
Goddess Has Risen..76
Thirteen Blessings: *Welcoming a baby to the Goddess community*...........77
A Menarche Ritual: *Honoring our daughters' first bloods*.....................79
The Coming of Winter..80
Invocation...83
The Grandmothers Speak: *Honoring the spirits of the ancestors*............84
For All Those Who Have Died: *A rite of remembrance for the Burning Times*.......86
Ritual for Mary K..87
The Power of the Queen: *A fourth aspect of the Goddess*.......................88
Dissolving a Coven: *Every ending is a beginning*.................................89
A Parting of the Ways: *Marking the end of a relationship*.....................92
For the Goddess of the Desert: *A women's seder for Passover*..............93
From Harmlessness to Right Livelihood: *A Pagan perspective on work*.......99
Rose Blessing to Venus...105
From the Heart of the Goddess: *A group blessing ritual*.......................106

Part 3: Deepening

Inanna: *Dark journey to the center*..109
Confessions of a Scry Baby: *Learning new magical skills*....................114
Circle Casting..116
Living the Dream: *Finding myth and meaning in every day*..................117
Ix Chel: *A Mayan Moon Goddess*..120
A Moon Mirror: *Making a magickal tool*..124
Sounding Sphere...125
In the Dolphin Dreamtime: *Tales from the sea*...................................126
Hestia: *Bringing the Goddess back home*...130
Blessings of the Corn Dolly: *The Goddess and the land*......................135
Talking to the Trees: *Connecting to the Mother in Elvish lore*.............137
The Stone Rosary: *Quiet and deepen*...139
Your Magickal Name: *A vision quest*...140
A Blessing of Wheat: *Magical crafts*...142
Working Alone: *Simple daily spirituality*...144
Entering the Underworld: *Journal writing for deepening*.....................145
Brigid: *Spirituality at work*..146

Resources..150

Introduction

Maiden Goddess, keep me whole
Let thy power fill my soul.
Mother Goddess, keep me whole,
Let thy beauty fill my soul.
Crone Goddess, keep me whole,
Let thy wisdom fill my soul.
Shekhinah Mountainwater

The re-emergence of the Goddess. The Goddess movement. Women's spirituality. The inevitable next step in the second wave of the women's movement (remember when we called it women's liberation?) is bringing women back to the Great Mother. Connection with the divine feminine within, celebrating, as we say, the Goddess in every woman. In less than twenty years, we have gone from a few esoteric books on Wicca and archeological or mythological treatises on goddesses (small "g") to perhaps hundreds of books on every aspect of women's spiritual quest. And we now offer you another one.

Much has been written about the phenomenon of women's spirituality, why the Great Goddess is returning now. In my six years as a Goddess publisher and editor, I have seen the Goddess movement grow at an amazing pace. Living in California, it was a revelation for me to receive letters from *SageWoman* readers all over the world, including bastions of conservatism and religious oppression. For many of these women, *SageWoman* and other publications and books are their only connection to what might be called the congregation of the Goddess. This connection helps assuage the feeling of isolation that can come from having the thing of most importance in your life be something completely unheard of – or perhaps frightening – to your friends and community. Now, as the Goddess movement comes into the mainstream more and more, women are finding it easier to find others of like spirit in their communities – and perhaps even in their homes, as men also open to alternative spiritual practices and belief systems.

And just what is this belief system we call the Goddess? For me, one of the most important elements of Goddess spirituality and Neo-paganism is the lack of dogma. The Goddess has 10,000 names (at last count!) and as many aspects as there are women to

embody her. As Joseph Campbell says, "Revelations of the Great Goddess, Mother of the universe and of us all, teach compassion for all living beings." My dream for the Goddess movement – and what I tried to foster in the pages of *SageWoman* during my tenure as editor – is a forum for the differing beliefs of all women who have opened their hearts to the Great Goddess. Through an open and compassionate sharing of spiritual experience, we can come to see that the heart of our sister is not that different from our own heart. And, as Campbell continues, "There you come to appreciate the real sanctity of the Earth itself, because it is the body of the Goddess. When Yahweh creates, he creates man of the Earth and breathes life into that formed body. He's not there present in that form. But the Goddess is within as well as without. Your body is Her body . . ."
(From *The Power of Myth*)

This book is divided into three sections, based on the symbolism of the Triple Goddess: the Maiden, Mother and Crone. The Maiden aspect of the Goddess is represented by Empowerment, as we begin to realize just how the Goddess manifests in each of us. Trying our wings, we seek out tools, techniques and experiences that will help us tap into the source of Goddess-power the Maiden gives. The Mother aspect of the Goddess is here represented by Community, gathering together to share Her love. Working with others, moving out into the real world to work our magic. The Crone brings Deepening, as we study the Goddess in Her infinite forms, learn to draw out Her wisdom from deep inside. From empowerment to community to deepening to empowerment, the circle is never broken.

The ways of women are steeped in mystery, but one thing is ever clear. We connect. We connect the daily to the eternal, the personal to the global, and the mundane to the magical. We connect with each other. We are aware of the web of energy that ties all life together, weaving a pattern of interdependence and mutual respect that is the true vision of Women's Spirituality. To know that you are the daughter of the Great Goddess, and that all creation is part of that Goddess, is to feel connected to all the magic and mystery of the cosmos. Then you know that, truly, you are *SageWoman.*

Lunaea Weatherstone
Dark Moon in Aries, 9993

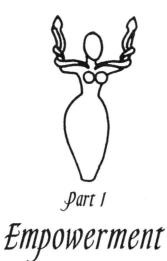

Part 1

Empowerment

We encourage women
to be transformed by their power within,
to surrender to the wisdom
that comes from change,
to awaken their own magic and creativity,
with the protection of the Goddess around us all.

Blessing by Lunaea Weatherstone

A Maiden, Two Mothers and a Crone

Interviews with the Triple Goddess

By Lunaea Weatherstone

Bethany Martin is ten and a half years old. I interviewed her on a hot September day in Southern California, sitting at opposite ends of a big squeaky bed.

Lunaea: What are some of your spiritual experiences? Have you been to any rituals?

Bethany: Thousands!

Tell me about some.

Well, my mom got into Goddess religion, and I told her I wanted to go to rituals with her. That's been about three years now. We had a ritual when I was the Lucia Maiden with candles on my head, and I thought it would burn my head off, catch my hair on fire! Sometimes I get embarrassed in rituals when we all go around the circle and say, "I am Goddess!" I always tell myself I'm going to say it really loud, and then I whisper, "My name is Bethany and I am Goddess!"

I do that, too.

At the Midsummer Madness ritual, I liked the way the priestesses talked about fighting racism. My mom says that I'm different from a lot of people because I don't litter and I care about the Earth. I have a friend who litters, and I tell her I feel sorry for her because she wants to litter the Earth. I saw a water pipe broken once and the water was shooting up in the air, and I started to cry because they were wasting all that water. It hurt so much that they were wasting that water. I cried when I watched "The Color Purple." At the ritual they said, fight against the people who are hurting the Earth, fight against racism. And I liked the dancing afterwards.

Are you into the Goddess the same way your mom is?

I like the idea of the Goddess, but I don't call it my religion. I like not having a religion, and then if I want to have a religion when I get older I won't have to be worrying about one I already have. I don't want to go to church. When I think about God or Goddess, I want to think about Him or Her the way I think about it, not the way someone else tells me to think. Once I told my dad, "I think that God is a him and a her and everything there is, all put together!" When I try to sort that out, it's confusing . . . but it's the way I want to think about it. Sometimes I say, "Mother Earth, protect us please!" I also have a stuffed cat that I kiss when I feel sad. That comforts me a lot, and sometimes I cry into it.

In the books you read, what Maidens do you like?

I like the Babysitters Club books. I like the way they know how to call 911, and take care of themselves. There's a book called Sarah and Katie, about really good friends. They have a big fight, but by the end of the book they are friends again, and I like that. I have a lot of good friends.

What kind of person do you want to be when you grow up?

In a book I read, they talked about adults who were neat and adults who were boring. I would like to be a neat adult. I know I can't stop all the things that go wrong, but I want to try. I want to be organized and clean. I like cleaning – sometimes when I'm really mad I clean! And I always want to feel it's okay to tell my age and not be ashamed of that.

What sort of things do you admire about your mom and other women you know?

My mom is funny, and I'm not afraid to tell her things. My grandma is really neat, and she always

> Sometimes I say, "Mother Earth, protect us, please!"

has the right answer. So does my mom. They do a lot of things for me, and care about me a lot. They're always willing to do things for everyone else. Personally, I think my mom works too much.

How would you like to be different from older people you see?

I know I can't stop all the things that go wrong, but I want to try.

I *don't* want to work too much! I don't want to put down other people because of the way they look or act. I want to be happy and make other people happy. But even while I make other people happy, I want to make sure that I make myself happy first. Not that I want to be selfish, but I keep saying that I'm going to set aside time for myself, to listen to these meditation tapes my mom gave me, but I never have the time! And then when I get bored, I never even think about that. So that's one thing I want to be sure to do when I get older.

If you could get into the habit of that now, while you're young, it would be much easier than to try to learn to take care of yourself when you're my age!

Like Joann says that on Sunday mornings she takes time to read and drink coffee in bed, and I think that's good.

Are you looking forward to growing up?

I'm not really excited, but I'm not feeling like, "Oh, no, I'm going to grow up soon!" I was talking to my mom about dying, and she said that I should hope that when the time comes to die, I'll be ready. And I said, "I hope I'll live forever!" But I always

say to myself that when I get to be old, a crone, I'm never, never just going to sit in my old granny rocking chair and just rock! Just stare and out the window and wait to die! If I wanted to go sit and look out the window, that would be different than just sitting there and saying, I'm going to die soon, I'm going to die soon, I'm going to die soon. I don't want to do that. If I do that, then I *will* die soon! I want to do all the things I didn't get a chance to do. Sure, sometimes I'll want to just sit and rock and look out the window, but I'll be thinking peaceful thoughts.

Part of being a Maiden is when you start to have your periods, when you start to bleed. You haven't yet, have you?

No.

Does it embarrass you to talk about this?

No.

Does that have any special meaning for you?

It's the same thing I feel about dying – I'm not excited, but I'm not down either. Probably when it happens, I'll feel like I want to, but now I say, another five years will be fine! I know some people start at eleven, though. It's not something I worry about. My mom asked me if I want to have a ritual in her circle when I start. I read about one in a book, and that sounded neat. I saw some red wrapping paper in a catalog, and I said to my mom, "Period paper!" But when I have my period, I'll see how I feel about a ritual then. I'm not going to worry about dying, I'm not going to worry about having my period, I'm not going to worry about growing up, I'm not going to worry about anything right now. I just want to have fun.

Sometimes when I look in the mirror I don't look like how I feel. Thank goodness people can't read each other's minds. Sometimes I feel I don't want to grow up. Sometimes I feel like I want to be a baby, so I could be pampered and carried every-where. But I also couldn't be as independent. If I had a choice, maybe for a little longer I'd stay this age and have fun. I want you to write this at the end of the interview: When you're a maiden I think it means you can be independent and fun! ○

Illustration: Bethany as the Spring Maiden, by Joann Powell Colbert

Two women, both in the Mother phase of their chronological lives. Joann Colbert is the mother of two boys. Judy Tolley has chosen not to have children. I offer you a distillation of those interviews, musings on the Mother by two wise women . . .

Joann Colbert:

When I was in high school and college I was into the culture and the music and the free thinking of the sixties, and I was reading everything, reading, reading, reading. I was experimenting with Eastern religions. My mind was open. I had an mystical experience at the age of twenty of encountering a being that I identified as Jesus, and so I became a born-again Christian. After being totally immersed in the Jesus freak scene for a year and hungering for more, a deeper knowledge of spiritual things, I married a man two weeks after I met him because he seemed to me to be a spiritual teacher. At that time I was looking for a teacher other than myself, because that's what we're taught in patriarchal religions. I got pregnant right away because we felt we were supposed to, that God wanted us to have a baby right away. I became a mother, before I had even fully explored being a maiden.

I had been an honor student at the University of California, getting awards and a lot of recognition for writing, but this religion told me to lay down my brain and stop thinking. I stopped reading and stopped thinking and could only do bible reading and bible study or listen to the pastors and to my husband, who considered himself to be more spiritually evolved than the church leadership. In this patriarchal religion, a fundamentalist church, there is the underlying assumption that you need to be led. You are sheep and there's a shepherd. And of course, Jesus is the ultimate shepherd, but, for a woman, her husband is her immediate shepherd. I was there to be a wife and a helpmate, and my world, which had been the university and brilliant scholars and poetry and art and music, was gone. When the two babies came, my life became even more circumscribed. During the ten years I was in the church, I stayed home, doing handicrafts, gardening, canning, baking bread. I have good memories of those things, but what I remember the most was how my real life was submerged. It was so suppressed that sometimes I would see a book or I would remember something that would touch off a memory in me of what my life had been before this,

and I could barely even bear to look at it. I was surrounded with bible ideas and bible oriented things. Other things were considered demonic. As a housewife, you don't meet anyone except the people in the church. I was very isolated.

When the boys were little, I had a great time being a mother, doing all the preschool stuff, reading to them, introducing them to the world. But there are two kinds of mothering, the physical parenting of a physical child, and mothering in the sense of creativity. It wasn't enough for the only outlet for my creativity to be cooking, gardening, or sewing. Eventually, because of financial stress, I went to work outside the home, at a textbook publishing company. For the first time in five years, I was in contact with non-church people. At first, I was scared to death. I thought I had walked into Sodom and Gomorrah. It seems very bizarre now. My whole world had been the church and the people in the church.

A major change in my life came when I was made supervisor of the art department. I was shocked that they had seen leadership potential in me. I had spent so many years being told that women follow. They don't lead. In my previous life, I had always excelled, but no one in the church knew me as a scholar or a spiritual seeker, they only saw me as a meek, quiet, housewife who did some nice drawings for the church newsletter. My self esteem began to grow by leaps and bounds from that moment. I began to think in terms of career. I went back to school. *Ms.* magazine was my lifeline, but I couldn't even buy a copy or bring it home – I had to sneak into the library and read it. Then I read *From Housewife to Heretic* by Sonia Johnson, which just blew the lid off everything.

Within a year I couldn't go to church anymore. I had no friends left. My children were in the Christian school. It bothered me that many of the teachers were not credentialed, and I began to look more closely at the curriculum. I read a section in the high school history book about the Transcendendalists, Emerson and Thoreau. Now, Emerson and Thoreau were my heroes in high school. And this book said that Transcendentalism was Satanic, an anti-bible philosophy. I became like a mother bear with cubs. Maybe I could lay my dreams aside for years, but I did not want my sons growing up in an environment where they would be told what

I became a mother, before I had even fully explored being a maiden.

philosophers are Satanic, especially when these are philosophers who are teaching you to think for yourself. They were feeding them repression, and there was to be no deviation. You were not to discover these truths on your own, which had been the sweet part of the Christian experience for me, that I came to it on my own, and then I was indoc-

As parents we have to nurture the children to follow their own dreams.

trinated afterwards. But with the children, they weren't going to have a chance to come to it on their own. I was not going to let my kids grow up in that kind of repression. I pulled them out and put them in Montessori school. What a difference!

I think it's good for kids to learn about all kinds of religions, visit churches and temples and choose for themselves. My younger son came to me last year and said that he wanted to go to a bible study class his friends were going to, and I sort of went, GULP. I said, you can go, but you have to keep a critical open mind, and you do NOT believe everything they tell you, and if you have questions, you come and ask me about it afterwards. And he said, Mom, they're going to play games and have food! (laughs) And here I'm going through this big serious thing. So he went a few times and it wore off. What is good for kids, as well as for us, is the sense of community that a church can provide. Perhaps we can create the community in a different way.

When my husband and I split up, my older son went with his father, and my younger son came with me. My spiritual interest shifted from Christianity to establishing myself with women's groups. Because I had male children, and was in

women-only groups, I could not incorporate my children into the spiritual life of the community. I couldn't bring them to rituals. That was hard. I know that this is an ongoing dialogue in the Dianic craft, and I don't really know what the answer is for the movement as a whole, but for me it is to create a community where there are Goddess-loving men as well as Goddess-loving women, so that my sons have male role models in their lives who are not just football coaches. Steven is coming up on his thirteenth birthday, and we've been wracking our brains trying to come up with a rite of passage for him that he won't turn his nose up at. I'm a bit envious of Judaism, that there is a whole cultural celebration for the children at thirteen. It's an issue that's close to my heart right now, not only creating rites of passage for the girls, with menstruation rituals, but doing something for the boys. What can we do for the boys? A big rite of passage for boys in this culture is getting their driver's license, as it symbolizes independence and mobility. So maybe we'll have the big celebration for Steven when he's sixteen, and do the rites of passage in stages.

There's a lot of joy that comes from thinking that something of who I am and what I believe is going to rub off on this boy, and he will grow up to not be racist and not be sexist, and to honor the earth, and to know that there's a lot more to life than patriarchal religions. He's grown up from the time he was six hearing about the Goddess. He has an altar in his room with his precious things on it, crystals and feathers . . . That part of mothering is really neat. You just need to remind yourself about that stuff when the report card comes home!

It isn't easy to be a parent. As parents we have to nurture the children to follow their own dreams. When the boys were about nine and six years old, I led them on a guided visualization to meet a spirit guide. Afterwards, everyone shared who they got on this vision. The older boy, Jake, got a kind of Moon Goddess, whose name was Salomar, and she was made out of moonlight. Steven got a female unicorn with wings and a golden horn, named Toddy. As time went on, I would occasionally hear them say those names, and I would think how nice that was that they remembered. Every so often, when we would pray, Steven would pray to Toddy. Several months ago, at ages twelve and fifteen, they were playing together with the ouija board, and they got their spirit guides! As we were talking

Illustration: Self-portrait as Artemis, by Joann Powell Colbert

about it, it turns out that both of them have had ongoing relationships with their spirit guides all these years. What a blessing! The joy that you feel when your child does something or says something that makes him happy – there's nothing quite like that. It's not the same as the joy that you get from following your own bliss, but it's as intense and wonderful in a different way.

A few years ago, I began to experience my creativity apart from mothering my children. I discovered my bliss, my work that makes me happy. I began to create artwork of mythological archetypes, mostly Goddesses. I drew six Goddesses in two months, Artemis, White Buffalo Woman, Mawu, Cerridwen, Dolphin Woman, and Hecate. I took them to a Goddess-class I was taking and hesitantly said, "I have these drawings . . ." and everyone went WOW! Now I have a list that gets longer and longer every day of pictures I want to draw and paintings I want to paint and things I want to make and classes I want to teach. I discovered I have a gift for turning other women on to their own creative potential, and have midwived other artists, who are now producing stunning work, which I look at and say, gee, I wish I could do that! (laughs) My work with Long Beach Womanspirit, creating Goddess events and faires and workshops is another kind of mothering that's exciting. Mothering is any time you have a tiny seed or flash of inspiration, and you nurture it all the way through the magical process until it's manifested in the physical world. This could be an event or a drawing or a child or a ritual or a magazine – it's all creative, its all mothering. And then you let it go, and it takes on a life of its own.

I use my friends as models for my Goddess drawings, and when I drew myself, I drew myself as Artemis, who is a maiden, not a mother. She is everything I wasn't at the time, independent, free, focused. But a psychic friend once told me that the deer I am so fiercely protecting is Steven, so the mother energy is there as well. The next drawing of myself will be as the Queen of Pentacles, a woman in her maturity, a woman who knows who she is. I'm in a very prolific and fertile phase of my life, with a cornucopia of things spilling out, all this abundance of creativity. I feel like for the rest of my life I'm going to be running to catch up, to get everything on my list done. I don't have much patience for people who say, "I'm bored." I believe

the most important quest for anyone is to find your passion, and the gift you have to give to the world. If you don't know what that is, I think that your number one priority should be – I know we're not supposed to say "should," but a mother can say "should"! – to find out what it is. You do that by paying attention to what really makes you happy.

Not what you think should make you happy, and not what makes other people happy when you do it, but what really makes you happy. Not just happy, joyous. Pay attention, and then don't discount it. And after you've identified your bliss, find a support system that will help you nurture it. If I hadn't had the circle of women who praised me and encouraged me to keep doing more drawings, those first six drawings would have been stuck in a drawer somewhere. Maybe the maiden's quest is to find her bliss, and the mother's quest is to act on it, and the crone's quest is to be filled with it, to rest in it, to look back on a life that was filled with following her bliss.

Judy Tolley:
When I think of the Mother, the Great Mother, she's very old and almost voiceless. She's not a Diana or an Artemis or a Demeter. She's not that eloquent and polished, the archetype of Mother I respond to. She's darker and more mysterious and more earthy – it's like she's a scent of rich moist soil, the fragrance of the lavender when I crush it. She's the first mother – she has no form, she's infinite. As if I were inside her, engulfed – it's all around you, it pulses and is the rhythm of your life, but you're not conscious of a separation. The first

I've had to deal with motherhood feelings through choosing not to be a mother.

Illustration: Judy as Joan the Greenwitch, by Joann Powell Colbert

concept of a higher power was a vast faceless female form. That's the artistic impulse that went into creating the Venus of Willendorf and some of the other early deity images. They are all faceless, as if She by being faceless could receive every single projection, and She would be right for every single person that came to Her. She's all faces, She's whatever you want her to be. That is Her vastness.

In our society, we have a cultural idea of what "mother" is, and it's usually the mother on "Father Knows Best." Because I'm a feminist, I realize that that is a product of patriarchal determinism for women who grew up in this culture, and I can't buy into that. On an emotional level, that's what I grew up wanting, and expecting to be myself, as a child in this culture. But I've chosen not to be a mother in the literal sense. I had my tubes tied when I was 35; I was sure I didn't want to have a child.

So I've had to deal with motherhood feelings through choosing not to be a mother. Through Jungian therapy I'm working with the world of poetry and mystery and myth, bringing those images up and seeing how certain archetypes of the Mother relate to my own feelings and self-knowledge. Through the women's spirituality movement I've had the opportunity to learn and experience these archetypes like no one has been able to do until this generation, because of the work that women are doing in reclaiming those archetypes. I'm learning how to mother myself.

There's a free flow of mothering care, in times of real dire need.

I think mothering yourself contains more honesty than mothering someone else, because it involves more self-awareness. The better you learn to mother yourself, the better you know yourself, and that means that you are revealing to yourself both the light and the dark side. You are going into the unconscious and starting to look at things that you put back there that are perhaps not flattering, or that sometimes may be frightening. Things that you've repressed, memories or personality traits. And when you can be that honest with yourself and continue to mother those parts and give them what they need, you've reached a place of self-awareness that you don't always have when you mother someone else. When we mother other people we tend to project what we think they need, what we think a good mother should be.

There's another kind of mothering, the kind I've found with my women friends. That for me is the richest, most feminine mothering. That's when I feel closest to being in touch with the archetype of the Mother Goddess. It doesn't have a lot of strings attached, as it does when you agree to mother children or spouses. There's a free flow of mothering care, in times of real dire need, with women we aren't ashamed to cry in front of, or to feel really vulnerable with. They don't have to have the answers, there is just kindness, openness, a willingness to listen and to provide what can be reasonably offered. For example, one day I was upset, and a friend showed me a sign she keeps above her worktable, which says, "Sometimes the only way out is through." And she told me to just think about that. It was true mothering. She gave me guidance, she gave me reassurance, she gave me hope. She could stop right there and listen. That's a beautiful kind of mothering we can give to each other.

"No strings attached" is important, I think – you don't get much of that from mates, and certainly not from children. You get it from your girlfriends and you get it from your pets. I'm a very nurturing and mothering kind of person. At work, I have a feeling of wanting to teach what I know, to guide and shape, so that new employees don't have to go through what I went through. So I can give some of my mothering energy that way, too. I have my pets, my friends, my husband, my garden, my workmates, my cooking, my artwork, and myself – all those things that I pour Mother energy into, consciously, because I did not choose to mother a child of my own body.

I do think of having a child, and what I would be doing with a child. I get those flashes once or twice a week. I think about raising this imaginary child, who is really myself, and giving her the wisdom and encouragement I wanted when I was that child. But it's important to me to stand up and defend the idea that two people can comprise a family. You don't need to mother a child to mother, and you don't need to have children to have a family. We can invoke the Mother aspect when we need it, or the Maiden or the Crone, at whatever phase of our lives we are in. We can hold all three simultaneously.

I feel sometimes that motherhood is overrated. Other times, I feel that mothers are totally misunderstood. There are times I think that mothers are the unsung heroes. And a lot of the time I'm glad I'm not a mother in the literal sense, and that I have the freedom to explore other forms of mothering. You can't do everything. Thank Goddess we have choices. ○

We interviewed Frankie Haller in her home, surrounded by books, projects in process, papers piled on every surface – signs of great activity and energy. We laughed as her little dog, Kwan Yin, added her energy to the room, frantically greeting us with wags and licks.

Frankie: Animals are a big part of a Crone's life after the mothering has ended, as a focus for parenting feelings. It's very important for those of us who have strong attachments to our mothering aspect. My life has been one of activity and caring for others, and sometimes caring more for others than for myself. That's something women have to cope with.

SageWoman: You've had a very busy and productive life. Was there a turning point when you turned to women's issues, women's spirituality?

It was an evolutionary process. Both my husband and I have always been political and social activists. Social activism is more inclined toward the masculine. One of the things that came up in the women's movement is that women learned through experience that social activism was relegating them to servant status, even among activist men who wanted to make a better world. That was one thing that led women of my generation, and the younger generation, to feminism. Another turning point in my life was the death of my daughter, as the result of a heroin overdose. That really focused my attention on causes and made me check out the world of religion – how patriarchal religion plays a part in keeping people from realizing their full spirituality. That was in 1973, and it's gotten worse since then, but we may have reached a turning point in the patriarchal focus. People can no longer tolerate it. It's my daily ritual to read the newspapers every morning and I can see the changing trend away from patriarchy.

Do you have spiritual practices in your daily life?

My life is my spiritual practice. I do feel a need for formalized ritual, but I do very little, unfortunately. My spiritual practice has become my daily activities. Right now I'm the chair of the National Women's Political Caucus; our primary focus is parity for women in public office. Having women

I began to identify more with compassion and mercy than with grief.

be visibly equal with men in public office will change the consciousness of the people, so that we will have a balance of masculine and feminine energies. That's my spiritual practice.

Are there Goddess archetypes you relate to?

Demeter is an archetype that I relate to very profoundly because of the loss of my daughter. Demeter is a very powerful image for me, as well as for the planet as a whole. We are seeing a return of the daughter and a rebirth of women's spirituality, an awareness of women, women being more visible, more vocal. My dog came to me in the ninth year after my daughter's death, and I named her Kwan Yin because I began to identify more with compassion and mercy than with grief. I think we're entering an era of compassion and mercy, of women's values. Women's values are more nurturing and caring and cooperative than male values. We need a balance.

What are some male values?

If you have an imbalance of the masculine energies, you have aggressiveness in men. You have people escaping into drugs and crime, houses are barred,

Illustration: Frankie as Hecate, by Joann Powell Colbert

people aren't safe in their own homes. There's a general feeling of fear. That's because of the imbalance of male and female energies, which has been going on for centuries. But just lately you see the feminine emerging, the female values, even in the mainstream press. Another aspect of the return of the Goddess is this very strong concern for ecology, for the earth, the air, the fire, the water!

What does it mean to you to be a Crone?

The Crone has the benefit of having the experience of the Maiden and the Mother, which enrich her in her old age. I'm sixty-five now. I have to tell you, this is the most productive period of my whole life, working full-time for the women's movement. I feel very fruitful. I do newsletters, I organize events, do political consulting.

Do you have Crone role models?

The masculine culture does not value age and wisdom. You can't really value age when you're going to send your young men off to war. We, as aging women, must be our own role models. We just have to do it one moment at a time, one day at a time. It's not easy. To Crone successfully is to be yourself, to be who you are. Some Crones wouldn't be doing what I'm doing, political activism, they'd be meditating or travelling, and I think that's great. I know a Crone who is 85, who went to Europe not that long ago. Another Crone nearby is 100 years old, still so sharp and smart, and she has no reservations about saying what she thinks! And it's right on target! Both of these women are older than I am, and I care about them very much. They are, in a way, my role models.

In your experience, are Crones outspoken?

Oh, yes, we tell it like it is, without holding back, when younger women don't. We don't have anything to lose! You're still into your careers, defining who you are, but when you're one hundred, you *are* who you are!

Do you look back over your life and have regrets about one path chosen over another?

No. The death of my daughter taught me that whatever you do is right. Whatever decision you make is the right one. I would not be the person I am today if it were not for my daughter. Blames, regrets – a waste of energy. Live as fully in the moment as you can. You have to have compassion for yourself. Realize that there's time for everything.

At our age, early thirties, we often feel that time is passing us by, that there is so much to do, so many projects – how will I get it all done? Do you feel like that?

As a culture, we're very time oriented, especially in the Mother phase of your life. You're building careers, you have children who have to go to school at a certain time, they come home for lunch at a certain time, they come home at night at a certain time, so you're very time oriented. There's no way out of it. But it makes a difference when you don't have to gear yourself to time, and that's one of the privileges of being a Crone. Your maiden and mother lives are time structured. Crones' lives are not structured so much according to time. I have choices about the way that I want to structure my life. I'm still working on structuring my life in a way so that I don't feel pressured. No sooner am I done with one thing than I'm doing something else. But these things, these projects, are my choice. I don't have to do them in order to bring food to the table. Maidens and mothers have fewer choices than Crones have, less freedom. There are far more constraints for you than there are for me. Things loosen up when you become a Crone.

It's good for us to hear that. Sometimes we think that if the pressure to get things done is bad now, it must get worse as you draw toward the end of your life. You're telling us that's not the case.

This masculine culture, because of its devaluation of life as a whole, tells us that we become less as we get older. That's not so, not at all.

Do you think about death?

I think more in terms of evolution. I believe that when the spirit leaves the body, the spirit evolves. So does your body evolve – it goes back into the earth and becomes part of something else, perhaps another body. I don't think of death as an end. Women have more connection with evolution and change, through our bodies. Women have more of an evolutionary spirit than men do. We experience

Live as fully in the moment as you can. Realize that there's time for everything.

it in our bodies. Giving birth is a very profound experience, which men can never have. Men don't have a profound experience of change during their lives. That's a limited perspective, which is why we live in a limited culture.

Do you have any last words of wisdom for women who want to become great Crones?

I would say, love and let go.

How do you know if you're letting go too soon?

That's part of loving and letting go. You have to let go of the doubt, too. Love and let go. ○

Editor's note:
About a year after the above interviews took place, Joann Powell Colbert's 15-year-old son Jake died in a fall during a camping trip. SageWoman readers are familiar with Joann not only from this interview, but also from her artwork that frequently appears in SageWoman and other publications. The outpouring of sympathy and support was a beautiful indication of how strong the web is between daughters of the Great Mother. Joann responded with a letter we published in SageWoman, and we offer it now as an epilogue to her interview – one mother's experience of grief.

I cannot tell you how blessed I have felt over the past few months to receive your cards and notes after the death of my son. Your wisdom and your expression of caring has moved me deeply. I thank you for the trees that have been planted in his memory, and I thank you for the prayers and energy sent my way. I feel as though I am being lifted up by many sets of arms.

I want to share with you a dream that I had on Beltane Eve. I had gone to therapy that day and had expressed to my therapist how hurt I was feeling because so many people were experiencing Jake's presence in dreams or psychic flashes, but I was feeling nothing but an empty void. I longed for a dream because of the healing dream I'd had after my mother died. My therapist, Flor, asked me, "What do you think Jake still wants from you that he never got?" The answer came, "He wants total acceptance and approval of who he is, just as he is." A hard one for me – I didn't *like* his smoking, his filthy mouth, the heavy metal music. She suggested

I go home and work at my altar by lighting a candle for him and affirming, "I totally and completely accept you and approve of you just as you are." After spending some time at the altar set up for him, and some time at my Beltane altar, I went to sleep. And the dream came.

I must preface the recounting of the dream by telling you that I never saw my son's body, except on the four o'clock news the day he was found. Because his skull was crushed, I chose not to see the body before it was cremated. At the time, I thought this was the best decision, but I have since wondered if seeing the body isn't extremely important for closure.

The dream: Jake's body is brought to me and laid on my couch. My house is filled with the same friends who were there the day we waited to hear if the searchers had found him. But they leave me alone as I hold his body, gently washing it, singing to it, combing his hair and anointing the body with scented oils. I get up and walk away from the couch, and when I come back, Jake sits up, yawns, and smiles his sweet smile. He looks very sleepy, but happy. I am ecstatic and joyful, because he had been dead, but now he is alive! I get on the phone and call a couple of friends with the news, then see the energy lines light up and down the coast; just as the news had spread that he was dead, so now does the news spread that he is alive.

I was euphoric for several days after this dream. Even though I am still dealing with sadness and loss, the soul-searching, the feeling that he is well and happy has not left me.

Thank you, sisters for your warmth and kindness and love. May the Lady return it to you a hundredfold. ○

You have to let go of the doubt, too. Love and let go.

Love and the Altar Space

Loving the Goddess, loving yourself

By MaryScarlett Moon

Is there an image of yourself there? You are Goddess, too.

I try to surround myself with beauty – lush greenery, sparkling glass, glimmering candles, Goddess images, gemstones, family photos, cools colors, warm woods. Being an urban-on-the-go kind of witch, this is no small task – yet neither is it a luxury. In the creation and appreciation of "beautyspace," be it my home, my car (my second home), my office, or any other place that I spend more than an hour a day of my precious earth-time, I remind myself of who I am . . . not just the above-average housewife, mother, or teacher, but a proud and glorious daughter of the Goddess.

It is hard to write that. Proud, ok, but glorious??? No. Yes. Yes!

And this is the point. It is indeed difficult , too difficult, for many of us (most of us) to stand tall, and declare ourselves glorious . . . or beautiful. Or sexy. Or intelligent. Or powerful. Or, or, or. These kinds of declarations are essential goals along the healing path, the Goddess path of wholeness, and these too are not luxuries. Before we can cast a spell, change the world, or reshape our destiny, each of us must be able to recognize "who I am" – the divine one, the Goddess within, she who can move mountains with the right data base! And, more importantly, learn to love her.

Every flat surface an altar

The altar is the perfect place to begin this concerted process of learning self-love. We have a saying in my circle, "Every flat surface an altar." Walls, window sills, bookshelves, and table tops are, of course, prime candidates for altar sites. Some of us even have hide-a-altars, poised beneath beds on breadboards for easy access and quick concealment. Our altars are crammed with magical tools, sacred symbols, images of the Divine Mother; we go there, daily, weekly, monthly to honor Her, to work magic, to feel our connection to the universe. But all too often, our work, our reverence goes without. And if the old maxim "as above, so below" is true, then speaking for myself, the universe must be a mess! At least sometimes.

I tend my altar like a garden

In using the altarspace to learn self-love, one must honor her personal preferences. Many sisters construct theme altars, depending on the magic at hand, the Goddess they need to honor/explore/appease, etc. Of course, learning self-love at the Aphrodite altar makes perfect sense to me, but Aphrodite may not always be willing to share Her space, no matter how worthy the cause. Listen to the Goddess within, She will guide you. (Remember, one of the reasons you got into the Goddess was that you could worship sans dogma.) Whether we create new altars for the task, or utilize our all-purpose ones, we must embrace the altar as safety zone, hallowed ground, Heaven on Earth. Proclaiming that the pantry, northwest corner, east wing or garage workshop is now your sacred domain can also be an important step on the path toward self-love. This tells the universe, and your family, that you matter enough to you to demand space to practice your craft.

Let us tend our altars like a garden, enveloping our hands in the icons, images and artifacts as if they were the Mother's own soil, to reconnect, rejuvenate, reclaim our place in this wild world. Look upon the beauty of your altar . . . that beauty is a manifestation of you, whether your altarspace is as simple as a small table adorned with only a single candle of your favorite color, or an elaborately appointed showplace. Look upon it with fresh eyes, see it. Is anything missing? Is there an image of yourself there? You are Goddess, too. Place images of yourself, and other real-life "heras" that you may have, alongside those of the Great Mother. Honor yourself in all of your aspects . . .

to full-length; honor yourself through the transformation, appreciate where you are now. By placing the image of Self alongside the image of Goddess, we will begin to bridge the gap; as we love the Goddess, so must we love ourselves.

Go to your altar, light a candle upon waking or before bed at night. Touch each and every tool, stone, tzotchke, charm, see the beauty of the Goddess, feel her love all around you. Take that love inside. Tracing the image of yourself in your many aspects with your fingertips, say "I tend my altar like a garden, my love for myself will grow and grow."

Make a list of what you love about yourself, keep it on your altar, and read it everyday. If you are too shy, create an exercise in your circle where you write your name on the top of a piece of paper and pass the paper around the circle clockwise; your sisters will write the affirmations for you, "I love my voluptuous thighs!" for example. When the paper returns to you, read the "I love my" affirmations out loud to each other, and keep that manifesto of self-love on your altar.

The Goddess goes everywhere you do, and so can your altar. Remember, the goal is to achieve self-

By placing the image of Self alongside the image of Goddess, we will begin to bridge the gap; as we love the Goddess, so must we love ourselves.

beautiful baby, sports star, graduate, lover, warrior, ritual celebrant. By displaying images of our triumphs, we will honor our accomplishments. When we display images of the not-so-triumphant moments – for example, on my altar I have a photo of myself taken right before the birth of my second child, a time of separation and painful turmoil – we will remember to have compassion for ourselves, too. Also, put a mirror on your altar. Start with a small one and work your way up

love all the time, not just as you tend the garden! A few reminders may be all it takes (as well as being the most prudent measure for the real-world) – a stone, a shell, a snapshot of you at the company picnic, an "underground" Goddess image. A Katherine Hepburn glamour glossy, perhaps? Marilyn? The Virgin Mary? Even the local card shop carries any number of beautiful female images. Use your imagination, find whatever you need to help you feel connected to your love for Mother and to

Madison Avenue and its unattainable ideal of feminine beauty, to the medical profession that practices misogynist medicine, the very structure of the patriarchy and its institutions are predicated and perpetuated upon our remaining self-loathing, not becoming self-loving. We are taught that only through outside sources, only through serving others, automatonic consumerism, and maintaining traditional, acceptable values can we be loved. The world economy itself is based upon the insecurity and self-loathing of the global population – that with a new dress, or a new car or a new weapon we will finally feel good about ourselves.

We must love ourselves, truly love ourselves if we are to return the Great Mother to her place of honor.

Again, we must turn to the altar . . . and it becomes active,

the precious love that you are developing for yourself. So when the going gets tough, the boss is in an uproar, the deadline is past, the copier is broken (again!), you can soothe yourself at the in-office/workplace altar, and remind yourself of who you are, that you are loved. If you work in an environment that will not allow for personal belongings about, you can still take your altar with you in the form of an image of the Goddess or a pentagram around your neck, next to your heart, resting on the beautiful shelf of your bosom.

As we tend our altars to learn self-love, we must keep in mind the importance of this great task. Self-love is more than an airy, new-age notion; the pop-psychology cliche that we "must love ourselves before we can love another" smacks of a certain condescension. The truth is that we must love ourselves, truly love ourselves if we are to return the Great Mother to her place of honor, and to reclaim our place as women in the world. From

transformative, alive. Here is where we alter our ways of seeing ourselves and our world. We must awaken and change. We are all proud and glorious daughters of a wise and infinite Mother, and our path is one of action, of responsibility. If we do not love and honor ourselves, we cannot love and honor the Goddess. Dancer Martha Graham captured the essence of learning and practicing love of self, as she explains to Agnes DeMille, "There is a vitality, a life force, a quickening that is translated through you into action, and because there is only one of you in all time, this expression is unique. And if you block it, it will never exist through another medium and will be lost. The world will not have it. It is not your business to determine how good it is, nor how valuable it is, nor how it compares to other expressions. It is your business to keep it yours, clearly and directly, to keep the channels open."

May your garden of self-love bloom and thrive! ○

Photo of MaryScarlett at her altar, by Jim Payne

Making Medicine Shields

Magical crafts

By Carol Jean Logue

For weeks, we looked forward to the workshop. Every event, every interaction, every stone and feather was grist for preinstruction. As we gathered totems, sacred bits of our tangible lives, our guiding spirits also gathered for the appointed Saturday. We assembled on the sidewalk outside the community center, grinning and hugging in hopes that Spring's chilly wind would blow away our nervousness before Andrea showed up. Even her being late was part of the initiation.

It took our moving into the sun, making peace with waiting, for her to drive up with her car full of our workshop. Each grabbed an armload and we found our ways into the basement room where we were to make hallowed Shields. Unfolding chairs and tables, we chose our places and indulged in cursory introductions. I sat with Eva, organic gardener, student of the plant world, and with Ginny ("I never was a Virginia," she explained, "Too much of a tomboy.").

Once Andrea purified the room with a smudgestick of sweetgrass and sage, we settled to a bit of information about Medicine Shields. Personal Shields are to be as balanced as possible. In the Native American tradition, they aren't used to ward off enemies. Shields are more a declaration of one's inner Self, and where they are carried into battle, they are seen as symbols of the strength that comes of being centered in one's true nature.

Most often, Shields hang at the entrance to one's dwelling. They announce, in subconscious imagery, who lives within. "Subconscious is a key word here," Andrea clarified, "as our intellects have very little help to offer in creating Medicine Shields. We must invite them to relax out of the picture."

To facilitate this relaxation, Andrea suggested we lie down or get as comfortable as possible in our chairs. She guided a meditation, far from Saturday's basement room, deep into the woods of our souls. She invited us to approach our Spirit Guides of the four directions.

"Begin in the South," she murmured. "This is where your inner little girl can be found. She speaks to you of trust and innocence. Picture your little girl as clearly as possible. Ask her name. See what she has to give you. Give her something in return."

Gently, encouraging us to take our time, to see and feel the details, Andrea continued, "Move to the West now. Here you can meet your adult woman. She speaks to you of emotion and introspection. Picture your adult woman as clearly as possible. Ask her name. See what she has to give you. Give her something in return.

"Move to the North when you're ready. Here's where you meet the adult masculine energy inside you. He speaks of mind, ideas, logic. Picture your adult male as clearly as possible. Ask his name. See what he has to give you. Give him something in return.

"Now, move to the East. Your inner little boy dwells in the East. He speaks to you of illumination, lightening up. Picture the little boy within as clearly as possible. Ask his name. See what he has to give you. Give him something in return."

When she "brought us back" to our workshop scene, Andrea suggested that we refrain from conversation, to let the imagery of our Spirit Guides come to conscious awareness, much as we linger in waking to recall the drama of our dreams, to seek their meanings. But she reminded us that "meanings" are tasks of the intellect, whose talents were not invited

Our intellects have very little help to offer in creating Medicine shields.

to help with our Shields. Not just yet.

Next, she directed our attention to the far wall, where she'd arranged perhaps two dozen alder saplings in a row. Our next job was to find out which of these was our personal sapling. Some of us knew right away. Some of us spent some time with the sticks, five feet tall, each with a personality of its own. As we cradled our green wood back to our places, we were astonished to hear our next assignment: to bend the trees, while holding mental circles!

They were two inches thick at the bases. I despaired of ever bending mine into a round. "Notice," Andrea suggested, "everything about this process. There are no accidents in making a Shield." I doubted I had the strength to begin. I glanced at Eva. She ran her hands tenderly along her sapling, as if to ask for its consent. Then, very gently, she began to bend it against her hips, to arc the alder across her shoulders, to become intimate with her Shield's frame.

And so, because there was nothing else to do, I confronted mine. Eventually, the room was the scene of grunting, gyrating, unabashed struggle. We were sweating, to a person, and invoking various forms of the Goddess. Ginny was especially vociferous, cursing her sprig, nicknaming it the Hulk.

I pricked my finger more than once, and smeared the blood near the hole at the south edge of my shield.

Andrea meandered among us, saying she was looking for a particular sapling, the one that had put up a struggle in her respectful harvest earlier that day. Although it seemed to volunteer for the holy job, it had felt like a particularly feisty energy. We begged her to tell us who had it. At Ginny's next outburst of frustration, Andrea nodded.

While I worked, and it was work, I mused over the encounter with my Spirit Guides. My little girl had given me a dewy rose. I'd given her a hug. My adult feminine had felt awesome, somewhat threatening. She was dressed all in black, announced herself as Mahatma, gave me a pearl. I gave her a deep, reverential bow. My adult masculine had called himself Storyteller. He gave me his skill. I gave him my work. My little boy, the least familiar of my Guides, had peed a bright yellow arc into my cupped hands! He was audacious, as if to say "All things are permitted here! Loosen up, C.J." I brushed his soft blond hair.

As my sapling began to really bend, Andrea circulated near me, saying, "There was a very yellow little boy over here during the meditation." I was stunned. I waited to see if anyone else might have had a yellow little boy. But no. Stammering, I confessed to the blond urinator. Needless to say, my trust in Andrea's guidance grew to a new level.

Across the room we heard a crack and a wail. Someone had been too bossy with her sapling. As I drew my alder into its round, others had already selected the tanned hides that were to form the shields' canvasses. Even though Eva was still gently coaxing hers, I was impatient to get on with mine, and was too rough, bending the last foot, the thickest part of the little tree to get the job over with. It creased, crushing tissue. "How like me," I reflected, lashing the teardrop into place with sinew. "I begin in doubt and despair, get the job almost done as I forget myself in the enterprise, and rush into carelessness at the end, just to be finished."

The deerskins were soft and pliable, some gleaming white, some shades of tan. I selected a white one from the pile and spread it out on the floor among others who were cutting shapes to fit alder frames. I studied the skin. I has drawn to the hole, as big as a child's palm, that must have been the perforation that took the gentle life.

Andrea saw me linger over the space. She said, "Feel free to use the holes any ways that seem right to you. They won't fray or ravel over time." And so I cut around the hole and began to peel sinew into strands thin enough to slip into the eye of my needle.

While others selected beads, feathers, claws, talons, pieces of fur, pieces of stick whose spirits beckoned them to the table, I spent the rest of the afternoon sewing the pure white hide to my teardrop. It was slow going. I wanted the stitches to be even, lovely in themselves. I pricked my finger more than once, and smeared the blood near the hole at the south edge of my Shield. An opening, a wound in my willingness to trust? No meanings yet.

By the end of the day, Eva had groomed her alder into a perfect circle. Amazed with her patience, we were chastened as she quietly described her intention to make the face of her shield from botanicals, pieces of birch bark and reeds, so as not to take animal life for her art. We began to lament the fact that we would have to finish at home. How would we see each other's Shields? Andrea suggested that we get back together in a month. And so we dispersed to a day considerably warmed by our basement efforts.

At home, I hung the teardrop on the wall of my room. Some days later there was a card from Andrea in the mail. It said, "Awaken your Shield in Song and Ceremony." We were invited to her place, far out of town, along the creek. In four weeks, could I design my four directions and relate them to my center?

That night, after work, I stopped at a fabric store and bought a piece of cotton with a rose print. It was a few more days before I made time, before my Spirit Guides were ready, to cut two roses, press the irregular edges, glue the cloth to the south of the hide, near the hole, near the blood, dried brown by now, and edge the piece in red ribbon, for grounding energy.

Then my life got busy. I had all sorts of excuses to keep me from facing Mahatma's pearl from her oceanic depths. As the two roses seemed more balanced than the one the little girl had given me,

I sought an image of pearly balance. In a crafts shop, I chose iridescent berry beads in all colors. Holding a string that seemed most "real," most "natural," it was clear that I should also have a black strand. Driving home, I saw the beads sewn into a yin/yang symbol.

Beginning with the white beads, I sewed a perfect curve of pearls along my pencil line in an embroidery hoop. Where creative energy met receptive energy, I threaded black pearls onto my needle. At the feminine edge of the round, black beads seemed to stagger into space, beaded muslin meeting hide in more chaos than order. No meanings yet . . .

My mother was interested in my process. She

I sewed iridescent butterflies along the ribbon, for former lives.

Illustration: "White Buffalo Woman," by Joann Powell Colbert

wanted to know everything I could tell her about the Medicine Shield of her eldest daughter. I explained how the frog is one of my totems; how it stands for dramatic metamorphoses; how I'd found a perfect specimen, squashed flat and dried along the road; how it seemed to be preserved in storyteller position: one arm to heart, the other outstretched, until something bigger had come along; how I'd kept it, wondering why. She protested, urging me to use something far prettier than a squashed frog in the center of my Shield. Good ol' Ma.

Each holding a large disk, some turned inward, toward their breasts, some facing out to greet the world.

The night before our Shields reunion found me uncertain about the north and east edges. So far I had fabric and glass beads on the hide. If I could balance these, I could represent animal, vegetable and mineral kingdoms within my psychic portrait. How to show Storyteller's gift? I found some ribbon, blue for communication from the throat chakra, and formed it into the continuous line of the encircled pentacle, leaving a trail to dangle as long as the red ribbon, for grounding. Then I sewed iridescent butterflies along the ribbon, for former lives. The berries weren't right for this project.

I had saved the brassy top to a can of whole wheat kernels. From this, I cut two moon crescents, attaching them with sinew, so they dangle in the east, waxing and waning. They were as close as I could come to my little boy's significant arcs of yellow. Gluing my small dried flattened frog in the center was the final touch. She seems to reach for the butterflies. She seems to sing from my focal point.

The next morning saw me wrapping my Shield in a red towel, heading out in the rain for our ceremony. It was fun to find Andrea's place, deep in the woods, at the end of miles of dirt roads, beside Rapid Lightning Creek. It was fun to meet my sisters again, each holding a large disk, some turned inward, toward their breasts, some facing out to greet the world, just as we are as individual personalities. In drizzly rain, we formed a circle beside the creek.

Andrea smudged us to welcome Spirit Guides, and invoked the four directions, Mother Earth and Father Sky. As we presented our shields, holding them high, Andrea drummed and sang of the powers of the four directions, of Mother's

nurturing, of Father's creativity, and the rain stopped. She whispered, "Thank you, Father Sky." Then we set our shields on the ground and began to dance to Mother's heartbeat, recalling our connections to the ancestors, to wisdom of the ages, asking for insights into our Selves and beseeching understanding of the universe around our centers.

As our circle broke up, some went for the vegetarian potluck fare. Some of us stood around cooing and exclaiming over each others' Shields. Some listened, and some told the stories of their symbols.

Now is time to begin looking for meanings. ○

The Earth is my mother
I shall not want.
Her hand brings forth the green pastures.
She tarries within the still waters.
She sustains my body.
She leads me in fields of fruitfulness
for my Glory.
Yea, as I walk through the summer of life
unto death,
I will not be afraid,
for You are with me.
Your womb in the earth
will enfold me.
You prepare a harvest before me,
and bless my home with children.
You fill me with milk and honey.
My cup overflows.
Surely, goodness and beauty will nurture me
all the days of my life,
and I will become part of the earth
forever.

Karen Dzubur

Ovulation Magick

Celebrating your egg-time

By Sola

Many bleeding ceremonies have been published, but I know of none that mark egging. If magick is about moving energy, this is the time. I can feel waves of it inside me, roiling and boiling, as steam sizzles from my prickling fingertips. This is the full moon of the body – let's celebrate it!

First, you have to find out when you ovulate. If you're practicing fertility awareness for contraception, you already know; if you're not, start learning, just to get in touch with the patterns of your body. I notice changes usually ten or twelve days after the last bleeding began; for you, it may be nearer fourteen or sixteen days, depending on the length of your cycle. The most visible sign is prolific, clear, slippery cervical mucus, like eggwhite, which is technically known as spinbarkheit. Often there's a slight rise in body temperature. If you do internal self-examinations, you'll notice that your cervix is probably softer and more open. Or you may feel different, more sexual or more energetic, for example. Learn to identify these changes in yourself and take time to rejoice in them.

Set aside an hour one evening when you're ovulating to honor this phase of your sacred cycle. Use the time to perform a creative ritual, a ritual of creation. If you want to conceive, ask the Goddesses of fertility to help you: Celtic Cerridwen, Greek Aphrodite, Norse Freya. And then make love, or inseminate yourself, or pray for parthenogenesis. Even if you don't want to conceive, make love if you're feeling sexy, for the sheer exuberant joy of it. (If you're heterosexual and your lovemaking includes penetration/enclosure, be sure to use lots of contraception.)

Bring a pen and paper into your sacred space and see what inspiration floods down to you through your open energy channels. If you can get outside to a lonely place, and the spirit moves you, run, dance, sing, howl. And ground this bubbling energy, that you may have it to draw upon when you're at a lower ebb.

Celebrate yourself, your womanhood, your potential, your creativity. If you're calm enough to meditate and concentrate, sit and think about the unfathomable wonders of your body. Take a great glorious gob of your fertility goo and play with it between your fingers. See how strong and elastic it is. Rub it into your skin and absorb its endurance and resilience, or give it to your favorite plant, a very literal way of grounding the energy. (If you're doing this in a group, keep your secretions to yourself in these years of caution.)

There's a theory going around that it's "natural" to bleed at the new moon and ovulate by the light of her fullness. That's all very well if you do, but if you don't, this belief serves only to make you feel "unnatural." Instead of pushing your body into a rhythm that it doesn't seek out by itself, enjoy your own individual dance around the month.

By the way, if you're on the Pill for some reason, think about getting off it. If you're firmly convinced that it is for you, you may want to recognize a phantom ovulation day, to tune into the energies your body is being chemically forced to suppress. You'd better use another method of birth control for a couple of days, in case your body responds more vigorously than your mind intended. Happy egging! O

If magick is about moving energy, this is the time.

The Moon Lodge

A place of woman power

By Spider

My sister the Moon sings her song to my womb, We dance in the spiral of life.

If you sit quietly, slow your breathing, and put your hands together on your womb, you will begin to create the sacred space of the womb-lodge or Moon lodge. Bring your awareness down to your hands, make friends with your womb, and allow her to teach you about the flow of your cycles. There is a medicine wheel in your womb. As you travel around it in monthly cycles, keeping in awareness will put you in touch with your inner cycles of healing and wisdom during all times of the month.

The cycles of the Moon influence our monthly cycles of bleeding. Before our wombs were distracted by artificial stimulation, the light of the Moon brought about ovulation (release) at the time of fullness, and the darkness of the new Moon brought about our flow (dreaming within, the time of inner healing and introspection).

The Moon is a manifestation of the Earth-Mother. We celebrate her cycles because they bring our bloods, and also because, of all the species of female animals that bleed, human women are the only species that experiences a 29-day cycle like the Moon.

At the full Moon, we celebrate with the community. Singing and dancing around the sacred fires, we lend energy to our clans, communities, and to the healing and preservation of the Earth herself. During the time of the new Moon, the women gather in the bleeding space of the Moon lodge to become quiet and enter the place of the spirits.

The days of bleeding are the times for women when shamanic awareness becomes our reality and work with the spirits brings many messages of healing and wisdom. Women quite naturally draw away from normal everyday activities during bleeding. It is to the space of the Moon lodge that we retreat to celebrate and hear the wisdom of our wombs. We give ourselves gifts, we bless and heal each other. Within the sacred space of the lodge, we reclaim the power of our blood, transforming our monthly cycle from a time of pain and inconvenience to a time of honor and healing.

Let yourself create a special place to celebrate your unique Moon cycle. Take some time off during your bleeding time to be there, either by yourself or with other women. Make or give yourself a present, dress in shells to represent your connection to the Moon's cycles, do divination work to get answers to any specific questions or just to receive messages from the spirits. Connect with your womb to feel your power. Wear your blood and make offerings of it to heal the Earth in a place special to you. Or better yet, sit directly on the Earth and let your blood flow right into her womb. Sing the song of the Moon's cycles to celebrate. And honor yourself, for you are a manifestation of the Goddess in her most abundant form! ○

Her darkness
leads me to
dreaming
within,
Her brightness
brings me
release.

My Sister the Moon

Composed by: Spider
Transcribed by: K. Younger

strongly accented beats
* repeat: final time repeat chorus 2x's to *fine.*

Birth Empowerment

Birthing from Goddess wisdom

By Jane Hearren

We who revere the Goddess should know that She has given us what we need to give birth.

In our Goddess tradition, the world is created by the act of birth. The details of the myths and stories may vary, but the world is born from the body of the Great Mother. And because the world is the Goddess, she is in effect giving birth to herself. The cyclic act of birth and rebirth reflects our Witches' cyclical world view, but unlike the patriarchal stories of rebirth, the Goddess does not have to die to be reborn.

The patriarchal world has done its best to take the power of birth away from women. A system that has tried so long and hard to control women's bodies has almost succeeded in depriving us of the knowledge that we have the power to give birth. It is heartbreaking to see women who have taken responsibility for so many aspects of their lives turning back to a patriarchal system for assistance at this critically powerful time in their lives. We who revere the Goddess should know that She has given us what we need to give birth. We need to remember that we are of the Goddess who gave us the power to mirror Her act of creation.

As we begin to reawaken the Goddess, let us honor her by taking back this sacred act. Many of our fears are inspired by patriarchal lies. We can confront them with the tools we use for psychic empowerment. I offer here an outline for a Goddess-centered process of empowerment in pregnancy to make possible an empowering birth experience.

As our Goddess-centered world view is cyclical, so is the nature of self-empowerment. We achieve power, use the power, and emerge more powerful than before. In the process, we use knowledge, affirmation, meditation and ritual to achieve trust. In the women's health movement we say, "Knowledge is Power." We reclaim knowledge of our bodies in order to begin to reclaim control over our physical experience, and when we begin to reclaim that control, we also begin to achieve power.

Begin by learning all you can about the physiological processes of pregnancy and birth. Remember to focus on normalcy. Avoid patriarchal texts that contain judgements of women's ability to give birth on their own. If you are using medical books, remember that they are written from a perspective that sees pregnancy as a disease state in need of treatment. Question these texts with the same critical attitude with which you would question a medieval churchman's treatise on witchcraft.

If you are fortunate enough to know a birth attendant who works outside of the medical model, talk with her. Ask her about dangers, complications, problems. In my own experience, I have seen very few women who would be safer in a hospital than at home, and very few complications that cannot be handled outside a medical setting. Understand that many complications are variations from an average, but not dangerous, simply different.

Learn also the patriarchal nature of the need to control. The birth process can only be controlled by extreme interference and invasion that create more problems than they solve. But the patriarchal mandate to control women's bodies is so strong that the medical world ignores the problems it creates.

Apply this knowledge in affirmation. Witches know that affirmation is a powerful psychic tool for bending and shaping reality. Affirmations made with reverence for our bodies, that affirm our power to create, that help us explore our relationship with pain and joy, are all forms of prayer. Each affirmation is a thanksgiving to the Goddess, who gives us strength for our work. Some affirmations for pregnancy might be:

My body is strong and beautiful.
My body is nurturing a strong and beautiful baby.
My body has the strength to bring my baby to birth.
I confront pain with grace and courage.
I see past pain into joy.

Birth is a crucible in which the physical and spiritual are fused, and powerful physical and spiritual experience is often painful. The nature of pain is complex, and difficult to comprehend. Pain and fear are closely intertwined; they feed one upon the other, increasing together. But pain is not always accompanied by fear. The creative process, whether it be spiritual or physical, can be intensely painful, but the joy of creation outweighs the pain. So it is with birth. Pain, like joy, like birth and death, is a mystery of the Goddess. We can approach pain with reverence rather than fear, and use the same psychic tools of trance and meditation to comprehend it.

Deep relaxation, trance and meditation are all powerful allies in working with, as opposed to fighting, pain. Extensive creative meditations which incorporate visualizations, focus on breath, and relaxation can be used to prepare for birth. "Moon Mother, Moon Baby" incorporates these elements.

Moon Mother, Moon Baby

Ground, center, and protect yourself. Use relaxation techniques you have found helpful in other meditations or trance states. As you become deeply relaxed, visualize a starry night. See the moon drift into your view, the full moon that is the Great Goddess in her Mother aspect. Allow your breath to become softer, deeper, more regular. As you breathe, see the moonlight as the Mother's life-giving energy, entering your body to surround your baby with love and power. The moonlight illuminates the baby in your womb. The Full/Moon/Mother supports and empowers you with Her light/energy/power. You may wish to chant or sing,

"In thy Power, Mother Moon, I put myself again."

Think of Mother Moon pulling the waters of the oceans toward Her in the tides. Envision Her pulling your birth waters in the same way, the ebb and flow. Feel the power and the pain in the tidal pull, as Mother Moon draws your baby toward its birth. Focus on the pain, on releasing your baby

into the Moon's power. As your breathing continues to be deep and regular, release with each breath.

Now see each inhale and exhale as drawing and releasing the Moon's light and power. See yourself connected by your breath to the power of the Mother. Draw in her power with each breath, and as you sigh on the exhale, visualize her light and energy exhaling not through your nose or mouth, but through your vagina, empowering and energizing the birth passage. As the image/vision begins to fade, release it, thanking the Goddess for her help and the power she sends to birthing women.

Knowledge, affirmation, and meditation come

The creative process, whether it be spiritual or physical, can be intensely painful, but the joy of creation outweighs the pain. So it is with birth.

Illustration by Wahaba Nuit-Cat Heartsun

together in ritual. Rituals of empowerment are a fundamental part of the Craft, and a ritual for empowerment at the birth time can be one of the most joyous and beautiful of our tradition. Many of my sister midwives follow Hopi tradition by holding a Blessing Way for expectant mothers. I have moved away from that practice in creating a ritual based on a more European tradition. The Hopi Blessing Way welcomes the pregnant woman into the Community of Mothers in a very special way; it confers grace and serves as an initiation. But the Blessing Way is focused on the process of becoming a Mother. My Goddess Birth ritual is more focused on the act of giving birth.

The heart of the ritual is empowerment. In this instance, power is directed to the birthing woman by her sisters in the forms of courage, focus, grace, and joy. In my own circle, which is largely composed of midwives and other women involved with birth, the ritual follows this pattern:

Each woman brings to the circle a green candle (green for life) and a gift. She may, of course, bring any ritual objects to lay on the altar that she wishes. The high priestess lights three green altar candles, then brings the Mother candle to the woman standing to the left of the expectant mother and lights the candle. Then, going clockwise, each woman says her name as she lights the candle of the woman to her left. In second, third and often fourth rounds of the circle, each woman calls the name of absent women to be present with us in spirit. This is our casting of the circle, creating sacred space.

Power is directed to the birthing woman by her sisters in the forms of courage, focus, grace, and joy.

At the end of the rounds, the high priestess brings a white or purple Goddess candle to the expectant mother, who lights it with her green candle. The Goddess candle is returned to the altar, and the high priestess takes the ritual salt, incense, candle and water to call the directions. Finally, she invokes the Goddess, specifically asking for a blessing on our circle from the Mother aspect.

At this time, we sing one or two special songs, and then begin the rounds of giving. First, each woman gives a prayer for the safe journey through the birth process. In the next round, each gives a story about an empowering birth. Next, each one gives her gift – which might be a poem, a drawing, a treasure bag, a crystal, a basket or a plant. Mine is usually a

painted box with lavender potpourri. When the gifts are all given, another song or two are sung, and then we share food and drink, and "social time." Then, we thank the directions and the Goddess, and open the circle.

Witches are perhaps in the best position to trust our bodies to do their work, even as we do work in our circles, because we have already turned our backs on patriarchy. Patriarchy has indoctrinated us since the day we ourselves were born with distrust – helplessness, inability, fear. We have been taught that we are unable to do this work of giving birth without the interference of men – men who are determined to control us in our most powerful times. I believe that these men are approaching birthing women with terrible fear in their hearts, and that they can only overcome this fear by placing women in complete physical control. It is to this end that patriarchal medicine advocates the use of drugs, hunger and surgery in childbirth. We can only reject this practice when we have perfect trust in the strength and power of our bodies.

Finally, a word about babies. As a midwife, and as a Witch, I envision our babies as between the worlds. The journey from womb to arms is not necessarily dangerous or perilous, but it is dramatic. Again, the patriarchy has used our love for our babies to threaten and control us – more than a few women have told me with tears that their doctors asked them, "Do you want to kill your baby?" when they tried to gain some kind of comfort measure for labor. The loss of a baby at the birth time or damage to the baby is indescribably painful. I can only remind women that it happens when the medical world is in charge, too. The power of trust extends to our babies. We must trust ourselves to know what is right and best for them, and remind ourselves that we love them. Mothers do not sacrifice their babies for some peculiar notion of what might be a fun way to give birth. On the contrary, mothers love their babies enough to hold deep respect and honor for the process of bringing them to birth. It is that respect and honor that empowers us to give birth with love and joy. ○

Birth from the Sea

A healing and renewing rite

By Mer-Nuit

To be done just before sunrise on a Monday or Friday during a waxing crescent moon. In a freshly cleaned, uncluttered bathroom, set up your altar. If possible, position the altar so that when you stand in front of it, you are facing the nearest seashore. Set out seven white candles upon a sea green cloth. On the cloth, arrange a white lily for purity, a pearl for wisdom (a smooth white stone will work as well), and sea shells of your choice. You will also need a bowl containing about half a cup of salt.

As the tub fills with warm water, concentrate on the purity of your spiritual purpose. Empty the bowl of salt into the water, then swirl your hand through the water in a spiral pattern. Ask the Goddess to put you in touch with your deepest psychic patterns, knowing that they will carry you always in the right direction.

Darken the room as much as possible while you soak in the womb-waters. Release your angers, fears and frustrations. Tell yourself, "I forgive, forget, let go . . ."

Release your angers, fears and frustrations. Tell yourself, "I forgive, forget, let go . . ."

When you are ready, light all seven candles. Use a rich coconut soap to bathe yourself from head to toe. Visualize your woman spirit transforming the negative into the positive, as the oyster transforms the grain of sand into a pearl. Rinsed and dried, dress yourself in new garments that enhance your sense of wholeness and inner power. O

Illustration by Katlyn Miller

I Am a Gift I Give Myself

A self-esteem ritual

By Shana Morgan

It is our vision of our self that puts the limits on our achievement.

I am a gift I give myself. Why do these words feel so good to read, but so hard to say, especially in the company of others? Why is celebrating yourself an activity that seems to require justification? Are there any personal problems, or even problems in the world, that cannot ultimately be traced back to a lack of self esteem? Our self image is the basis for everything in our life. It is our vision of our self that puts the limits on our achievement. How we feel about our self is what we project to others, and our need for self protection is what builds the barriers we erect around us.

Surely, something so vital to our happiness we would cultivate and control carefully. We would meticulously fashion the highest of self-esteem levels and vigilantly monitor this precious image, instantly weeding out anything negative as soon as it appeared. Or would we? When receiving feedback from others, most people will rationalize and dilute the positive and simply accept the negative. Any failing in our self image is reinforced even if the facts have to be stretched to do so. Unfortunately, all too often, we do not even have to stretch the messages from our family, friends or society to reinforce feelings of inadequacy.

To prepare for our ritual, it's important to look at the sources for your low self esteem. Specifically, what messages did you receive in the past that gave rise to negative feelings about yourself? Write these messages down. What people in your life, right now, reinforce a negative self image? What messages do you receive from them? Write all these down.

Then think about what you want in your life, in your relationships, in your image of your self, in your feelings toward your self, and write a declaration of a new self. Describe yourself exactly as you want to be, but make sure you write in the present tense, not future. Instead of saying, "I will feel more confident," say, "I feel more confident." Make sure you include statements of unconditional acceptance of yourself, such as, "I feel good about every part of my self." Spend some time working on this statement, writing and editing, Try to be concise but inclusive.

Up to this point, all the work in changing your self image has been conscious and intellectual. But that is not enough to effect a life change. You must also engage your unconscious, your feelings and your higher self. Performing a ritual is one of the best ways to do that. You can judge if the ritual should be solitary or with a group. The one described here is solitary, but it could be easily adapted.

Select a time and place for your ritual where you will be undisturbed for a couple of hours, perhaps the last hours before going to bed on a night of the full moon. You will need the following:

- A cleansing incense and charcoal (sage or a blend such as this one for purification, healing, strength and removing negativity: equal parts frankincense, dried bay leaf, dried fern and sandalwood)
- A flameproof container or cauldron
- A bowl filled with dirt
- A large white candle and a smaller black candle
- A glass of water
- Each negative message written on a separate piece of paper
- The name of each person who is a negative influence on you, written on small pieces of paper (it should be noted that you in no way intend any harm to come to these people; you simply want to change the way the person treats you)
- The declaration of your new self

Music can often give a ritual fullness and engage

your "feeling self." If you are not comfortable singing alone, a cassette recording is a useful tool as long as you have each cassette ready to play with minimum fuss. If you want to use songs from several tapes, one method is to copy each song onto a blank tape in the order you will use them. Several songs seem appropriate with this ritual, such as Susan Haist's "Song of Courage" ("Warrior Goddess, come to me"), found on Lisa Thiel's tape, "Songs of Transformation;" "The Earth, the Air, the Fire, the Water" and Linda Udelow's "Higher," both found on Libana's tape, "A Circle Is Cast."

Also think about what higher powers you may want to invoke. Among the many titles of Au Set or Isis are "Source of Healing, Almighty Lady of Wisdom and Restorer of Life." She would be appropriate to invoke for healing and wisdom. Athena can also bring both wisdom and victory to she who asks. In Native American traditions, the medicine of the moose is self esteem, and frog's medicine is cleansing. The bear is a very powerful medicine force for introspection and healing.

your whole aura being washed and energized. Sit down, spend a moment or two breathing slowly and deeply, until you are centered and relaxed, then call the corners as you are accustomed. Sitting back down, feel the difference in energy now that you are "between the worlds."

Light the black candle, put a pinch of incense on the charcoal, and picking up the first small paper with a negative message, read it out loud. Allow

Instead of saying, "I will feel more confident," say, "I feel more confident."

The best way to prepare for this ritual would be to take a bath with magical herbs. (For purification, strengthening psychic powers, courage and healing, place dried rose petals, lemon peel and a spring of thyme in a piece of cheesecloth and steep it in your bath water.) If bathing is not practical, you can steep herbs in water and rinse off your face and hands. Visualize the water washing away any cares, worries or negativity. Feel the healing energy of the water and herbs entering your body.

Light the charcoal and place a pinch of incense on it, cupping the smoke, directing it toward your body from feet to head and back to feet again, visualizing

yourself to feel the weight of the words as they linger in the air, then touch the tip of the paper to the flame. As the paper burns, refute the statement out loud and drop it into the bowl with the incense. Do this with every negative message, adding small pinches of incense as necessary.

When all the negative messages have been countered and burned, stand up and wash your aura all over with incense again. This is a good time for a song, perhaps "Higher." Re-center and sit down again. When you feel the energy flowing through you once more, pick up one of the papers with the name of a person who tears at your self esteem.

Illustration by Joann Powell Colbert

As you hold the paper, speak out loud to that person's higher self. Explain that you do not want to be treated in the same way any more, and explain clearly how you do wish to be treated. Know that the person's higher self has heard you. Then visualize an encounter with the person where she treats you in the old, negative way and you simply, but effectively, tell her that is not how you will be treated anymore.

Finally, visualize the person treating you differently. Take the paper and bury it in your bowl of earth, envisioning Mother Earth embracing and transforming that person. Do this with each name. When you are done, light the white candle from the black and extinguish the black, placing it in the bowl of earth. Add more incense, stand up and wash your aura thoroughly, perhaps while playing the "Song of Courage." Sing along, dance, feel light and free of all negative influences.

Take the paper and bury it in your bowl of earth, envisioning Mother Earth embracing and transforming.

Center in again, sit down and pick up your declaration of a new self. Pass it through the smoke, then face the East. Call upon the powers and gifts of the air and feel the powers of discernment and clarity of thought flowing into you. Pass it through the flame, face the South, call upon the power of fire and feel energy and the will to change igniting you. Sprinkle it with a little water, face the West, call upon the power of water and feel compassion and love for your self bathing and permeating you. Touch it to the earth, face the North, call upon the power of the earth and feel wisdom and patience with your self anchoring you. Raise power by singing "The earth, the air, the fire, the water," and charge your white candle, your declaration and your self. Acknowledge the change by reading your declaration out loud with the absolute conviction that as you will it, so must it be!

Take some time to experience this new feeling of freedom and power before you ground the energy and thank the directions. Save the white candle and the declaration. Mix the water, the ashes and the earth in your bowl, then bury all of it. Each day following your ritual, take at least ten minutes to re-light your candle, re-read your declaration, and reward yourself with positive reinforcement. ○

This is the Age of Kali
The New Age of feminine force.
Who do you think she is trampling now?
Again the recumbent male
Of ignorance, seclusion, oppression
Lies under her feet.

Destroyer of worlds, eater of demons
The Gods themselves once begged your protection.
Armed with weapons and grace
All who see you, fear the flashing blades
The severed heads and hands
Of your careless play.
Laugh again, slash through
The deadlocked dualities of our time.

Black visage of awe, Smoky One
Embrace the inert Shiva
Corpse of our old ways.
Birth a new universe of balance
The moving force of creation is yours,
Joyous Mother of Time.

Dance into our power, My Mother
My Shining One, Kali.
Dance in the strong virgins, the warrior women
Wise Crones and teachers.
Manifest in your daughters,
Make us also terrible
            and dark
                  and lovely, as you.

Gretchen Faulk

Making Empowerment Necklaces

Magickal crafts

By Judith Tolley

When considering the idea of empowerment, there is nothing that conjures up the image of the witch or shaman better than the making of one's own craft tools. When creating ritual objects and magickal devices, it is essential we begin by setting the stage for our projects with spiritual intent. When we begin to build an empowerment necklace, we start with an idea about who we are and what we want to emphasize about who we are, or in another vein, we think about how we may want to change ourselves and enhance our image. For individuals who work with magick, this is not a new idea, but for those of you just starting on the inner path, let's look at some methods for enhancing self-awareness.

I usually work with postcards of Goddess images, hanging them on the wall or placing them on my work table where I can readily glance at them. This helps me channel that particular Goddess energy into the piece I am making. Sometimes I light a candle and meditate on the Goddess image. Going into a light trance, I let my mind free-associate with the images that rise and fall behind my closed eyes. When I feel at peace, centered and calm inside, I am ready to begin my artwork, letting the Goddess move my hand or direct me to whatever materials I must choose to form the piece. In this way, I feel my artwork is inner-guided and speaks from my higher self.

Play music in your work room that inspires you and allows you to relax and shift consciousness. Beginning to build ritual objects can be stressful at first because there are powerful messages about who can and cannot be artistic. These negative inputs have to be left behind you – only when you can honor your right (rite!) to make art will you feel the flow and power of your artistic nature. We all have our own signature that must be at peace with the images that come from our brain and the results of transforming those images into actual reality. Be

gentle with yourself; love yourself and the wonderful substances that will metamorphose into your personal ritual objects. The necklace will especially reflect your own style and vision. I have never seen two alike, as they reflect the 10,000 images of the great Mother Goddess.

There are techniques that are helpful to use when choosing materials for your necklace. I see the making of every empowerment necklace as an adventure that begins with the collection of the charms, amulets and beads which are strung to form the necklace. These objects can be collected from your own jewelry box (such as using a single earring or old pieces that have meaning to you, parts of jewelry that were gifts or inherited form your woman-line), from trips to garage sales, swap meets, antique stores, or from the many craft stores that sell the raw materials used for our ritual objects. It is fun to swap beads and materials with friends, thereby putting their energy into your piece, not to mention reducing the initial cost of building up a supply of materials.

When you are searching for objects to string onto your necklace, you can invoke the Goddess to guide you to those objects. You may read the tarot cards to receive images of power. It is especially helpful to use the medicine wheel to locate power animal images. By keeping a record of your strong impressions, you are tapping into your personal symbology. If you are working with a group, it may be helpful to do a guided meditation or vision quest before beginning artwork. This can create an atmosphere of magickal energy where the muse descends and guides all involved. Often our ideas need to be sparked by looking at pictures – explore books that contain Goddess images, animals, portraits, scenes of exotic lands and people. You never know just when and where you will be blessed by Brigid's gift of inspiration.

We start with an idea about who we are and what we want to emphasize about who we are.

Here is a list of objects that can be collected for making ritual and empowerment necklaces, and also used when making fans, masks and other power crafts.

Beads: Glass beads, clay beads, Indian beads, pearls, costume jewelry, brass and silver beads, bone beads and buttons, fish bones, plastic beads, handmade beads of Sculpey*.

You never know just when and where you will be blessed by Brigid's gift of inspiration.

Miscellaneous: Bells, Goddess figures, amulets, charms, crystals, rocks, metals, animal figures, sea shells, pieces of wood, seeds and seed pods, leaves, tiny pine cones.

Fabric: Yarns in many colors, metallics, fuzzy and wild, jute, hemp, fur, leather (scraps are great), cotton and calicos (used like in rag rugs), cording, gift wrap ribbon, lace trim, any kind of ribbon.

Equipment: Scissors, white glue, glue gun (optional), glue sticks, crochet hooks, large needles and heavy thread (I use waxed linen thread which will string beads without a needle; purchased at leather stores), beading needles and beading thread (size A), pie tins to hold beads and charms after stringing.

While I am gathering my objects for an empowerment necklace, I store them in bowls on my altar. They become enriched during daily ritual and begin to store up power. I plan a necklace by thinking of the Goddess it is to invoke, by collecting images that will reflect her image, and by empowering the necklace with charged objects and colors that will visually communicate the necklace's purpose. I work with these three aspects until it is time to birth the necklace. When I have collected enough (and you will have to intuit this), I begin to string the beads and amulets, usually using about thirteen strands that will dangle from the main cord (see illustration). I feel numbers are an important part of the magick that goes into the necklace. I tie knots three times, and use beads in multiples of three, invoking the triple aspect of the Goddess.

You are now ready to assemble your empowerment necklace.

First, there is a question of what kind of base your necklace will be built on. I use polyester cord, the kind used for making braided rugs. Check out your local fabric and craft stores for suitable materials. These cords should be cut long enough to tie securely with a knot (worn at the back of the neck and wrapped with yarn, leather or fabric to hide the knot ends and match the body of the necklace). After knotting the ends together to create the desired length – I prefer to wear my necklaces long, lying upon my breasts and covering my heart chakra – you will now begin wrapping the cord in whatever material you have chosen.

Start at one end and work toward the center. Reverse your colors (if you want to) at the center and work backwards with the colors until both sides are even. I usually wrap about eight inches of the cord if it is already covered with fabric. If the cord

Illustration by Joann Powell Colbert

is raw, I glue and wrap fabric around it. This gives texture and interest. It is possible to wrap your cord in ribbon or yarn; embroidery floss is beautiful when wrapped. Use a small crochet hook to pull the ends inside the wrapped area, thereby hiding the ends. Take your time and go slowly – wrapping is tedious and you will have an urge to hurry. This will be the foundation for your necklace and your magic, so do it with "intent." If you have glued your wrapping onto your cord, let it dry overnight. It could slip if you start to tie on amulets before it is secure.

Lay your necklace cord on a table top, facing you as if you were looking into a mirror or the reflection in a lake. You will work on this flat surface while trying out what arrangements you like of the amulets you've gathered for this particular necklace. I like to attach strips of fabric and/or leather to the cord, creating a fluffy and primitive look. I then tie on amulets and embellishments on top of the fabric. I may spend an hour or more arranging and rearranging my magical assortment of beads and amulets. Use your imagination and feel free to call on your inner guides to lend you inspiration. Now is a good time to work with music or meditation. Sometimes I feel the flow so strongly that I cannot stop applying my trinkets, but if I feel stuck, I go away for awhile to clear my head and free myself of garbage.

When you have settled on an assortment of amulets, etc., tie them on front to back, hiding the knots as best you can. I use several strands of waxed linen thread to string my beads on, but you can use fishing wire, thin wire, heavy beading thread, anything that will go through the beads, as long as it is sturdy and can take the wear. The beads and amulets, especially heavy ones or metal charms, will cut through the thread with time. Over the course of wearing the necklace, check your amulets for signs of wear, and replace them as needed or just restring them. Again, use a crochet hook to fit the ends of the thread under the wrapping or behind a piece of fabric. Try to stay neat without cutting our thread too short. It is best to leave a quarter inch above the knot for safety.

After the amulets and charms have been secured, try on your necklace and trim it to the desired shape. Now you can attach special magical items such as feathers, ribbons, large beads, glitter, puff paints, sea shells and twigs. I always like to have one or two special items tied onto my necklace, like a "The Earth is our Mother" button from an Earth Day ritual I attended, or several mockingbird feathers I found near my home (these were glued on and the ends secured down by a button). The necklace is a growing thing; you will want to add talismans all the time. The abundance or simplicity is up to you – this is your magic and it should look like your manifestation of power, not anyone else's. Be happy with yourself and what you create. Every necklace is a unique, one-of-a-kind masterpiece!

Caring for Your Empowerment Necklace in a Sacred Way

- Don't get your necklace wet or try to wash it if it gets dirty. It's better to trim the soiled part off and reweave a new piece of cloth, leather, feathers, etc., into the necklace. I try not to wear my necklaces direct on my skin, as the sweat of a healthy pagan discolors the material and begins to wear and disfigure it.
- It's best to store the necklace hanging from a hook, on the wall, etc. They look great hanging over altars.
- Don't limit yourself to just one: create a gallery of empowerment necklaces for each elements or aspect you wish to invoke. Be on the lookout for new ideas and new kinds of materials that can be used to express the Goddess in you through your ritual jewelry.
- Things do fall off, get caught on surfaces or just break once in awhile. The necklace is constantly evolving – be open when a piece of it bites the dust, and just add something new. We learn through our mistakes!
- The empowerment necklace makes a great gift for special occasions, for coven members, spirit-sisters and family members. It's a way of giving magic and power to those we love and cherish.

Honoring the Completion of the Necklace

For those of you who enjoy ritual (and which of us doesn't!), you can create a completion ritual to honor your necklace. This could be as simple as smudging the necklace with burning sage or incense, and calling the four corners to empower the necklace with their aspects. If you have made your necklace with friends, it is a beautiful experience to sit in a circle together and "show and tell" your necklaces. Introduce the necklace to your circle sisters, tell of the images you received when

Call on your inner guides to lend you inspiration.

making it. Tell of your hopes and aspirations that have been woven into the piece. Name your Goddesses and invoke them into the necklace with song, music, chanting or silence. We are what we manifest, and we live as our potential selves – each act of ritual bridges a present reality we wish to experience. And so, our necklaces move us to an image of ourselves we wish to attain.

As in ancient times when art techniques – basket weaving, pottery, loom work, etc. – were passed on from woman to woman, tribe to tribe, we in contemporary times have re-established this network through what could be called the womanspirit oral tradition. The techniques for making empowerment necklaces were shown to me by Laura Hines-Jurgens, who learned it from Gwen Gibson. ○

Regarding homemade beads and amulets made from Sculpey: there are several brands of plastic modeling clay available in hobby and craft stores (also in art supply stores) which can be used to make unique beads and molded and sculpted amulets and Goddess figures. The directions are on the package and it is simple to create your own personal empowerment figures and symbols from this medium. You will find material that can be used as molds or imprinters everywhere, from buttons to kitchen utensils. What's important is the look and message – this is where the power starts to become generated.

> *Name your Goddesses and invoke them into the necklace with song, music, chanting or silence.*

Epitaph

Sitting in Circle, we spoke
Of what irritated in life
What we wished changed in a new age.
Grandmother's turn:
"I'm serious now, don't laugh
Have you ever noticed the obituaries?
I'm tired of reading (and I quote)
    'Preceded in death by her husband
    Beloved Sunday School Teacher,
  Nursery Leader, Relief Society Worker
       and Door Greeter
     She was a homemaker. . .'"

We groaned at the standard formula,
but what's to be done?
"Take it back!" she said. "Write your own!
That's what I'm doing.
Forbid that loving family to print
Other than what you wish. Think of the
possibilities."

So say of me when gone ahead:
      She so loved the Goddess
Ever were raised her arms in the moonlight.
    Many were her altars
      And husbands
    Always love in her life.
   Studied well to bless and cure
  Raised up sons to honor the Earth.
Played with her dolls and was happy that way.
     Blessed be."

Say of me when gone ahead,
she loved the Goddess well.

Gretchen Faulk

Once in a Blue Moon

Wishes come true

By Kris Fawcett

Often the rituals or spells we weave bring results that are inconclusive, or only approximate the effect we had in mind. So I'd like to share with you my experience of being involved in a ritual that proved to be more powerful than any of us suspected at the time, of a spell cast under the light of the Blue Moon and how it worked itself out beautifully.

"Once in a Blue Moon" is how we describe something that happens only once in a very great while. A Blue Moon is the second full moon in a single calendar month, and is a rare event indeed. When one of my women's circle sisters who shares my love of astronomy discovered that May 1988 was just such a double-blessed month, she called me to propose that we create a ritual to celebrate the occasion.

We wanted the tone of the ritual to be light and joyous in keeping with the anything-goes spirit of the Blue Moon, beneath which anything can happen. So we invited everyone to come to Renee's house an hour or so before the ritual was to start, to bake cookies in shapes that symbolized our wildest dreams, those things we dared ask for only "once in a Blue Moon."

Blue was the theme for the evening: blue ritual attire, blue cookie dough, blue Kool-Aid to drink, blueberries and blue corn chips and bleu cheese dip to munch on. While the cookies were baking, we went outside to gaze at the rising moon through a blue filter I'd improvised, just to get us in the right mood.

With circle cast, we lit blue candles and went in a round describing our wildest Blue Moon dreams. My cookie was in the shape of a stone trilithon, because I'd longed to visit Stonehenge since I was a little girl. And the more I learned of women's spirituality over the years, the more magickal places in the British Isles called to me: Avebury, with its complex configuration of Goddess-related neolithic sites, its long barrows, Lammas mound and great stone circle and avenues. Glastonbury Tor, the priestesses' isle in *The Mists of Avalon*. Ireland, with its Bridget-blessed hills and little folk and spiraled Newgrange barrow. The list had grown impressively over time, and I boldly voiced my wish to see them all, to learn what I needed to learn from each place, to deepen in my understanding of the Goddess and her places in the world. And, I added as a practical afterthought, to be able to accomplish this magickal journey in such a way that I wouldn't be left bankrupt! Blessed be, chimed in all those in the circle, weaving our spells on the Blue Moon tide.

Three days later I received a brochure in the mail, printed on blue paper, describing an upcoming Women's Mysteries Tour of magickal sites in Great Britain, including Stonehenge, Avebury, Glastonbury Tor, Newgrange and other Irish places, and more. As if the Goddess was just making sure I got the connection, on the front of the brochure was a drawing of a Stonehenge trilithon with a (blue) moon rising over it.

Have you ever felt the flow of your life literally curving toward something? Now I know why our craft is called wicca, from the Old English word meaning "to bend," as in a river, as in a reed. By the time I'd finished reading that brochure I no longer had any doubt: this was the next step on my path, this was the journey I'd been waiting all my life to make. When the Blue Moon decides to act, I marveled, she doesn't waste any time!

Still, there remained the seemingly insurmountable financial obstacle. Where was I, who couldn't manage to save even a hundred dollars for any length of time, going to get the $2600 needed for the trip (and in less than six weeks' time)?

Blessed be, chimed in all those in the circle, weaving our spells on the Blue Moon tide.

I knew I could probably qualify for a loan, but that seemed unwise in the extreme for one who was already living from paycheck to paycheck. Yet how could I let this perfect opportunity pass?

One of the worst things you can do to a Libra is force her to make an important decision in a short time. After listening to me agonize over the

It was outstanding! Our all-woman group of thirteen (!) pilgrims, three guides and two English college students we hired as drivers visited all the places I'd dreamed and quite a few more besides. Magickal occurrences abounded, wondrous sights and beings presented themselves everywhere, and all-in-all the experience was about as close to perfection as I've ever come.

Magickal occurrences abounded, wondrous sights and beings presented themselves everywhere.

Heading back to the "real world" wasn't as bad as I would have thought, because the experience had changed me and I saw everything with new eyes. Still, there were the inevitable financial consequences of my loan to face. Where I'd always just gotten by, now I teetered constantly on the brink of budgetary disaster.

But wait, there's more: the story has a happy ending, for the Blue Moon wasn't quite done working her magic after all.

This spring, the company I've worked for for seven years decided to terminate its employee profit-sharing plan. Each of us had the option of taking control of our vested amounts, or leaving it in the common pool until we retired. Can you guess which option most of us chose?

The bulk of my money will be rolled over into an IRA to avoid tax penalties, but I kept enough to pay off my loan, which

situation, my friends and family nearly to a person gave me the same basic advice: Trust the Force, Luke. If this trip meant so much to me, they said, then by all means do it, and have faith that the Goddess would provide me with a way of getting by. Then I turned on PBS, and there was Joseph Campbell talking about how those who follow their bliss find that doors will open for them.

Well, who am I to argue with Joseph Campbell? (Not to mention the Goddess.) So, to make a long story short, I took a deep breath and did something completely illogical, financially irresponsible, and absolutely right: I borrowed the money, and three months later was on a Venus Adventure in England and Ireland.

puts me back where I was before all this began. An especially nice touch: I received my profit-sharing check on the day of the full moon in late May – exactly one year after our Blue Moon Ritual.

So the wheel has turned full cycle, and I'm once again financially stable, and immeasurably richer in spirit than I was a year ago. I've learned that sometimes the best thing to do is just turn off that logical rational voice that keeps coming up with Good Reasons why you shouldn't take leaps of faith. Like the Fool in the tarot deck who steps blissfully off the edge of a cliff, with the help of the Blue Moon you might just find that you can fly. ○

Illustration by Wahaba Nuit-Cat Heartsun

She Changes Everything She Touches

Body change as ritual magic

By Lunaea Weatherstone

The Goddess comes in all shapes and sizes. We honor each other and ourselves as living images of Her. She is the Maiden, light and energetic, slim and small-breasted, Artemis and Kore. She is the Mother, abundant and lush, round and soft, rooted to the Earth, Demeter, Mawu. She is the Crone, the changing body, incorporating wisdom as its strength, maturity as its grace. We love each of these images, and encourage our sisters to appreciate their own unique physical beauty, whatever their shape or capabilities. We are not all Amazons, we are not all Earth-Mothers; we are all beautiful.

However, there may come a time on your path when you choose to change the body you inhabit. Whether we want to become rounder or thinner, stronger or more limber, it is often a time of conflict for sensitive women of spirit. Wanting to change your body may bring up feelings of confusion. Anger at the society that insists we be thin and hard may keep you from losing weight doesn't feel right anymore. Fear of being disapproved of by that same society may keep you from letting your body gain weight to a point that feels safe and comfortable for you. And because you know you represent the Goddess, because you know you are the Goddess, a desire to change the body you are in may feel like a rejection of some aspect of your spirituality.

I've been experiencing some of these feelings and conflicts for a long time. While I love and honor my large woman's body, a symbol of abundant grace, in recent moons I've been needing to know what it feels like to be smaller, after so many years of being large. This brought up a lot of "stuff" for me. Having been shaped like the Venus of Willendorf for as long as I can remember, and being an outspoken advocate of that image of beauty, how could I even think about losing

weight? Was this a rejection of the Goddess, of my large sisters whom I honor so much, and of my own values and self-respect?

One of the first obstacles for me was in truly understanding what I meant by "The Goddess comes in all sizes." I'd been saying that for a long time, but I hadn't really come to terms with the fact that one of the sizes She comes in is "Small," as well as "Medium," "Large," and like me, "Extra-Large." I am probably typical in that I've been seeing the Goddess in my own image, and when I wanted to change the image of myself, it seemed to be a negation of myself as Goddess. Wanting to manifest a different aspect of Her became okay once I remembered that every woman I see on the street is the Goddess. A lot of them were smaller than I was by about 100 pounds, and they are Goddess, as much as I.

Changing the body seems to me to be a magical working, alchemy, a transformational mystery. As magic, it requires that all five elements (Earth, Air, Fire, Water, and Spirit) be part of the process.* Using the pentagram as a symbol for this work, I began to see each arm of the star as equally important. I offer these thoughts to you, for use in making physical changes of any sort.
* Thanks to Shekhinah for this inspiration.

Begin with Air, the element of the mind. The first step in magical workings is a clear vision of your intentions. How do you want to be different? Have a photograph, drawing, or other inspirational image of the change you are making. Use meditations and visualizations that reinforce those intentions. Tapes and videos can be very useful as tools to aid you in keeping a clear focus on your goal. Hypnosis, which is a technique of relaxation and repeated positive suggestions, is a good way to strengthen your own visions of change for your body. I have

One of the first obstacles for me was in truly understanding what I meant by "The Goddess comes in all sizes."

been helped by subliminal tapes, which have messages too soft to be heard by the conscious mind, but which are absorbed by the unconscious. Some of these have soothing music, and some have a sort of "white noise," such as waves breaking, which can be played quietly under normal conversation or while you work.

One of the most powerful magical tools is affirmation. Many of us use affirmations every day, as well as in ritual magic. For changing your body with self-love, it is important that these be tuned to the moment, as well as to your long-term goal. For example, it is not enough to say, "I have the body of an Amazon, strong and powerful." That's a great affirmation, and a wonderful image to hold of yourself. But you also need the daily affirmations, such as, "I love my beautiful Goddess body," "Everything I eat turns to health and beauty," or "I have all the energy I need to move my body today." Write these daily affirmations on small pieces of paper and tape them up around your house and workplace. Put one on your dashboard of your car, on your computer, on your television, on every light switch. Change them often, so that you don't start looking right past them, or, if you live with others, have a friend or family member change them without telling you, so that you will be surprised by a new thought some morning while brushing your teeth.

Another important aspect of Air is speech. Speak your intentions to those who are closest to you. Ask for verbal support and encouragement. Let them know that you also need to be honored for the body you have now, not just for changes you want to make. Understand the power of the spoken word, the energy and intention it carries – when someone asks you how you are doing with your new body project, try saying, "GREAT!!", no matter how that day is going. It may change your energy enough to help you focus on your goal or run that extra mile.

Air is the element of beginnings, intentions, visions, inspiration and plans. We need those to start us up and keep us focused. Now we move on to Earth, manifesting the change.

We are incarnate, in a body, and we need to give thanks for that. Wanting to change does not, and cannot, mean that we do not love our bodies now. I don't believe it's possible to make a permanent positive body change from a position of self-dislike.

We are incarnate, in a body, and we need to give thanks for that.

So, with the Earth arm of the star in mind, remember to celebrate the body you are in now. Touch and stroke your own skin. Pay attention when your lover touches you. Feel the roundness or the thinness or the softness of your body as it is now. While you are working to create a body change, be extra-sure to do the sensual things that give you pleasure, such as bubble baths (my own personal favorite, as anyone knows who has ever tried to get me on the phone), naps, massage and/or self-massage, clothes that make you feel good at each stage of your body-change, and other sensual treats for the outside of your body.

The inside of your body relates to Earth as well. Choosing the foods that feed you and the movement that feels right for you are ways that we ground our intentions in physical reality. Learn about nutrition, about anatomy and healing. Ask your body what it needs, and listen for the answers. Maybe you need to eat meat, or maybe you need to only eat live foods. Maybe you need quiet walks in the early morning or maybe you need a sweaty aerobic workout twice a week. To make a physical change, you will need to do something you are not in the habit of doing now. While it may be possible to just wish yourself thinner or stronger or healthier, I've never known anyone who's done it! (If you have, let me know, quick!)

Your body is the Earth, and the Earth is your body. Honor that connection with the most gentle loving care you would give to any beloved friend or child. The physical, earthy reality is that, even though we are spirit, we are in a body for a reason. We are animals. As animals, we have emotional feelings and desires, as well as physical needs. This is the Water arm of the pentacle.

In order to have a positive and successful body change, you must want it. To wish for something is an important step in any magic work. Working through doubts, letting feelings flow through you, has to happen. The trick is to not let them trip you up, so that your body-changing project comes to a halt. For example, if you are in the habit if eating for comfort, as I am, then there will be times when that seems to be the only way that comfort can reach you. And so sometimes we will surrender to that, and that's okay. We are not trying to be saints, just to be healthy! Self-love and acceptance are part of the watery you.

But it is also possible to either find other comfort (perhaps in the Earth arm of the star, with its lovely bubble baths!), or to just let those watery emotions and needs and fears flow over and through you. Just watch them, dive into them, go with that flow, even if it seems negative. You don't have to have that doughnut so that you won't be sad. You don't even need to do intense work to figure out why you're sad or to fix it. Just be sad. Be needy. Want the doughnut – it's okay. Grieve for the old bad habits as they fall away from you. Cry, sigh, sleep, sit and stare at the wall and be bored. Let all the fears about changing your body, the arguments and insecurities, come out, and then sit there and look at them.

When we feel all awash in doubt and nebulousness, a spark of discipline and will is sometimes needed to help us get back on track. Does this sound scary? Do you feel that you don't have the discipline to make this change? Fire – will power – is the one magical thing that our society focuses on to excess. They forget the other four arms of the pentagram and think that all you have to do to be strong and healthy and perfect is to take charge, quit stalling, and get down to business. "Just do it." "Shape up!" Well! I don't know about you, but my will power often needs help. When it's a choice between cooking a healthy dinner when I'm tired or stopping for a quick fast food fix, it's my will that has to take control and get me home. Sometimes I offer up my will to my Spirit Guides. "Help keep me focused, keep me from being distracted from my goals," is a frequent prayer.

Fire is the generator of courage and endurance, as well. The flame that keeps us moving, whether running or walking or stretching gently. Fire is the part of us that takes a risk, makes the leap of faith that moving into an unknown physical realm involves. If you have always had one kind of body, and you are changing that form, it's scary. It's a death, in a way. Where is the old you? Is that lost forever? The courage to change, the will to change, the endurance to change . . . and to know that the Spirit is the same, whatever the packaging.

The fifth arm of the star is Spirit. The part of us that understands what is meant by "This body, this temple, this is the Goddess in me." The work you do at your altar, the prayer and rejoicing for being in a body at all, and for being in this body in particular, at every stage, this is Spirit work that is essential for successful change. Give thanks to the Mother for birthing you. Give thanks for the earth that nourishes you, the air that inspires you, the water that cleanses you, the fire that warms you.

This body, this temple, this is the Goddess in me.

Surrender to the knowledge that whatever you do is right, and failure is impossible. If you truly love yourself and desire to change your body, it will be done. Simple as that.

If, as you work through these changes, you discover that the change you thought you wanted doesn't feel right, let it go. The most important change you can make is the change to self-love and acceptance. To see yourself as beautiful, just as you are, is to give thanks to the Goddess, and to show Her to all you meet. ○

Illustration by Joann Powell Colbert

A Red Tape Ritual

Working through obstacles

By Guusje Moore

"I see the red tape becoming red strawberries that adorn the top of a red cake."

My group, which grew out of a "Cakes for the Queen of Heaven" class, formed several years ago. Most of the members are self-employed or somehow work outside the mainstream. However, in the course of our various business endeavors, we all deal with the patriarchal society on a regular basis, and thus have frequent encounters with red tape. One week, a couple of us were having severe problems; projects were being choked and delayed. So we created a red tape ritual.

As we always do, we gathered on a Thursday at Sue's apartment. Her altar, which occupied a good portion of the dining room floor, was ablaze with candlelight dancing off crystals. We greeted each other with hugs and cries of welcome, and took some time to catch up on everyone's activities, loves, joys and sorrows.

Seating ourselves cross-legged around the altar, we cast our circle, invoking the four directions, the crystals of the Earth's core, and the galaxies of the universe. A red fireproof plate, intended to receive the red tape, was placed in the center of the altar. Each member took a strip of red construction paper, symbolizing the red tape that we wished to unscramble. We began with a word association – tossing phrases from one to another – "red tape," "I'm sorry, they're in a meeting," "bureaucratic snarls," "he's at lunch," "the computer is down." The clichés of our time bounced from one woman to another and took on energy of their own – "federal holiday," "she will call you back," "fill out form 4X1 in triplicate," "that's not my department," "let me transfer you," "that line is busy." On and on the words came – "it's in the mail," "that file is misplaced," "maybe tomorrow," "call me next week," "no, that information is incorrect."

Then, each of us took her strip of paper and visualized what we would like it to become.

"I see a large red dragon that sprouts two heads for each one that is lopped off. A strong woman appears with a sword and drives it back into its lair, where it falls in submission."

"I see the coils of red tape slowly unwinding and unraveling and falling away from our work."

"I see the red tape weaving itself into a red velvet carpet that will carry our projects to their fruitfulness and fulfillment."

"I see the red tape becoming red strawberries that adorn the top of a red cake. All of us gather round and partake of it, and thus the red tape vanishes." That visualization was greeted with a chorus of "ummms" and "ohs."

"My paper is all knotted up, and as I speak, I unwind and smooth it out, as the roadblocks will smooth out. It is now a spiral, showing how the work will continue upwards in a smooth path. I then fold it in half and light both ends to show that it will completely disappear."

As each of us finished speaking, the other members intoned "so be it." We touched our papers to a candle and dropped the burning strip into the plate. The strips coiled and twisted and smoldered, and we silently watched them turn into ashes. The room was calm, and we could feel the energy spiraling upwards with the smoke symbolizing the red tape that we knew would begin to unravel itself during the upcoming week. We opened the circle, invoking blessings upon our projects, our wishes, and those members who were not resent. We ate bread and cheese and chocolate chip cookies, and then we parted, to meet again the following week.

Over the course of the two weeks following the ritual, the bureaucratic morass began to untangle and work was able to proceed. Blessed be! O

A Magic Mirror

Creating your own Tarot images

By Claire Jones

A fairy tale heavily interwoven with classical Wiccan lore, "Snow White" offers the notion of the Magic Mirror. I have often wished for such a mirror. It would reflect to me not only what is real, but what I want to see in myself, and what I would like for others to see. Imagine having a mirror showing you all that is inside, as well as outside, reflecting for your eyes the reality as well as the "glamour" that surrounds you. And perhaps reflecting a pathway for healing and transformation of old wounds and scars. Or a Magic Mirror serving as an eye into the future of what can be.

As a girl, I would often wear my grand purple velvet cape my stepmother made for me and prance around the yard, pretending to be the fairest of them all. Running inside to see myself in the full-length mirror . . . running out again to show all the world (that is, the bees and the insects and dogs and cat in our yard) what a beautiful queen I was. An image of power and glory in my purple cloak. It was a wonderful fantasy.

Of course, the process of conforming and aligning to what is a socially acceptable female in the United States of the late 20th century took away all my fantasies of the Magic Mirror. Took away the image of power and glory I was as a seven year old playing in my cloak . . . the Magic Mirror became a sweet but archaic childhood notion.

I was an adult of 32 years when I began studying Tarot. I slowly began to unravel a part of my child brain that had been tightly bound and stored in a dusty corner of consciousness – the mind of myth and symbols. I found it difficult at first to understand the images on the Motherpeace deck. My teacher patiently encouraged me, coaxed and pulled that part of me that had been chopped up by the swords in my head. Communication in pictures instead of words became a part of my thinking once again. It was a long process, but incredibly healing.

At one lesson, my teacher gave me an assignment: "In pens, pencils, crayons or whatever, make a Tarot card of yourself. Use an image of what you would like to be. Include some things that you are now. Include symbolism of who you are in your life, such as a mother. Place your image in the middle of the card, with your name at the top, and your title underneath. Maybe something like 'Priestess of _____' or 'Daughter of _____.' If numbers are important to you, choose an appropriate number and place it at the top of the card as well. You can use this card to show yourself the issues you are struggling with in your life now, or you can use it to reflect a future you want to create, or a tool to shun a past you wish to discard."

The Magic Mirror lives! What an incredible opening it can be to construct your own image. To see the past, present and future of your life on a sheet of paper, drawn by your own hand. My mind was filled with possibilities. Images flashed by me; almost immediately I knew some of what my card would contain. The resulting Tarot card, "Claire: Priestess of Longing and Pathos," was an astounding representation of my life at that time. Portions of the pain of my past, a projection of the future in the hazy image of a little pink bundle who is now my daughter (drawn more than a year before her conception). My love for my precious son, born to the blue moon of 1985. I photostatically reduced and used Motherpeace Tarot images, powerfully effective character symbols for three people who dominated my subconscious during that time. Included symbols of aspects of my character I viewed as disturbing to my inner harmony – just to make sure I would take a good look at them! Each of those aspects of my personality have substantially modified since that time.

To see the past, present and future of your life on a sheet of paper, drawn by your own hand.

45

Her mirror

is dark,

the four

corners

filled with

mystery.

The Tarot is both a complex and simple form of communicating with the Goddess. She will speak to you through the Tarot; you can speak to her. Whether it be through the images of a published deck or your own hand-drawn symbols, it is not so much a system to learn as it is principles to grasp and grow from. As has become so obvious in our television/computer screen/video-oriented world, visual image can be powerful in altering and shaping human consciousness. Drawing images has also become a recognized form of psychotherapy and is encouraged along with the more traditional forms of journal and diary writing.

Whether or not you think you can draw, whether or not your card is aesthetically pleasing to you, creating your own Tarot image can become a regular part of your introspection process. It can become a tool for projection and transformation, a meditation, a method of prayer. It is a tool ripe with potential. ○

Madonna Mia

Her bedroom is dark,
the four corners
filled with mystery.
In the center of one
wall is a dresser
between stiff, wooden
chairs. On the dresser
is a crocheted scarf,
the color of tea. On
the scarf is a square,
flat, silver-plated, long-
handled brush and a comb,
its mate, dug into its bristles,
a hand mirror and a little
papier-maché box of hair pins.
In the center of the dresser
is a statue of the Virgin,
between long, thin candles.
Before the Virgin is a short,
round votive candle
in a thick glass cup.
On the wall over the dresser
hangs a mirror. Tucked into
one bottom corner is a
palm cross to keep away
mal occhio. Tucked into
the other bottom corner
is a picture of her daughters,
to see the future.
Hung over one top corner
is a string of rosary beads,
circle of the Virgin. Hung
over the other top corner
is a scapular, to be worn
against her skin for protection.
Her mirror is dark,
the four corners
filled with mystery.
In the center of the mirror
is another Goddess
image – my grandmother's
brown and wrinkled
face, as she combs
her wispy gray hair.

Rose Romano

Illustration by Wahaba Nuit-Cat Heartsun

Earthworks

Pentacles in the Tarot

By Lunaea Weatherstone

Hundreds of tarot decks have been published over the centuries, and we all have our favorites. The most popular traditional deck is probably still the Rider-Waite Tarot, illustrated by Pamela Colman Smith, and the most powerful and popular of the women's decks is undoubtedly the Motherpeace Tarot, by Vicki Noble and Karen Vogel. If you went for a tarot reading twenty or more years ago, a reader using the Rider-Waite deck may have interpreted your cards differently than the reader of today. By studying other decks, such as Motherpeace, readers who still prefer the more traditional decks can gain a freshness of interpretation, a more contemporary or more archetypal interpretation. For example, comparing the suit of Pentacles in each of these decks gives us a new slant on the age-old concerns of work, prosperity and material well-being.

The suit of Pentacles has evolved over the years. In older decks, this suit was often called Coins, and represented the merchant class, specifically dealing with money and work. The attainment of personal wealth and mastery of one's profession has always been an important goal, and an abundance of Pentacles in one's reading was considered auspicious, a sign of good fortune to come. This is the general interpretation of Pentacles in the Rider-Waite deck – the attainment of your place in society through the acquisition of money and saleable skills. The Motherpeace deck has a slightly different approach to this suit, as we shall see. In the Motherpeace cards, the suit of Pentacles is called Discs, and is illustrated by Native American images. The focus is still on wealth and the attainment of success, but personal success is not measured by the society's opinion as much as by one's own self-satisfaction.

To begin, lay out your Pentacle cards from the ace through the ten (we will not be dealing with the court cards in this discussion). Take a moment a walk through the story they tell. Examine the images, see what metaphors the symbols bring up for you. Are there cards that you are attracted to or cards you feel repelled by? Where are you in the cards? Where would you like to be? After reading this article, take another look at the cards before you, and choose one or two to place on your altar, perhaps to represent the work you are doing now, and one to represent changes you would like to make in your work situation.

Let's compare the two decks, one card at a time, beginning with the Aces. In the Rider-Waite deck and in the Motherpeace deck, Aces represent a gift, often a divine gift. The Rider-Waite deck shows a hand reaching out of the clouds, offering a gold pentacle. There is a path leading from this gift, a path that leads through an arch of red roses off to a distant mountain range. The traditional interpretation is that of "the most favorable of all cards." This is the attainment of perfect material contentment, wealth, ultimate success. The culmination of golden prosperity.

The Ace of Discs in the Motherpeace deck also represents an earthly gift. But here, instead of symbolizing the culmination of material success, the image of a baby on the card represents the beginning. You are given the means to success. The power is within you. Vicki Noble says that Aces mean a "Yes!" from the Goddess. So if you are asking a question about a gift, money, a baby, something materializing on the earthly plane, this card is a Yes. In a more general position in your reading, this card shows that you are ready to receive abundance, and that you have the gifts you need to manifest what you need. This card relates to the Major Arcana card "The Magician" – the gathering of tools to manifest your desires. The Ace of Pentacles or Discs lets you know that you have

By studying other decks, such as Motherpeace, readers who still prefer the more traditional decks can gain a freshness of interpretation.

the blessings of the Goddess. Move forward with confidence.

The Two of Pentacles shows a young man dancing as he juggles two Pentacles within an infinity symbol. The stormy sea in the background rocks two ships, mirroring his rocky dance of balance and survival. The traditional interpretation of this card is gaiety and recreation, and yet there is the

in the movie of life-death-rebirth, and that this, too, shall pass. The trick, in both decks' images, is to remain balanced (literally in the Rider-Waite card and spiritually in the Motherpeace card) while life's storms rage around us.

The Rider-Waite Three of Pentacles is a picture of a master craftsman showing his work, in this case ornamentation on a church, to two men, a monk and

The message of the cards is to let go of your worldly worries by turning to the spirit.

a hooded merchant. The card symbolizes pride in achievement, attainment of public recognition for skills, and mastery of one's craft. As such, it is a card of success, a positive card for those undertaking a task. While this craftsman is showing his solitary work to the community, the Three of Discs' women are building the temple of the Goddess *in* community. There is still pride in achievement, but it is the pride that comes from working in cooperation, admiration for another's work as well as your own. This card shows that building the

potential for bad news, perhaps from those ships. The juggling act is always precarious, and the gaiety could be short-lived. The Two of Discs illustrates this same precariousness with a young mother of twins, each with its own demands and desires. She stands grounded on the green grass of abundance, and a waxing moon shows her willingness to undertake this new task, knowing that this is just part of the infinite cycle of life. These babies will not be young and demanding forever. The two-headed snake passing through the movie reels shows us that this is just another scene

temple is as spiritual as worshipping in the temple, making this a powerful image for honoring work in the world.

The Four of Pentacles and the Four of Discs both show people holding fast to what is theirs. In the case of the Rider-Waite card, what is being held is money. This has been variously interpreted as an inheritance, a gift or knowing that your money is secure. In the Motherpeace card, what is being held is solitude. The inner self is what is being preserved here, and it is time, as the image shows, to close the

Illustration: "The Sybil," by Joann Powell Colbert

door and shut out the world for awhile. While the Four of Pentacles has also been interpreted as selfishness and greed, the Four of Discs is selfishness in a much more positive sense. If we don't take alone-time for the self to renew and center, the work we do in the material world will suffer. This is not a permanent withdrawal, but a short time apart to think, plan, talk to the Goddess, and emerge richer in spirit, so that that the work may go on.

The Five of Pentacles shows two beggars in the snow outside a lighted church window. The Five of Discs shows a woman working with clay or dough. Both cards symbolize a return to the spirit after a time of trouble. The Rider-Waite card shows people who have suffered materially from hunger and cold, being comforted by the light of the spirit. The Motherpeace card shows a woman who has suffered emotionally seeking comfort through a meditative act of creation. Working out worry and stress through the hands can achieve the same ends the beggars seek from their church. In both cases, the message of the cards is to let go of your worldly worries by turning to the spirit, and also serves as a reminder that spiritual growth often happens through material and emotional hardships. While the Rider-Waite card shows a turning from the earthly to the spiritual, the Motherpeace card, in true womanspirit fashion, shows a turning to the spiritual through the earthly, in this case through work.

The Sixes of Pentacles and Discs both illustrate the giving of blessings – the Rider-Waite card the blessing of alms, and the Motherpeace card the blessing of healing energy. The traditional meaning of the Six of Pentacles is of immediate prosperity that could change – a reminder that while you may be the giver of wealth now, you could be the beggar soon. This is a call to vigilance, a warning to pay attention both to your wealth and to your duty to your fellow humans. The Six of Discs gives a similar message, showing two people, one healing and one receiving. The card's position in the reading will tell you if you are the healer or the healed, the changer or the changed, but the meaning goes deeper. Someday you will need to give healing, someday you will need to be healed. The scales the merchant holds, and the polarity treatment being given by the healer, remind us to seek a balance of give and take, to avoid a co-dependent relationship, but to accept and surrender

to interdependence. Just as the Six of Pentacles shows the wealthy merchant putting stock in his heavenly future by the giving of alms, the Six of Discs shows that the giving and receiving of blessings assures us of a blessed reward.

The Seven of Pentacles indicates worry and fear regarding material abundance. A young man leans on his hoe, gazing at the crop of Pentacles he has been cultivating. Will his work be good enough? Will he be able to pay his bills? Will his business fail? These are the traditional interpretations for the Seven of Pentacles – worry about one's ability to manifest on the earthly plane what one needs to survive. The Seven of Discs, on the other hand, also comes up in a reading where there is worry about material wealth or work, but the message here is clearly, Don't worry; things take time. The pregnant woman in her melon patch knows that the baby must be born in its own time, just as the melon must ripen on the Goddess's schedule, not hers. If you have done your work well, like the man with his Pentacles and the mother-to-be with her melons, then the results are out of your hands. Trust in the Goddess to provide for your material needs. You have done the best you can.

The Eight of Pentacles shows a man happily at work making Pentacles – what a great job! He is an apprentice Pentacle-maker, and they just keep getting better and better. This is valuable work in his society, and he works in the assurance that, as his skill grows, so will his prosperity. This knowledge makes his work lighter, as he anticipates material reward. The Eight of Discs also shows craftspeople at work. Like the Pentacle-maker, their work is valued by their society. But the pleasure they take in their work comes not only from the anticipated financial reward. Rather, this is the happiness of Right Livelihood. When the work you do gives you joy, as the creation of pots, baskets and Pentacles gives the workers in both cards, then the material reward is just icing. Do what you love and the money will follow is the message of both Eights – for the love of your work increases your skill even as it enriches your spirit.

The Nines show another kind of love. Loving the things you own, the things you have brought to you through your work, is one of the joys of life. The Nine of Pentacle's woman has realized perfect peace and plenty, and is rejoicing in the beauty she

The giving and receiving of blessings assures us of a blessed reward.

has created around her. Her gown is decorated with symbols for the planet Venus, symbolizing the importance of grace and beauty in spiritual well-being. The Nine of Discs shows a woman celebrating that grace and beauty in another way, though the creation of a sand-painting. She has retreated from the world, like the Pentacles woman in her walled garden, to celebrate beauty. She loves her creation, and yet it is by its nature temporary, as is the woman's garden. These cards tell us to love what we own and to let it go in its time, confident that we have the skills to bring to us whatever we need for our material and spiritual abundance.

The Tens represent the fulfillment of material joys. The Ten of Pentacles shows a multi-generational family gathered together at home, enjoying their prosperity and resting from their labors. This card is interpreted as the ownership of property, the gaining of a material base and the security of home. The Ten of Discs also shows the security of home: as a community of loving friends. This card pictures a woman in the act of giving birth, surrounded by the protective, loving energy of women holding empowerment shields. They sing as she gives birth to – a child? an idea? a new project? a new job? The message is that of support and encouragement, not competition and jealousy. Each woman is empowered by the success of the others, as the Pentacles family is strengthened by the foundation of the home and continuity. The culmination of the Pentacles/Discs suit, therefore, is the gaining of emotional, familial and financial abundance.

Using these archetypal images, we can begin to explore what it means to have abundance, to succeed on the earthly plane, for Earth is the element of Pentacles/Discs. When we are grounded in Earth, we can then experience the emotions of Cups without drowning, the energy of Wands without burning out, and the challenges of Swords without being wounded. ○

The culmination of the Pentacles/ Discs suit, therefore, is the gaining of emotional, familial and financial abundance.

The Cowry Wish Charm:
A spell for nurturing our ideas and wishes

By Katlyn Miller

Take a fairly large cowry shell, such as "egg shell" or "leopard," and cleanse it thoroughly. Then rub it with fragrant oil and place it upon a green cloth. With red ink or blood (your own), write your idea or wish upon a small slip of parchment paper. This is placed next to the shell. Now put seven drops of milk and five drops of honey into the cowry shell. This symbolizes fertilization of the womb where your wishes will grow. Carefully fold the slip of paper with your wish on it, meditating upon your desire and seeing in your mind's eye the wish being born from the realm of ideas into the material world. Next, place the slip inside the shell entirely, saying:

> Born of Water
> Born of Earth
> Mother, give my
> Wishes birth
>
> Mead of heaven
> Seed of love
> As below, so
> As above
>
> Mother Shell
> Womb of the Sea
> This wish is born
> So mote it be!

Kiss thrice the shell and bury it in the Earth, the body of the Mother. Know your wish is taken care of and will be born within the year. When it has been realized, you may unearth the cowry shell and it may be used again for another "birth."

The Moon in Me

Life in the moonlight

By Deep River

It's been another busy week in the city. I'm exhausted. I wonder how I'll get through this last evening at the third of my three part-time jobs. But when the light of the full moon shines down upon me through the cool night air, it is easy to remember who and what I really am: beloved daughter of Gaea; sister to her other animal life, plants and rocks; witch – transformer of energy – priestess; celebrant of the wheel of life. As I let the moonlight remind me of these truths, the weariness drains from my body and I am aglow with Selene's silvery essence. I joyfully take responsibility for my part in the dance of life-death-rebirth upon Gaea's face. Instead of the heaviness I have felt all day, I am now energetic, confident, at peace. I leave my car in the dimly lit parking lot and walk across campus toward the classroom where my students wait. The stares I draw make me giggle. I'm dressed like any other instructor, am weighted down with the ordinary number of books and papers. Despite my feeling of lightness, I am reasonably sure that my feet really are touching the ground as I walk. I'm certainly not the first woman they've ever seen, and not even the prettiest. So why do they stare? They must sense that I have some special secret . . . perhaps one of them suspects the truth . . . that I have the Moon in me! ○

Illustration by Wahaba Nuit-Cat Heartsun

The weariness drains from my body and I am aglow with Selene's silvery essence.

Looking Within

Transforming yourself, transforming your life

By Pam Sekula

My power started to grow when my world crumbled and I had to look within and meet the woman I am.

Intentions, behavior and what it really looks like when my insides match my outsides. A couple of years ago, my beautiful daughter Barbara bleached her hair, wore ragged jeans, a black leather jacket and went through a "personality change." She also had a boyfriend who "didn't talk" (to her) but who carved his initials into her arm. This person also tried to burn down our house by throwing gasoline at it. I strongly suggested that the order of the day would be to get into treatment for alcohol and drug abuse and start to straighten out. One of the things she couldn't get over was how I knew something was wrong.

You may chuckle – I can look back and shake my head (it will be a long time before I chuckle about it). But very often we operate on the principle that everyone knows our good intentions and therefore should make allowances for the outrageous behavior. I know, because I, too, operated on the good intentions/bad behavior premise.

My "insides" (how I felt about myself) always compared themselves with your "outsides," how you looked. 99% of the time, I fell short. You had it all: brains, looks, popularity, enough of everything. So, I "faked it." I bought the bill of goods . . . the clothes, the make-up, the "right stuff." My insides knew the difference . . . my guts knew . . . but my head did not. I was old enough or sophisticated enough to know how to fake it, try to cover it up. My daughter fortunately didn't have that luxury . . . her insides and outsides matched. You could tell by looking at her how she felt about herself, life and everything else. It hurt.

My power started to grow when my world crumbled and I had to look within and meet the woman I am. I didn't like her. I had to go further back, to the child I was, and that started some of the healing.

I transformed myself into a single parent with three daughters and found myself sitting at the kitchen table one night/morning in a lot of pain . . . psychic, emotional, agonizing pain. I knew that I did not want a drink or a drug; I knew that my children and I were in trouble; I knew that I was going to have to change and I did not know how. Moreover, I was going to have to get rid of my false pride and ask for help . . . ask how to do some new things . . . ask how other women had done it.

The next transformation had to do with a formerly dependent woman turning into a gardener, making arrangements for the house to be insulated, having it painted (and being "taken," I'm sorry to say). I turned into a parent who cared enough about the lives of her children to make them very angry . . . so angry that there was a chance that they would leave and never come back. It was scary. I took that chance and still have their love . . . and gratitude. I found out that I liked garlic and raw onions, silence, Heavenly Hash ice cream and linguini with clam sauce (not necessarily all at one sitting). I loved the feel of white cotton and for awhile looked a lot like Nehru, all in white.

It wasn't just outwardly that I changed, although I was trying to match those outsides with what was growing within . . . strength, confidence, courage and direction

There were days and there were long, sad nights, when I was on my knees at the side of my bed sobbing into the mattress . . . the inner pain, again. One daughter was a runaway . . . out on the streets of who-knows-what city, sick and sad . . . the religion of my youth kept whispering, "Mea culpa, mea maxima culpa!" By day, I was fooling people into thinking I was coping . . . by night, I wanted to die. I did not die. I changed. Another transformation. I began to look within and not be afraid of who and what I found . . . and I began to love that strong/weak/happy/sad/loving/angry/kind woman . . . and pretty soon, inside and outside looked more and more alike.

One of my daughters told another woman, "My mother can do anything!" "Not everything," I laughed. "Well," she countered, "almost everything!"

I believe that no real change, no transformation of any magnitude, can occur without gut-wrenching, agonizing back-up-against-the-wall pain. We can learn without pain, we can learn and be motivated and enjoy ourselves . . . but my biggest challenges and successes are things I would have passed up, thank you, had it not been for the motivation of pain and the faith that pain has a beginning, middle and end. Good always comes from the effort.

You see, taking life on life's terms, "going with the flow," was something I always intended to do, yet ended up fighting and struggling every inch of the way. My intentions were to be the perfect mother-daughter-sister-wife-employee and, in so doing, end up the best beloved of all the people involved in the aforementioned categories. As you well know, the job of perfection is 24 hours a day, non-stop, no vacations. I intended to do many things, promised that I would and was not able to come across . . . I did that time and time again. My intention was to communicate with my family, but every time they received a letter from me, they were afraid to open it . . . seems I'd only write when I needed money, or when I was drinking.

When I said, "I love you," it was suspect. There was always a reason; I didn't think I was that kind of person, when, in fact, I was. Other people can spot it a mile away . . . why did they let it go on? Because they loved me and didn't know how to confront me, thereby enabling my behavior to continue. It's easier to confront a child or teenager, it's part of the responsibility. It's difficult to say to an adult, "Your behavior is atrocious, you'd better do something about it or else we can't have you around here . . . it is too painful."

What goes around, comes around. Some things did not change in my life as quickly as my attitude toward them did. There was a great deal of wreckage to clean up, there were hurt feelings that would not heal by a simple, "I'm sorry." I had to do more than mouth the words. I had to do more than read about what a good idea a right-minded attitude and life would be . . . I had to live that way! I had to act that way! One day at a time, I examined my motives, tried to live in what I found to be a more

I wanted to die. I did not die. I changed.

comfortable way and began sharing with others about how I felt, who I was and listened to who they were and how they felt. I was not unique in my being human; I was unique in my talents and abilities, my personality and inner self. I was sober.

It was necessary for me to make a decision to look even further within . . . Because of my childhood and young adult life, I had learned to "cope" in unhealthy ways. At six years sober, I went to a 28-day program in Minnesota and was introduced to more of who I am. My counselor said, "Get with the women! You need to do that for yourself." It occurred to me that what I most wanted to do in my life was to help other recovering women (all women, for that matter), increase my spirituality and write; I didn't know exactly how that would all come about, but I had a feeling that it was going to happen. This was Summer '86.

There are no coincidences. During the Winter of 1987, I designed some needlepoint canvasses and had lots of nice yarn left over. With them, I began a blank canvas and was happy with what emerged: a Native American scene, sky, sand and various symbols. It was abstract, yet not.

At the same time, I received the Llewellyn New Times and the tarot books caught my eye. I had been using a traditional deck and after reading about the Motherpeace book, felt that I would like a more women-oriented slant to my readings. There was no picture and not much description, but I was drawn to it and sent away for the book.

I finished the needlepoint and framed it. UPS dropped off a package and instead of the book, they had sent the Motherpeace deck! I decided to keep it and took the cards to my craftroom for "bonding."

While going through the beautiful cards one by one, I came to the 9 of Discs and there was my needlepoint picture! It was so similar that I knew it was no mistake. It was a definite sign to me that I needed to know more . . . next came Diane Stein's *The Woman's Spirituality Book*. I used the bibliography as my "required reading list." I've studied and pondered . . . I've written letters to some of the authors and have made a few friends . . . I've found publications like *SageWoman* and want to be a part of what it has to offer. Having looked within, I've met, accepted and/or changed my Self . . . my intentions coincide with my behavior . . . the quality of my life is wonderful. Troubles, sure, some pretty painful, but WomanSpirit is how I live . . . and who I am . . . and everyone benefits!

At present, I am halfway through a Women's Mysteries course taught by one of the most loving and magical women I've ever met. I had expressed to a friend that I wanted to know more, learn more and was directed to my teacher as being "the real thing"! Indeed, she is. Magical doors are opening. Power from within is growing. Blessed Be! ⚪

Magical doors are opening. Power from within is growing.

The Belly Dancer

I saw Yasmina dance today
with flirting eyes and lovely breasts
skin of gold and hung with bells that
sound to her lightest step,
that glint as she glides and sways.

The scarf round her hair was
the color of moon-tinted purple skies,
black veils were layered with clouds of red
and sewn with sequins to catch
the sweep of circling feet.

Bracelets, earrings, hide and seek veils
belly of smooth fascination.
Arms like snakes, hips in rhythm
impossible to imagine her stilled.

Surely
this is how women have always danced,
dances of pleasure, dances of birth
dance for a Goddess above.

This is how we have always played
for pay, for each other
for love of the drum and flute.
Yasmina trembles and the stars stop awhile,
she could dance for Astarte herself.

Gretchen Faulk

Self-Blessing Belly Dance

A sensuous solo ritual

By Judith Laura

I intuit, as have others involved in belly dancing, that the dance originated in ancient goddess worship and is a mime of the birth process. In an effort to reclaim the heritage of the dance, I have devised the self-blessing belly dance ritual that follows. Each woman may wish to improvise her own choreography, using traditional belly dance movements as embellishments to the ritual.

The circle is closed, the four corners are blessed by extending arms upward, striking the zills once while speaking (or thinking) the first line. The dancer touches the designated part of her body three times, with her veil, which is draped over her head, as she speaks or thinks the first line of each verse. She then strikes the zills once and rotates her hands from the wrists upward in supplication. The second line of the verse is accompanied by the dancer drawing her hands down in front of her, elbows leading, palms facing her body. If any part of the body is ailing, the words, "and heal" may be added to the request for blessing. I have done this for the womb, but if the dancer has no problem with this organ, she may want to omit this Or she may want to add it to the blessing for each organ, as a protective measure.

Great Mother,
I ask for thy protection and blessing.
Bless my mind,
that I may always know thy wisdom.
Oh Great Mother, bless and heal.
Bless my eyes, that I may always see thy beauty.
Oh Great Mother, bless and heal.
Bless my ears, that I may always hear thy music.
Oh Great Mother, bless and heal.
Bless my nose,
that I may always smell thy fragrance.
Oh Great Mother, bless and heal.
Bless my lips and tongue, that I may always taste
thy goodness and sing thy praises.
Oh Great Mother, bless and heal.
Bless my touch, that, like thine, it may heal.
Oh Great Mother, bless and heal.
Bless my breasts, that, like thee,
I may nurture others.
Oh Great Mother, bless and heal.
Bless and heal my womb, oh Mother of All,
and bless the fruit of my womb.
Oh Great Mother, bless and heal.
Great Mother, thank you for your protection
and for blessing this dance.
The circle is opened. ◯

Bless and heal my womb, oh Mother of All, and bless the fruit of my womb.

Illustration by Wahaba Nuit-Cat Heartsun

Old Year, New Year

Egyptian new year magick

By Normandi Ellis

Hathor, who, in her manifestation as night sky, bestowed her gifts of love, light and joy for over 8,000 years.

No one more loved festival than the ancient Egyptians. Their tombs and temples vibrate with portraits of women dancing and playing music in the service of the Goddess Hathor. The art recounts temple feast days, throngs of boats sailing, gardens and banquet halls filled with beautiful men and women bedecked in jewels and sniffing lotus, eating, drinking, talking.

The ancients coordinated their many festivals with no less than three astrological calendars – the lunar, solar and Sothic cycles, which determined the month, day and hour when divine beings made their true self and will known. That star-studded sky which they observed was the body of the Goddess Hathor herself, patroness of astrology, love and jubilee. Life and death were her domain, and the full and crescent moons appearing on her diadem measured cyclical time.

The New Year began on July 19th, when Isis appeared as the rising Sothic star that heralded the annual life-giving flood of the Nile. The week preceding the new year was replete with festivals, reminiscent of the way we moderns celebrate New Year's Eve by drinking, eating and feasting, talking and blowing horns. But amid all the celebration, the ancients did not forget the spiritual reason for this great party. Priests and priestesses also spent time in meditation, focusing their attention on exploring the mysteries of life, death and rebirth.

My own similar New Year/Old Year ritual is simple and rewarding. During the last week of the old year, I spend an hour each day writing in my journal, marking my passage through the year, preparing myself for the year to come. By noting the cycles through which I have passed, I acknowledge the part She has played in the births, losses and rebirths of the year.

Eve 1 – The Night of the Mothers

By ancient calendars, December 24th is celebrated as the Night of the Mothers. It is dedicated to Hathor, who, in her manifestation as night sky, bestowed her gifts of love, light and joy for over 8,000 years. So ancient was she that all other Egyptian Goddesses fused with her, including Isis, the prototype of the Virgin Mary. She offered a peaceful respite from the blazing sun, and her dark body manifests the passive and intuitive feminine attributes. The stars suspended from her body were her children, both divine and mortal. A seven-thousand-year-old portrait of Hathor depicts her as a dancing woman, holding and uplifting the stars.

More often she is seen as a beautiful woman wearing two crescent moons like the horns of a cow upon her diadem. Between these horns she bears the circle, simultaneously the sun, the moon and the egg of the world. Poet priestesses dedicated many prayers to her, such as this Hymn to Hathor:

O Great One who became sky,
you are strong and mighty.
Every place fills with your beauty.
The whole world lies down
beneath you. You possess it.
As you enfold earth and all creation in your arms
So have you lifted up me, a child of the Goddess,
And made me an indestructible star
within your body.

One of Hathor's oldest aspects was as the full-bellied hippo goddess named Opet. With her swollen belly and tongue darting between her teeth, she embodied the laboring Great Mother, who ruled the in-between places of life – womb and tomb, the transition between birth and death. In ancient times her celebration coincided with the winter solstice. The longest night of the year represented a period of waiting, a time of longing and of dreams.

The Night of the Mothers is a period of potentiality. It is the woman about to birth her life and dreams. She is full of intention. The Goddess does not give birth by accident, but by design. She imagines full well the gods, humans, plants and animals she wishes to manifest. The secret to manifestation is desire and intention.

I use this night to meditate on the future. Taking paper and pen, I ask myself: Specifically, what is it that I wish to manifest in the coming year? What part of myself am I birthing – to achieve my highest potential, to be joyful and creative, but what exactly does that mean? A single, clear, specific statement of intent puts me in the frame of mind where I can reach my goals. As children of the divine creative matrix, we share in her magical power. We create matter ourselves. Knowing what one wants, and keeping it foremost in mind, is the most likely way to manifest what we desire.

Eve 2 – The Birth of the Son/Sun

As the body of heaven, Hathor arches above the Earth, her arms and legs reaching down to embrace east and west. She is also the abundant celestial water who gave birth to a heroic solar son, variously Horus or Ra. This ancient solstice celebration marked the return of light. At dusk each day she swallowed the sun, which travelled in darkness the length of her body before it was reborn from her womb at dawn. Throughout the day the sun sailed across her belly, until at dusk she swallowed it.

The sun crowning the Goddess symbolizes active ego consciousness, the driving force of the human vehicle that helps us to manifest the plans of the divine mother. Where the lunar aspect represents subconscious desire, the solar aspect allows us to name ourselves consciously, but it always follows the intuition that reveals the will of the unconscious. The sun is propelled on its path across the sky by the sacred winged beetle, Khepera, whose name means "becoming." It is Khepera, the breath of the mother, which propels us from darkness to light.

At his birth, the Goddess's solar child is called Nefertum, meaning "beautiful beginning." At dawn he emerged from the womb, symbolized by an opening lotus. At night the lotus closed around him and returned with him beneath the waters. The Great Mother lotus represented divine feminine wisdom. Its roots go down deep, hidden in the mud, its stem passes through nurturing water, and its flower opens into the light. So does Hathor nurture us in the unconscious, subconscious and conscious life.

The return to light and consciousness demands that we know exactly who we are in order to find the

As children of the divine creative matrix, we share in her magical power.

Illustration by Wahaba Nuit-Cat Heartsun

key to our becoming. Again, with pen and paper, I ask myself, who am I really? How have I spent my time in the last year? What being am I becoming? What are the results of the actions I have taken? I try to map who I will be by discovering who I am. I use this day to look back through my journals and write a time capsule of the year. This summary helps me chart how I unfold over time. By monitoring the content of my life, I am consciously applying myself to my own becoming.

How have I spent my time in the last year? What being am I becoming? What are the results of the actions I have taken?

Eve 3 – Isis and Osiris

Osiris and Isis – brother/husband and sister/wife – ruled as equal partners. Divine, mortal beings, they taught the art of agriculture and communal living. As the god of the Nile, the source of abundance, Osiris appeared as the annual flood that replenished the fields. He was what Robert Bly would call a male mother, symbolized by his pendulous breasts. Isis was both the dark, rich earth fertilized by the flood and the star Sothis which caused the waters to rise. But Osiris was also a figure of sacrifice, murdered by his brother, Set. In her grief, Isis erected temples throughout Egypt, and her temple at Philae, just below the first cataract of the Nile, was said to be the source of the Nile waters. Here she awaited her husband's return.

On this day, again with pen and paper, I recall the natural gifts of the world, thanking the universe for its abundance every day. What blessings and nourishment were received during the year? What seeds planted in the dark, fertile soil have come to fruition?

Eve 4 – The Imprisonment of Isis

After Osiris died, Set imprisoned Isis. Set was worshiped as god of wind and sand storms, whose sudden, violent appearance disrupted the flow of life. As the personification of the desert, he represents loss, restriction and sterility. A destroyer of forms, Set separates us from the old and makes way for the new. The imprisonment of Isis precedes her triumphant release and her movement into her true power as the great enchantress. It was because of her enforced isolation and meditation upon her loss that she came to supreme greatness. Even while imprisoned, she showed her jailer compassion. This is the true meaning of the alchemical dictum that the philosopher's stone teaches us how to turn the lead of our lives into gold.

On this night, I record the losses and restrictions of the year. As I read through my list of disappointments, I recall the lessons each taught me. I try to see the unfolding pattern and contemplate how each delay and sorrow has changed me through the year.

Eve 5 – The Birth of Isis

The birth of Isis is one of the most joyful days of the year. For nearly 3,000 years, she was worshiped as Queen of Heaven and Earth. One hymn to her reads:

Illustration by Wahaba Nuit-Cat Heartsun

Open heaven's gates, draw back the bolts.
I have come to sing for Isis.
I have come to praise her name, O Flame.
I have come to adore the Great Speaker of Spells.
How beautiful her face, happy, renewed, refreshed
as the day when her mother first fashioned her.
All praise to the Queen of Earth and Heaven.
All praise the Goddess Isis.

One myth tells us that Isis claimed her power as Queen of Heaven by turning herself into a scorpion and stinging the arrogant, patriarchal sun god Ra. She promised to cure him of his misery only if he told her his secret name, the name his mother gave him at birth, the name that resonates magical power. He retreated with her behind a cloud, where she penetrated his heart and learned his secret. In truth, Isis knew Ra's secret name all along, for as a sky Goddess she is a manifestation of Hathor; that is, she herself was Ra's mother. She simply used this ruse to remind the arrogant son of his proper place, which was subservience to her. The veiled Isis reminds us of her penetrating mystery and tremendous power when she says, "I am all that has been and all that shall be. And no man has uncovered my face. No one has ever lifted my veil."

Myths tell us that she was childless when Osiris was slain, yet after she recovered the body of her husband, she transformed herself into a hawk and lowered herself upon him, wherein his spirit passed magically into her. Thus, the conception of her son was magical and immaculate. Isis was a Goddess of love, health, feasting and dancing, aspects she shared with Hathor.

All hail, jubilation to you, Golden One,
sole ruler of the world
Mysterious one who gives birth to divine beings
who transforms the animals,
molds them as she pleases,
who fashions men and women.
O Mother, luminous one who thrusts back darkness,
who illuminates every human creature with her rays
Hail, great one of many names . . .
It is the Golden One!
Lady of drunkenness, music, dance,
of frankincense and the crown,
of women and men
who acclaim her because they love her.
Heaven makes merry, the temples fill with song,
and the earth rejoices.

On this night, I pause to praise Isis and to spend a moment recalling my enthusiasms of the year, my magical accomplishments, my creations, my joys.

Eve 6 – The Birth of Nephthys

Isis had a beloved sister, Nephthys, the last child of the sky Goddess. Sometimes called the Veiled Isis, Nephthys bears the emblems of the temple and the cup upon her head. Her name means lady of the house, but this is the divine house, the temple of the spirit. Where Isis ruled heaven and earth, Nephthys ruled the underworld, the world of dreams, the hidden mysteries and psychic phenomenon. A Goddess of the unknown, her power lay in the tomb where she assisted Isis in the mysteries of transforming death into life. She joined Isis in mourning and became the Goddess of women, especially of the woman healer who aids those in suffering. She brought healing dreams and comfort. To enter Nephthys was to enter into the adytum, the room of gold, the holy shrine where the darkest, deepest religious mystery transpired.

On this day, I spend time reviewing the dreams that have visited me throughout the year. By noting the pattern of the developing unconscious, I reap its healing messages. I also spend a moment recounting the amazing synchronicities of life, the calls of the psyche which bring transformation.

Eve 7 – The Seven Hathors

In ancient Egypt, the birth of a child was attended by the Seven Hathors, who functioned much as fairy godmothers do in European myths. They are sometimes thought of as the nine Muses of the Greeks, sometimes as the three Fates. They were aspects of the goddess Hathor and formed a part of the fortune-telling which attended all births. The seven Goddesses correspond to the constellation of the Pleiades. Sometimes the Seven Hathors are incorporated into a single image, the Goddess Seshat. She was the patroness of writing and des-tiny, the holder of the akashic records. As another aspect of the Great Mother, she records our actions on the leaves of the celestial tree of life. The flower headdress she wears is made up of seven petals, reminding us of the seven aspects of Hathor. On this day, horoscopes may be drawn, Tarot read, I Ching thrown, or, as I did recently, the drawing of seven Angel cards, which I took as my gifts from the Goddess for the coming year. I wish you the many blessings of the Goddess for the new year. O

All praise to the Queen of Earth and Heaven. All praise the Goddess Isis.

The Right to Choose

An empowerment ritual

By Donna Albino

Tonight, helplessness was replaced with empowerment.

Several of my witchy friends and I are concerned about the possible overturning of Roe vs. Wade by the Supreme Court. On the full moon in April, four of us gathered in Boston to work out our anger in ritual. Our altar cloth was a piece of plain white satin. In the east, we placed a smoldering smudge stick in a bowl of ocean sand. In the south was a fat white candle. In the west was a large scallop shell filled with sea water. In the north, we placed a quartz crystal ball on a bed of mugwort. In the center, we placed a statuette of the ample-bodied Mother Goddess. Two rose candles burned outside the circle. Flowers of all kinds were placed on and around the altar. At each quarter was a plain metal coathanger.

All four of us cast the circle, singing to the four directions and using smudge and a bright spring flower to mark the sacred space. Then we sat at the four corners and took the coathangers into our hands. As we handled them, feeling their edges and coolness, one of us said, "Tonight we come together in outrage of the continued lack of power women have over their lives. We hold one instrument in our hands as a symbol of the desperation women have felt in the struggle to control their lives. Restricted by pious laws, women have had to risk their lives to save themselves. Tonight we say, no more. We remember our past, the choices we and our sisters have made, and we transform our world."

We took turns talking about ourselves and the women we had known. One of us spoke about a friend from high school who had died from an illegal abortion. Two of us spoke about legal abortions we had, and the thought processes leading to these decisions. One spoke of repeated illegal abortions her grandmother had endured because of poor birth control education and lack of resources. As the stories flowed, our anger and frustration with the failure of "the system" to empower women

became focused in the hangers. Our hands were sweaty and tense on the metal. At the energy peak, we held out our hangers over the altar, and one of us said, "We are tired of being desperate, of feeling our bodies are our enemies, of feeling helpless. Tonight we say, no more. We will transform these hangers from self-inflicted weapons to symbols of love and beauty."

One of us took her hanger apart and fashioned it into a heart shape. Another of us was adamant about not taking her hanger apart, saying only in its whole state did it have desperate connotations for her. She pulled the triangular section into a circle. The third woman fashioned her hanger into a uterus and fallopian tubes, and the fourth formed a symmetrical, pleasing sculpture from her hanger. We passed the flowers and floral tape from woman to woman and covered our hangers with flowers. As the hangers transformed form ugly symbols of helplessness into beautiful garlands, we began to assimilate pain in our past into action for the future. We spoke about being active in anti-Operation Rescue protests. One of us vowed to take a Model Mugging class to feel more confident in her body. Another talked about a therapy group she was active in. We processed guilt and shame about our own abortions and began to love ourselves a little more. Our smiles came back. Our anger was transformed into pride.

When our garlands were finished, we placed them on the altar and held hands, chanting softly. One of us spoke, "Tonight, helplessness was replaced with empowerment, emotions were channeled into action, and trust in each other brought is more understanding. We love, we fight, we will survive. We celebrate our sexuality. Thank you, Mother Goddess, thank you, Aphrodite, for your presence here tonight." We opened the circle with a renewed sense of hope and love. ○

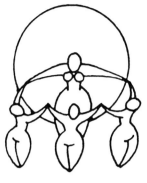

Part 2

Community

Blessed be the women who are wise and strong,
who heal with their loving hearts
and sing Thy sacred song.
For sisters united all are we,
spinning and weaving in harmony.
So let the magic now be cast,
to mend the sorrows of the past,
so together we may be
in love for all eternity.

Blessing by Priyamvada

The Lessons of Power

Daughters of the Goddess work together

By Shekhinah Mountainwater

The worst is sisters who have turned
Sending sisters to be burned
Betraying all we used to be
So we lose our harmony . . .

Power issues are generally a taboo subject in the women's movement, as well as in the neo-pagan movement. It's hard to admit that even those of us who consider ourselves "revolutionary" still have problems learning how to get along, to cooperate with each other, to share power. Every long-term feminist I know well can tell her horror story of betrayal and competition from sisters, of jealousy, back-biting, rip-off and very real harm. Many women are cautious, keeping to themselves, still healing their wounds. As a result, the movement wavers, becomes fragmented.

Where there is silence draped around a subject, there is usually concealed power as well. Recently we have begun to break some of our silences around such subjects as money and lesbian love magick. People are silent and make taboos because they are afraid, and of course the system of coercion and suppression benefits from our fears. When we break the silence, we are taking the first steps in the process of liberation.

Having been relatively powerless members of society, it can be quite a task for women to learn to understand power. This applies to any oppressed people. The first awakening usually entails the realization that "those guys" over there have more of something than I have: more goods, more mobility, more influence, more love, health, money, access, etc. The second awakening entails the realization that I myself have forgotten to take my own power, to make my own choices, to be responsible for my choices, to set goals for myself, to find ways to fulfill those goals. I have been controlled for so long that I have come to allow it,

to participate in it unconsciously. And the third awakening is the realization that most of us are unable to live as equals. We don't know how to share power.

Feminists and revolutionaries have developed a good deal of "theary" and praxis around the first two types of power awakening. The third type of power, which Starhawk calls "Power With" has only recently begun to be explored. We arc besieged by a barrier of splits between sisters: hurt, mistrust, jealousy, competition, estrangement. It seems we are no better than the system we claim to unravel, subject to the same problems and behavior patterns. How can we build a new world when we ourselves are still so much like the old one?

It is a painful thing for me to be saying this, writing this. I have held my tongue for years; I too have been afraid to publicly share my own experiences of hurt and betrayal. I am still reluctant to go into detail; afraid I will only alienate my readers. Perhaps it would be better to discuss the lessons I have tried to learn from my experiences.

In my early days of feminism, I was probably as naive and starry-eyed as the next woman. I had found the Goddess, fallen in love with a woman, and it seemed to me that I had found paradise. I didn't know then that we are all programmed by the patriarchy, that we all have deep scars and wounds from this. That the transformation promised could not happen overnight, because there is so much healing still to be done.

I was extremely innocent and idealistic. This was compounded by the fact that I had led a very unorthodox childhood. Raised by an artistic mother, I was encouraged to express myself freely, to shun such institutions as marriage and formal education, and seek fulfillment of my own creative potential. It

We are beseiged by a barrier of splits between sisters: hurt, mistrust, jealousy, competition, estrangement.

was a given in my reality that everyone had gifts to share, and that life is simply an opportunity to develop them. Surely it followed that one's talents would be welcomed in the world, that everyone would be supportive of one another's development.

Not so in most cases (though there are exceptions). I was shocked to discover that some of my sisters were threatened by my powers of self-expression; that they resented my freedom, my beauty, my gifts. I grew afraid to shine my light, withdrew and became isolated.

We are talking about a specific kind of power here; this is the power of influence and effectiveness. Judy Grahn talks about it in her writings on Sacred Blood. She uses the metaphor of the apple tree's ability to make apples. We are all like apple trees and can bear fruit that enriches or supports those around us, as well as ourselves. But because we have mainly seen abuses of this kind of power, we have learned to fear it, to suppress it, or to isolate it up on pedestals.

As a teacher, I have also experienced resentment and rejection from sisters. Often they would flock to me in the beginning, place me above and beyond them in estimation, then turn away in anger. I would be upset and confused by this pattern and become afraid to offer any teachings or classes. Meanwhile, I would see other women, who offered work that was similar to my own, garnering success, becoming "stars" and being placed on distant pedestals. Rarely would any of these sisters, whom I consider my peers, be able to offer me recognition or support.

I tried offering groups that were more "collective" in approach, but that didn't work either. "No one's in charge here," I would say, and we would all kind of wait around for someone to suggest a direction to go in. These groups generally drifted apart. It seemed that women still needed some sort of leadership, but that as leader, one risked continually the mis-understandings and rejections of the pedestal. Few women choose to take these risks, preferring to keep a "low profile" and preserve their status as "one of the folks."

I hear through the grapevine about how other priestesses and teachers who would appear to have all kinds of support and recognition are actually

"No one's in charge here," I would say, and we would all kind of wait around.

feeling as isolated and unappreciated as I. This too is a hush-hush topic, implying a "loss of face" if admitted out loud. Often I think to myself, if all the "women of power" were to give one another the kinds of support they feel are missing, the world would probably do a flip-flop of ecstasy! But we are not supposed to talk about these things. We aren't even supposed to admit that we want and need attention, let alone acknowledge that recognition is a matter of survival, not ego.

The subject of "women of power" gets us into another definition of power: the psychic power of magick and ritual. A woman of power is one who has developed herself from within. This too can be seen as threatening by the society at large. "Look out – she's a powerful woman," I have heard people say, as though this somehow implies that any woman who has claimed her own power must be a tyrant, out to control and intimidate others. So our true and good powers become confused and mistaken for the false powers of the patriarch.

Well . . . this is such a vast subject, and really needs to be dealt with in a book, in many books. Instead of going into lengthy analysis here, what I want to do is offer a few concepts and visual images that may help us to begin to build alternatives.

The Dancing Woman, Rune of Power

In my rune system, Womanrunes, this is a symbol of Power-From-Within, or, as I like to call it, Power-Of. It is the woman of power, the woman who takes power, the woman who has claimed direction of her own life, taken responsibility for herself, acknowledged her own abilities, validated herself as a sacred and important being. It is the woman whose ability to influence and affect the world around her is flowing freely. And it is the woman who has validated her magick: her psychic power, her passion and creativity. Every woman can be this woman; we all have gifts to share; we are all valuable.

The
Dancing
Women,
Rune of
Celebration

Put two women-of-power together and we have a new symbol, the Rune of Celebration. It is about "Power With" as Starhawk calls it; a sharing of power, a mutual expression of influence and will.

Link up any number of women-of-power and the message is one of solidarity, of a group or pair of strong people, working together in harmony. This and the previous symbol imply a situation where every woman involved is expressing herself freely, where there is equality of influence and no one is feeling limited or controlled.

Now, these are lovely ideas, and we have all dreamed of a world where they are the norm. Occasionally we have even experienced this kind of harmony. But we are still learning how to create such a norm for our daily lives, that will last and become the society we seek. What are the missing links, what do we still need to do to make this happen?

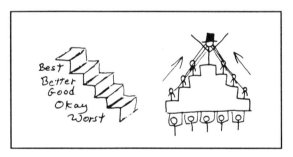

Here are what I often call the "Staircases of Patriarchy." On the left is the status stair, the inner system of comparison that is used to keep us separated and categorized. Most groups have a status stair; some show it outwardly, others express it more subtly, on a psychological level. We are taught to compare ourselves and one another according to its precepts, placing ourselves somewhere on its various levels of value. Those at the "top" are by turns admired and resented. Those at the "bottom" are by turns exploited and scorned. Everyone is either trying to "make it to the top" or maintain their position of "top dog" and keep at bay those who threaten to come up from below. This staircase tends to create a lot of jealousy among women because of the scarcity it imposes: scarcity of attention, recognition, security, self-esteem and so on.

On the right is the patriarchal stair of social structure, showing the way most groups are organized, whether it be families, schools, religious institutions, political structures and so on. At the top is the "leader" or "boss" or "God" with all his "underlings" in their places on the steps below. At the base are the slaves (usually women) who hold it all together. The lines drawn from bottom to top represent energy, communication, recognition, power. All of these lines are directed from below to above, so that most of the energy goes to the highest position. No lines are drawn between people on lower levels, to show how isolated we are and how little sharing there is.

Both staircases show a society based on the "one-up" idea, a dualistic thoughtform built on opposition and difference. We have all been conditioned by these stairs and are either "stuck" on lower levels, "striving" for higher levels, or attempting to maintain the highest at great cost to our health and hearts. Obviously, the first step we must take in recreating our uses of power is to step one more time . . . off the stair. How can we do this?

Many of us have had the experience shown above: it is what often happens when one has become disenchanted with staircases, and decides to step off. We find ourselves in a chaotic limbo where the lines of energy and communication have gone all awry. Some people fight, some become tyrants while others submit, some go off and form "cliques" that usually end up on their own

Problems of power usually stem from the dualism of self vs. Other.

staircases, some become "lone wolves" and decide to hell with all groups. Some get depressed and value themselves even less than before. Most often we end up returning to the old patriarchal staircase because nothing better has really presented itself.

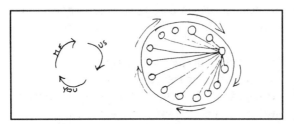

Those of you who have been reading my articles will probably find my circular "thearies" familiar by now. Circles are, I believe, the thearetical solution to most human problems caused by dualism. Problems of power usually stem from the dualism of Self vs. Other. One side receives, the other gives, one gets attention, the other is invisible, one recognized, the other made insignificant, one dictates, the other obeys, one has more money, the other less, and so on. The triadic circle on the left is a simple grid that can be used to replace such diads.

In order to replace the Self vs. Other diad, we need to make a circle of equality. This requires an understanding of the sacredness and value of each and every one of us. Me/You/Us says that each part of the circle is as important and necessary as the next. It says that each woman has the right to give and receive power, and that there is time and space within the circular flow for all. It also says that each of us takes responsibility, as well as receiving the benefit of others' responsibility.

The circle on the right is a model for group interaction. It is based on the pattern set up by such processes as Consciousness Raising and Passing the Rattle. The little circles represent people, the lines represent communication, energy, influence, and they can move in any chosen direction. At this moment, one woman in the circle has the rattle; she is the center of attention. She who holds the rattle holds the power; she who supports this woman gives the power. Everyone in the circle is on the same "level," all are visible and fully present. Givers of power lend energy, time, respect, focus, receptivity. Takers of power speak and express freely, give of their skills, insights, experiences. The arrows show that this is a changing situation;

Power becomes a matter of give and take, a circle of energy.

the rattle will move on. Everyone will have her turn to give and take power as well as responsibility.

Sometimes the rattle stays in the hands of one or more women for a prolonged period of time. This can be understood as teaching, performing, priestessing, nurturing, leading, organizing events, publishing magazines like this one, and so on. It can work harmoniously as long as it is based on mutual consent, and as long as no one gets permanently hung up in their roles. Power becomes a matter of give and take, a circle of energy. But there is still room for a gentle, enlightened leadership, an opportunity for each member to contribute as well as receive. In such a structure each woman has free choice as well; she can always refuse the rattle or take the rattle according to her needs and wishes.

This system works well when women are able to move easily from giving to taking power and back again. In patriarchy, our tendency is to do only one or the other. We either lead or are led, make decisions or have them made for us, speak freely or do all the listening, support or depend. We must become a new, more flexible sort of creature in order to share power, able to move freely back and forth, or 'round and 'round.

None of this can happen without the cultivation of those qualities represented by the Rune of Power within each of us. We need to become like the little woman shown, her arms upraised in free expression of all that she is: autonomous, independent, able to create life, to manifest abundance, to preside at her own rituals. In order to have a world of such women, it is necessary to have a mythos that supports and propagates it . . . a mythos based in the image of a Goddess as Self-Creating-Source-of-All. This is the image that has been torn from us, whose terrible loss has made us forget how wonderful and beautiful we really are. It is also the original image of Unconditional Love, the Mother Love that enfolds and accepts us, teaches us to completely accept ourselves, no matter what.

There is much healing and work to be done, of course, before we will see these things manifest on a large scale. We have all been hurt by the patriarchy in some way. Many sisters have low self-

Illustrations by Shekhinah

esteem, addictions, fears, illnesses of all kinds. These are the wounds we have sustained, living in a society that is itself unwell. We must be gentle and forgiving of ourselves and each other, and try to understand what has happened to us. The healing takes time and requires patience, self-discipline, commitment . . . all qualities implied by the Rune of Temperance below.

The Bowl, Rune of Temperance

Put together the Runes of Temperance and Power-With, and we get a new symbol which represents honour among sisters. Honouring one another,

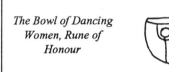

The Bowl of Dancing Women, Rune of Honour

being loyal, honest, respectful, faithful, keeping our commitments, standing by one another, working to find common ground, to create agreements: all of these require temperance, especially in times of adversity. And Honour is the basis for any true and lasting community.

Last winter, I taught a class in priestessing and worked with a small group of women to offer a Candlemas ritual for their community. Many problems of power surfaced during that time, and the runes of Power-Of, Power-With and Honour came in handy for use as visualization. At the ritual we had Power-With carved into our candles, which were placed on the altar along with the Tarot card of Honour. This card shows three women holding wands upright like staves, standing in a circle. Their left hands are on their hearts to show their pledge of commitment to themselves and one another. There is a Maiden, a Mother and a Crone; one is Black, one Native American, one White. These variations show that honouring is given through the generations and across all the artificial barriers drawn by the patriarchy.

When the ceremony had ended, I was packing up the altar things. I found that the Tarot card of

Honour had been damaged slightly. Somehow the heat of a candle must have melted one edge, blurring the word "Honour" and leaving the card somewhat tattered. I mourned a bit, and everyone agreed it was a sign; we still have a long way to go.

Later, something amazing happened. I re-examined the Honour card in my deck, and couldn't find the smear, the blur, the little bubbles of melted plastic. It had all smoothed out! No one is going to believe this, I thought, chuckling witchily. But that's okay. It means that something has mended . . . that Honour among sisters is still a good dream. Blessed be! ○

Honor is the basis for any true and lasting community.

Avalon

Before the sacred oak groves
Were destroyed by men,
Priestesses danced under starry skies
And divined the future
In the depths of dark green wells.
I remember these times
With sadness and love
Whenever women gather
To celebrate the beauty and power
Of our souls.

Mattie Coll

Circles of Self Love

Group support for opening your heart

By Deep River

Remind everyone to allow themselves to admit to their good qualities.

Surely it's no secret that the key to accepting the love of the Goddess into one's own heart and sharing it with others is self-love. The following are some activities for circles that provide group support for the work of opening one's own heart.

My Strengths

This exercise is not only useful for fostering self-love, but also for strengthening group bonds of love and trust. Create an atmosphere of safe space before you begin. Everyone is given a piece of paper and a pen. At the top of the paper are written the words, "My Strengths." At the very bottom, "I am Goddess; I am _____" where the woman writes in her own name. Filling up most of the paper is a large circle, with a smaller circle inside it, like a big donut. In the inner circle (the donut hole), each woman is instructed to write six of her positive qualities. These may be physical, personality, skills or talents; anything relating to her lovability or capability. Remind everyone to let down their guard a little and just allow themselves to admit to their good qualities. These can be as seemingly inconsequential as being a good driver or having a pleasant voice. It's important to stress that you don't have to be a world-famous chef to say you're a good cook, president of the League of Women Voters to say you're politically aware, or a professional comedian to say that you're funny.

This is very difficult for a lot of people. If someone just can't think of six things to write, give her permission to finish that part later. Spend at least five minutes for this first part, then explain that the papers will be passed around the circle so that everyone else has the opportunity to write what they see as your strengths. Comments by the other women will be written in the outer circle, the donut part. When everyone has had the opportunity to write at least one comment on everyone else's

paper, return the papers to their rightful owners and allow some quiet time for everyone to read and absorb what her circle sisters see in her. Women who know and love themselves well will find that many of their own inner circle comments are repeated in the outer circle, But there are almost always comments in the outer circle that the woman would not have seen in herself if she'd done this exercise alone. This exercise works with both adults and adolescents and is a precious gift for participants regardless of their current level of self-love and acceptance. It also strengthens the group bond by encouraging each member to recognize the many sources of strength with which she is interconnected.

A Letter from Mom

One of my circle sisters shared this with us when it was her turn to act as High Priestess. She, in turn, learned it at a workshop she attended with another group of women. My thanks to all who have passed this activity along. Each woman is given a piece of paper (we used pink) and a pen, then instructed to write a love letter to her daughter (a mythical daughter if you don't actually have a flesh and blood one), telling her whatever the writer feels that she needs to know. When everyone is finished, the letters are folded and paced in a basket (it's better if you don't tell them ahead of time you're going to do this). The basket is passed around, and everyone takes out a letter a random. One by one, each woman reads aloud what her "cosmic mom" wrote to her. Our group had some amazing results: everyone got the perfect message (why were we surprised?). One divorced women struggling to raise her three children told her daughter (a real live five-year-old) that the divorce wasn't her fault . . . the woman who received and read that letter needed to hear just that from her own mother. Another read that she really need to hang in there and stick with her schoolwork. . . exactly what she needed to hear.

The "coincidences" went on and on as each of the eleven women read their letter. Hey, when a group works well together, these things happen. My love letter from "Mom" has a place of honor on my altar.

The Goddess in the Mirror

This exercise shows up in one form or another in many writings on self-esteem and feminist spirituality. This is a great way to begin or end a group ritual. After the circle bonds and takes some group breaths, a woman (let's say Shelly) holds up a hand mirror, looks into it and proclaims, "I am Shelly, I am Goddess." She then shows the mirror to Marie on her left and says, "You are Goddess." Marie takes the mirror, gazes into it and says, "I am Marie, I am Goddess," and so on around the circle until the mirror returns to Shelly. Before putting the mirror down, she may want to quote a favorite passage about the presence of the Goddess in every woman, or just speak from the heart.

The mirror exercise may be recalled the next time you find yourself frowning at your reflection in your own bathroom or public restroom mirror – at the myriad of bodily "imperfections" you've talked yourself into despising. Tell yourself, "Snap out of it! That's the reflection of the Goddess! How dare anyone suggest that she's anything less than perfect!" Even if all it does is make you laugh, the magic of the mirror exercise has worked its transformation: you can't laugh and be mesmerized by your own "ugliness" at the same time. The mirror now invites you to look beyond the Madison Avenue image of beauty to the real face of the Goddess.

May the love of the Great Mother flow through you and your circle, too. ○

We have chosen to be together to learn from each other.

Illustration by Zelma of Halcyon Her Co.

Invocations for Winter Solstice
By Gretchen Faulk

During these invocations, as each brief passage is said, a candle is lit for that direction. At the center, light your altar candles.

The light of the East reminds us that in weeks to come, the daylight will grow stronger. The Sun will warm the Earth and our hearts.

The light of the South reminds us of the possibilities of the human spirit. We can respond to the universe.

The light of the West reminds us of the richness of community. We have chosen to be together to learn from each other. We honor our diversity.

The light of the North reminds us of the beauty within us and all around us. In beauty is strength, inspiration and joy.

I know that the Goddess is above me, I feel the Goddess under my feet. And here, all around me, I see Goddess! I salute you, beautiful Goddesses.

Each woman is made welcome with a hug, kiss and brief word, and the circle is cast!

In Praise of Santa Lucia

Lady of light

By Rose Romano

"In Italy, ancient pagan goddesses coexist with Christian saints. Or goddesses become saints."

Lucia lived in Syracuse, Sicily, around the year 300. Born into a Christian family, she vowed, at a very young age, to remain a virgin her whole life. It is said that her eyes were so beautiful, they attracted many would-be suitors and that, in order to discourage men from approaching, she plucked out her own eyes. She is today, in the Catholic church, the patron saint not only of Syracuse, but of all those who have trouble with their eyes. In most pictures, while she's shown with her eyes in her head, she holds a small tray with two eyes on it.

At one time, not knowing of Lucia's vow, and apparently before Lucia had plucked out her eyes, her mother tried to convince her to marry a young Pagan man who admired her. Furious when she refused, the man reported her as a Christian to the local officials and she was eventually put to death.

What intrigues me most about Lucia, besides the fact that "virgin" is sometimes used as a euphemism for "lesbian," are the stories that make her sound so much like the sun Goddess. Her very name, Lucia, means light. In *A Saint for Your Name,* Albert Nevins lists several name equivalents of Lucy, including Lucia, Luce, Lucien, Luz, Lucinda and Lucina. Lucina is mentioned by Z Budapest in Part II of *The Holy Book of Women's Mysteries* as the "Goddess Lucina, brilliant Sun of Healing." It seems appropriate that there should be a connection between the Sun Goddess of Healing and a patron saint who protects our eyesight. And in *Liberazione Della Donna: Feminism in Italy,* Lucia Chiavola Birnbaum says, "In Italy, ancient pagan goddesses coexist with Christian saints. Or goddesses become saints . . ."

Also suspicious to me is the fact that the stories of her martyrdom (the inability of oxen to drag her off to the "house of ill-fame" she'd been sentenced to;

an unsuccessful attempt to burn her – that is, her body wouldn't burn; her death by being stabbed in the throat with a sword) are now considered untrue according to official church teaching. Yet, although little is written about her in the books I've read, it's written respectfully. Whether Lucia is a saint or a Goddess, she is very important to Sicilians – and deeply loved by them.

Lucia was loved so much by missionaries travelling north, they brought her story at least as far as Scandinavia. It became a Swedish custom to celebrate her feast, called the celebration of the Lucy Bride. A young woman is chosen as St. Lucy – she carries martyrs' palms and wears white clothing and, on her head, a crown of candleholders with lit candles. Her feast occurs on December 13, just in time to prepare us for the coming of the Light of the World on Christmas – or the Winter Solstice.

Things Seen in Sicily, a book by Isabel Emerson, begins: "Sicily! Sicilia! . . . that stepping stone between Europe and Africa which partakes of the characteristics of both continents!" Because Sicily is, legally and politically, a part of Europe, it's sometimes forgotten how much Sicily is influenced by African customs.

But, in *Sicilian Ways and Days,* Louise Caico reminds us of this influence. She describes the forms, if not the substance, of many Sicilian customs. Most of the customs she mentions are spiritual – an accurate reflection of what is most important in matriarchal Sicily. For example, she discusses San Calogero, a contemporary of Santa Lucia and very important to Sicilians, and describes him as "the most mysterious of all Sicilian saints, and . . . always represented as a Negro."

Caico devotes a chapter to Santa Lucia's festival.

She describes the incessant beating of the drums through the village, all day and half the night; the procession of the image of Santa Lucia, in her hands a silver tray holding her eyes; the flaming torches, the bonfire, the people yelling and jumping. Although she never mentions the significance of this way of celebrating, she still conveys the excitement and intensity.

Her description made an impression on me, bringing up childhood memories of saints I had always regarded as goddesses and gods, although I never knew why. Somehow, Santa Lucia is a comfort to me, in how she fits in with both traditional Catholicism and Italian-American witchcraft – and in how she seems to belong just as easily in American feminist spirituality.

The poem that follows is based on Caico's description of the Sicilian celebration of the feast of Santa Lucia on December 13, as she saw it in the early part of this century. It will probably seem as much African as Italian, yet that's only because it's really neither – it's Sicilian. ○

Let us now praise Santa Lucia

Hear the thunder of the drums,
constant drums through the dark.
The villagers jump and dance,
holding their torches high
through the narrow lanes
between the rows of huts.
The whole village seems on fire
as the villagers jump and dance,
holding their torches high
as the villagers scream and laugh
holding their torches high
as the flames jump and dance,
the whole village seems on fire.
Hear the thunder of the drums,
constant drums through the dark.

Let us now praise Santa Lucia,
who would not be married to any man,
born in Sicily, in the city of Syracuse,
admired by all for her beautiful eyes
(hear the thunder of the drums,
constant drums through the dark)
who put out her own eyes
to turn away the eyes of men.
The whole village seems on fire
as they carry her, jumping and dancing,
through the narrow lanes
between the rows of huts,
on her head a crown of candles,
a crown for the sun goddess,
as the flames jump and dance,
her flames jump and dance,
her eyes in a plate in her hands,
the whole village seems on fire.
Let us now praise Santa Lucia,
who protects the sight of our eyes. ○

Santa Lucia is a comfort to me . . .

The special
attunement

women have

with the cycles

of the Earth

Mother.

Spell to Send Away
Mal Occhio

Tomato sauce bubbles
in the big, black pot.
Grandma stirs
with her long, wooden
spoon.
The scent of garlic
circles the room –
protection in the kitchen.
Pasta waits.
Grandma sits me
at the table,
draws the shades,
the room is gray.
Grandma lights the candles,
places a small bowl
of olive oil and water
on the table,
rubs the oil
on my forehead and
prays to the Madonna.
My headache is gone.
Now we eat.

Rose Romano

(*Mal occhio*: evil eye)

Illustration by Cris Palomino

Spring Planting Rite

Honoring the Earth Mother in community ritual

By Spider

In the Spring, the clanmothers lead the women into the fields to perform a powerful ritual to coax the great Earth Mother, Ata Bei (at-ah-bay), into once again giving her gifts to the people. "The women have within them the rhythm of the universe . . ." These sacred words of the Taino tradition speak of the special attunement women have with the cycles of the Earth Mother. Through our bleeding times, we know the powers of Ata Bei to give and take back life. Because of these gifts, women have the honor of performing the spring planting ritual.

This is a most festive event. Women from the circle volunteer to take on the roles of Ata Bei and the four food mothers. The clan mothers wear their special feathers and each one carries her unique clan staff, representing the gifts given to the six original children. Once dressed in special masks and wraps, the women leave the community circle to perform the sacred planting. There is much drumming and chanting as the men wait for us to complete our work.

We cleanse with salt water and smudge with the smoke of sage and copal. Each woman contemplates what she wishes to plant in her own life as she goes about the dance of planting for the community. We paint our faces with our menstrual blood or Beiha, a traditional Central American ceremonial plant. This painting represents the sacrifice made during the birth as well as the power women have through our monthly bloods to bring new life into being. Then the women prepare to dance the ancient dance of the Boa Constrictor.

In the Taino tradition, Ata Bei, the Earth Mother, is symbolized as a snake with her tail in her mouth. The eternal circle, for she is everything that has always existed, all that exists at the present, and all future potential. All creatures of Earth are her children, and we exist in the center of this great circle. The animals and plants, birds and stones, are our sisters and brothers. We honor and celebrate these relationships in the Caney Medicine Wheel, a circle of 28 stones representing Ata Bei through the 28-day cycle of the moon.

It is within our stone medicine wheel that the sacred dance begins. Each woman weaves her own strand into the creation of the Koa, or Ata Bei effigy. (Ata Bei, translates as "Mother Snake.") Singing the ancient shamanic chants, the women are joined by our grandmothers who danced on the Spring Earth in times before us. The dance becomes trance as the power of Ata Bei becomes stronger, as the snake is being woven.

When all is finished, our woven Koa is wrapped around the woman wearing the Ata Bei mask. We pause at the planting site so that each of the food mothers can plant her sacred seeds and ask for the gifts of her direction to come to us.

The food mother of the South steps forward and begins to part the Earth at the South of the medicine wheel. She will plant the sacred squash, bringing us the gifts of innocence and openmindedness. The food mother of the South is wearing a green mask. Green is the color of new life, the spring shoots, and seeking. The turkey is the bird of the South, the one that does not fly, but instead walks on the Earth.

The food mother of the West steps to the West and parts the Earth. She will plant the black beans, the food of introspection. The color of the West is black, the darkness within where we go to meet our spirit guardians. The bird of the West is the owl, the one who sees in the darkness.

The food mother of the North goes to the North and

Our grandmothers danced on the Spring Earth in times before us.

parts the Earth. Wearing the white mask of the North, she plants the cassava. (Cassava is the staple food and healing plant of the Taino people. It is made from the root of the yucca plant. In the Taino tradition, Ata Bei's son is Iocahu, Lord of the Yucca.) The North food mother wears the hummingbird feather. The North is the place of healing, experience and wisdom. The hummingbird is the bird who goes away in winter and is transformed by her/his experiences.

We nourish the seeds with our blood and gifts of herbs.

The East food mother goes to the East to part the Earth and plant the sacred corn. The East is yellow, and corn represents illumination, courage and strength. The East mother wears the hawk feather, the high-flying bird that can gain perspective on a situation by rising above it. The East is the direction from which the sun returns to us.

Each food mother plants her sacred food, asking for her direction's gifts and a plentiful harvest. We nourish the seeds with our blood and gifts of herbs before closing the Earth. The rain rattles call to the sky to bring the nurturing waters for the seeds to grow.

Our task completed, the women chant and dance back to the communal circle, where the snake will be unwound and dancing will continue long into the night. It is a time of special celebration, for the women have spoken to Ata Bei and we can all feel her favors coming on the Spring winds. ○

Prayer of Thanksgiving

For the beauty of the Earth,
Great Spirit, we thank you.

For the warmth of the sun,
Great Spirit, we thank you.

For the glory of the stars
that beautify the night,
Great Spirit, we thank you.

May we always be mindful
to live in harmony
with our brothers and sisters,
the plants, animals and crystals
And for our shared existence,
Great Spirit, we thank you.

For our families and friends
and the love we share,
Great Spirit, we thank you.

For the joy of today
and the opportunity to walk the Earth,
Oh, Great Spirit, we thank you.

Deanne Quarrie

A Birthday Ritual

Celebrate the gaining of wisdom

By Joanne Astraea

Seeking to honor a dear friend at her birthday, I asked the Goddess for a ritual that would show my friend how special she is to her sisters. What She sent was a blessing for all who participated. May it also bless you and yours.

Ritual Preparation – Altar Space

Prepare the altar to honor the birthday person. If she favors a particular flower or plant, that should be present. If someone she would like to be in the circle is not able to be there, represent that person with something on the altar (photo, jewelry, his or her name on a piece of paper, etc.). In representing the elements, use symbols that you feel the birthday person's energy in. You may also ask her to create a special altar for herself. If the people present wish to share physical gifts, they should be placed around or under the altar. Each person participating in the ritual should bring a candle to light for the birthday person.

Casting the Circle

Take some time to sing and raise energy. When calling in the specific directions, call in the elements, Goddesses, animals, etc. that you feel the birthday person is especially connected to. For example, I invoked the south, and my invocation went something like this:

"Hail powers of the south!
We call you to join our circle as we prepare to celebrate the birthday of our dear sister, Jemaia. We give you thanks for her wonderful energy that sparks our creativity. We thank you for her healing spirit that comforts us when we draw close to her in sorrow. Thank you, Hestia, for the warmth of her home, the blaze of her fireplace, the gentle flicker of candles glowing on her altar. Brigit, we praise you for the wonderful work our sister does, the beauty that you give her the will to create. She blesses our lives by showing us the beauty she sees.

"Powers of passion, thank you for her beautiful sexuality that shows us the loveliness of being a woman. Thank you, powers of the south, for our wonderful friend. We ask you, with all your energies and powers and passions to come to our circle, as we seek to honor her. Blessed be."

Similarly, call in the other directions, touching on

Light the candle you have for her to cast your wish . . .

Illustration by Wahaba Nuit-Cat Heartsun

the characteristics that are seen in the birthday person.

When invoking the Goddess, call in the Goddesses that are special to your friend, the ones you know she often calls on, and depends on to help her in her life. Also, call in the ones you feel have something special to offer to her at this time.

After the circle is cast, you might like to seal it by passing a sacred kiss around. You have now created a sacred space, unique and special to the birthday person. The Goddess and powers she relates best to have been invited to join in, and the altar is prepared as an homage to her.

The Ritual

Within the circle, each sister takes time to speak of and honor the birthday person. During this time, they offer to her whatever gift they would like to have evidenced in her life during her new year. For example, you may praise your friend's belief in her ideas and dreams, and wish for her the perseverance needed to see some specific dream come to fruition. Or perhaps you admire her ability to be strong under the difficulties she faces, and wish for her to have more humor and fun in her life. Whatever you have to offer, light the candle you have for her to cast your wish as a spell. If you have a physical present to share, do it after you have lit the candle. After everyone has shared and lit candles for the birthday person, give her the opportunity to share what she would like to, and to light her own candle. Raise the energy again, and bind your spells. You may wish to sing some songs that are favorites of the birthday person.

Thank the Goddess and the spirits from the directions for being present, and release them (of course, inviting them to stay and party, if they would like), open your circle, and continue your celebration as you wish! ○

Praise Her abundance, Praise Her creations

Goddess Has Risen

Words by Shekhinah Mountainwater (1st verse) and Lunaea Weatherstone (remaining verses). Tune: "Morning Has Broken," original words by Eleanor Farjeon, melody traditional.

Goddess has risen, Now is Her season.
She gives us reason to be and to give.
Praise for the Maidens,
Praise for the Mothers,
Praise for the Lovers,
Loving to live.

Sweet comes the Maiden, dancing through flowers,
Rejoicing in powers so free and so bold.
Praise for the sweetness
of her light laughter
returning after
Winter's dark cold.

Mother's love showers over the green Earth
She brings us a rebirth of fruit and of grain.
Praise Her abundance,
Praise Her creations,
All lands and all nations
Shall feast once again.

In Summer the Lovers, lips red with berries,
come singing so merry, come laughing so gay.
Give thanks to the Maiden
and thanks to the Mother
For blessing each lover
with passion's sweet play.

Goddess has risen, Now is Her season,
She gives us reason to be and to give.
Praise for the Maidens,
Praise for the Mothers,
Praise for the Lovers,
Loving to live!

Thirteen Blessings

Welcoming a baby to the Goddess community

By Shekhinah Mountainwater

In the familiar tale of the Sleeping Beauty, twelve fairies were invited to the celebration of her birth, and each asked to give a gift of blessing to the child. But, as we know, there was a 13th fairy whom nobody liked, who was not invited, but who came anyway. She came with a curse, not a blessing, because of her rage at being excluded.

This is, of course, a patriarchal story. As Nor Hall, a Jungian therapist, has discovered, the rejection of the last fairy is a rejection of the Crone archetype, which, in effect, creates a state of psychic numbness or the "hundred years' sleep." We are told that only the prince, our shining male heroic archetype, can rescue and waken us, and we wait passively for the miracle that usually never happens.

The Crone is the Dark Goddess who resides in us all. She is our deepest Power, and when we suppress Her she can become very angry and destructive. Since we are also taught not to show our anger, we can become passive and numb instead. Hence Beauty's prolonged slumber, which has lasted centuries.

But if instead we make friends with this Crone and allow Her energies to flow freely within us again, we can be made whole. The return of the Goddess in all of Her aspects represents this healing, in political, spiritual and social spheres, as well as in our psyches.

And so we find it natural to look again at the old stories that were told to us as children. In them are symbols that are full of beauty and meaning for us, if we can unveil their mysteries. Some of these symbols are oppressive, and we have heard many a feminist complain about the damage caused by fairy tales. But some of the images go back to the roots of myth, and if we can learn to understand them, we can find many important treasures. We can retrieve these lost parts of ourselves and bring them back into our everyday world, there to re-weave them into better stories.

I think often about the thirteen fairies, especially when someone I know is having a baby. When my brother's wife gave birth to little Mara, I thought it would be wonderful if she could receive all the blessings that the fairies offer, and so I composed for her the following poem. I wrote it out by hand and mounted it in a frame, so that she could keep it by her through her growing years. I thought perhaps the words would seep into her unconscious mind and help her to bring their messages into reality. I realized the poem could be used for other children as well, and I offered it once again to Chloe Rose, who was born to my friend Sandra's daughter.

Of course, there are more elaborate ways this poem could be used. Modern witches might want to have a celebration similar to that of Beauty, and perform a ritual in which the Thirteen Blessings are actually bestowed magically upon the child. Thirteen women could be Fairies or Goddess-Mothers and offer gifts that represent each wish. Everyone could help raise the cone and visualize in concrete images the gifts the Fairies offer. The poem could be chanted, the name changed:

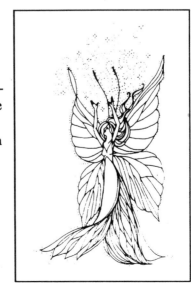

She could receive all the blessings the fairies offer.

The images go back to the roots of myth.

Thirteen Blessings for Chloe Rose

May you always be:
Beloved and loving
And glad of living
Freely receiving
And freely giving

May wisdom and beauty
Shine from your soul
May your spirit be free
To find your goal

May the glow of good health
Be yours for always
And Earthly abundance
Fill all your days

From evil or harm
May you always be free
Yet able to fight them
Should the need be . . .

And at the last
May you be ever blessed
With the power of Beauty's
Thirteenth guest

Whose loss caused her long
One-hundred-year's sleep
But whose gain bringeth wonders
of the psyche so deep –

Let the magick be yours
Sweet Chloe so fair
For you and all of
The world to share
So be it!
Blessed be . . . ○

Illustration by Wahaba Nuit-Cat Heartsun

A Menarche Ritual

Honoring our daughters' first bloods

By Nan Hawthorne

A daughter raised with the recognition of her own identity as the Goddess and as part of the Goddess will learn easily that the functions of her body are positive and even sacred. She will have an almost matter-of-fact understanding of them, a respect for her own impending womanhood. If you and she are part of a Goddess-identified community, perhaps she will have had the opportunity to watch other daughters reach menarche, the onset of puberty and the first menstrual flow, and look forward to it herself, avoiding the tension, confusion and misinformation our patriarchal society and the sanitary napkin and feminine deodorant spray industries foster. The following menarche ritual serves as an illustration of the art of ritual crafting with sexual cycles in mind, and offers a suggestion for a tradition to reinforce our daughters' understanding of the Goddess within them.

Menarche for an aware daughter of the Goddess will be anticipated and joyfully announced by her, so you will find it easy to commemorate it while she is still experiencing her first menses. If you have a Goddess community, contact as many of the women who have already passed menarche as you can and ask them to come to your home for the menarche ritual. If possible, include like-minded or open-minded female relatives. If you have not had one ready for her in the expectation that your 10-13 year old daughter will have her first menses soon, obtain some item of jewelry, a ring, a pendent, bracelet or earrings containing one of the following stones, all of which resonate with the root or belly chakras, energy centers for sexuality and menstruation: bloodstone, ruby, coral, carnelian or garnet. Buy a fairly long, 3-6 feet, piece of red cord or yarn, or three of these tied together at one end so that they can be braided.

This ritual is inspired by the menarche celebration of Panamanian Indian women, who venerate menarche as a bond between women and the Goddess. Greet your daughter's first menses with some pomp and fanfare, but, of course, be sensitive to her wishes on this. Let her choose the women attending and the extent of the preparations.

As soon as the daughter announces her first menstrual flow, consult her about the menarche ritual, then suggest that she spend a good deal of the time until the ritual in meditation. Tell her to pay close attention to her dreams during this time, and to write about them in a dream diary, or to use whatever artistic talent she enjoys to express her feelings and describe her dreams. Tell her that she may now choose a special name for herself, which she may keep a secret or share with the women of the Goddess community. In the meantime, prepare the ritual yourself, with the help of women relatives, if that's feasible. Have each woman coming to the ritual bring a gift that somehow represents what womanhood means to her. Prepare your daughter's favorite foods for the feast.

If you can, plan the ritual for out-of-doors, in a secluded spot covered low with tree branches or an overhang of a hill. A cave would be ideal. But a small room will do, such as the daughter's bedroom, dimly lit and draped with cloth to make it cave-like. If there are only the two of you, even sitting under a draped table will work quite well to simulate the womb of the Mother. If indoors, have a handful of earth tied up in a cloth bag handy.

When the ritual space is ready, bring all the women together in the next room or outside the grove or cave, except your daughter, who should be somewhere nearby meditating. Greet them, saying that you are all meeting as a society of maidens, mothers and crones to welcome your daughter into womanhood at her first bloods. Explain any special

She may now choose a special name for herself.

The Coming of Winter

But what if Persephone chose the underworld
as her only chance to run away from home?

After all, if your mother is a fertility queen
who controls every living thing on earth
and she sets you up as a perfect virgin
eternally teenage goddess of spring,
doomed to a circle of boring nymphets
and wimpy sorority dances in chiffon,
what the hell else can you possibly do
but turn radical?

You go out walking, pissed
(the other girls know
to leave you alone when
you're moody like this)
and the sunny field of flowers and
hummingbirds
is enough to make you sick. Up drives this
dude
in a funny helmet and a black convertible
nothing like the creep you've been warned
about.
He bows, grins, and asks if you'd consider
sharing his job, ruling the worlds of the dead.
It's subtle, challenging. You'd be great,
he says.
(You're ready to kiss his shadow.)
At least come down and look around, he says;
they'll never understand our type up here.

Your mother throws a fit when she finds out.
She hollers Rape, tears up the kitchen, calls
a planetary strike by every species
of tree vegetable shrub grass and fruit
but it doesn't work. Stoned on courage
inside your lover's cave, you drink the
darkness,
stroke a kitten's ghost and pity her.

The blood of joy which now flows to your womb in womanhood

observances you have planned, or the whole ritual if you have not performed it before as a group. Stand in a circle, holding hands, or simply be together for some minutes, smiling into each other's eyes, grounding individually or singing together to reinforce the group bonding. Welcome each woman into the prepared ritual space in order of age, eldest first, blessing each one with blessing oil or salt water, as follows:

Welcome, (name), to the celebration of (daughter's name)'s first bloods! I bless you in the name of the Goddess as you enter her womb. (Sprinkle her with oil or water, or touch oiled or wet fingers to her breast over her heart and her abdomen over her womb. Hug her and let her pass into the ritual space.)

Have an older family member or special friend stand out to welcome and bless you. When all have entered sacred space and have taken their places standing or seated in a circle, go to your daughter to bring her into the room. Perform a blessing on her, such as:

Welcome, my daughter, to the Womb of the Mother! I came from that Womb, as you came from mine, and I re-entered it to come forth again as a woman, as you do now, and as you may some day guide a daughter of your own into womanhood.

Bless your mind, clear and free as the soft breezes of summer. (Touch oil or water to her forehead.)

Bless your eyes, soft as a mountain lake or flashing with fire like the sun. (Touch her eyelids.)

Bless your mouth, sweet with laughter and the anticipation of kisses to come. (Touch her lips.)

Bless your heart, brimming over with the blood of joy which now flows to your womb in womanhood. (Touch her breast over her heart.)

Bless your belly, rounding now as you leave childhood behind, able to grow large and full now when you choose to be a mother. (Touch her navel.)

Hug her and bring her into the center of the circle, or if you are alone with her, sit across from her. Introduce her to each of the women, who should greet her and hug her.

Ask each woman to sit and relax. Lead them in a grounding and centering meditation:

Breathe deeply and slowly. Feel the inrush of breath like a deep, cool drink of water, pouring into you and smoothing out and cleansing your insides. Feel the air you expel wash away any distracting thoughts, any tensions, any worries you bring into this space from your day. Keep breathing, deeply and slowly, feeling your body and mind relax, feeling yourself begin to drift and surge, as if each breath were actually the push and pull of gentle waves. You realize that you are lying in a large lake. Look around and see the shore, the sky, the water lapping at your skin. You are securely buoyed up and cannot sink.

You remember that once, when you were above this lake, on a mountain, in a tree, flying overhead, you saw that this was not a lake at all, but the crystalline yet liquid body of a huge woman. Her skin, not resistant like a human woman's, is instead like a thick, viscous, clear liquid, so that a swimmer could enter and explore her body with ease. Feel her hands as they caress your limbs, buttocks, back and hair, like gentle waves. You feel utterly relaxed, utterly safe and secure.

You feel yourself drawn to this huge woman's womb, so you let yourself begin to sink. Your head fully underwater, you find you breathe easily in the fluid of her body. You swim down into the deepest part of the woman-lake, and can see as you pass through into her womb, can see that the spirit of the womb of every woman ever born, back to the one ancestral mother of us all, is there. It is so vast as to hold them all. Find the spirits of some particular woman or women, communicate wordlessly with each and share your woman wisdom. (Pause a few minutes.) You find that you are drifting out of the woman-lake's womb, through her birth canal, slowly, inexorably to the light. When you drift up and out of the lake, you find that you awaken from your meditation on the shore of the lake. You are clear, refreshed and focused on our celebration.

Cast the circle by greeting the directions, starting in the east and ending the clockwise circle at the north. Keep the circle casting simple, as the closing of the circle will be more elaborate, perhaps saying nothing more than, "Welcome, spirits of the (direction) to our joyful and loving celebration!"

Finally she sends this mediator guy
with cute wings, curls, and not afraid of snakes.
He spins out sparkling words till you agree
to visit Mom, spend half the year above
ground.
(The earth shifts.) You all decide on a story
of marriage vows and pomegranate seeds
to explain the other six months.

Before you know it
the animals, plants and weather goddesses
are following your rhythm, making a hollow
time for souls to rest between fiestas.
Your mother, her aching breasts swollen with
summer,
insists that the world is needlessly dying of
grief
but you and the approving spirits know better.
Even humans learn to shut up long enough
to notice their dreams and little mysteries
and folks seem happier that way.
Your man Hades,
proud of you and sweetly off key, roams
the caverns humming "You're not a kid
anymore."

From then on, you and Mom get equal
billing. (You start designing snow.)

Joanna Cazden

Tell her to pay close attention to her dreams.

To invoke the Goddess, ask each woman in the circle to stand and give a name of the Goddess. When each has spoken, begin a chant or steady drumbeat. Tell your daughter to watch each woman as you all move and dance in a clockwise circle around her, to look for the Goddess in each, to understand from their movements the meaning behind the Goddess she chose, and to feel free to imitate them, laugh with them, speak with them. Begin to move the circle, each woman singing or humming and dancing how she feels about being the Goddess.

For the Magickal Work, all should sit around your daughter as she lies down in the middle. Hold hands in the circle and concentrate on her. Place the handful of earth in a small cloth bag on her belly. Say:

My daughter, you are deep within the earth, within

she is here reborn a woman!

Illustration: "First Moon Blessing," by Cris Palomino

the womb of your Great Mother. We, your sisters, are there with you, preparing to be reborn as a woman. We have each made the journey, and we will lead you to your own womanhood.

Each woman, beginning with the eldest, should lay her hand on the bag of earth and say a blessing, tell a reminiscence of menarche, offer an affirmation on the beauty of the bodies of women, sing a song, or otherwise send her own energy and blessing into the bag. After each has done so, all should join hands again, leaning over the daughter, and hum a chant or random notes. Separate yourself from the circle, lean over and lift the upper part of your daughter's torso to a sitting position. Hug her tightly, then release her suddenly, as the humming of the women rises to a yelp of joy, in which your daughter should join. She is here reborn a woman! The women should touch and stroke her, smile, laugh and greet her. Returning to their places, again eldest first, each should present her with her gift, explaining its meaning. You should place the coral or other jewelry on her, stating that it is a token of her womanhood. Give her the red cord, instructing her to tie a knot in it each day, braiding between the knots if three strands were used, until her second menses arrives, to commemorate each day of the lunar cycle. Say:

Now you are a woman, and as a woman, you will share in that invention of womankind, the awareness of the passage of months, the calendar. Each day as you tie a knot in your menarche cord, feel the Goddess within you, say the name you have chosen into the cord, and when the first day of your next bloods comes, tie the last knot, count them, and remember that number: it is your own. You will find that your bloods most often will come to you in that many days. On that day, tie this cord around your waist to relink your body with the Goddess's. You are the Goddess.

Your daughter may take this time to speak, to ask questions of the others, to announce and explain her name. Feast together while she does this, paying attention to her, answering her questions.

To open the circle, your daughter should go to each direction, counterclockwise starting with the north, and thank and say farewell to them, telling what each represents to her, members of the circle adding correspondences and meanings as they wish. Let

your daughter thank and hug each woman, then join the circle to say, "Merry meet, merry part, merry meet again! May the peace of the Goddess go with you! Blessed be!"

Providing a positive environment, through love and ritual, for the daughters of your community, you will be fostering a strength in the new generation of women which will follow these first decades of return to the Goddess. Instruct her both in the traditions of her path, and in the autonomy she deserves to make her own choices, to trust her own intuition, and to find the Goddess within. ◯

Invocation

Diana, enfold me in your embrace.
Comfort me.
In the wailing of my heart
and the sorrow that wracks
my back and chest,
let yourself shine down upon me,
your moon self.
Hold me. Be with me.
Let me feel your loving presence.
Send the bird of heaven to me,
to enter my heart
and fill me with your spirit.

Francesca Dubie

You will be fostering a strength in the new generation of women.

The Grandmothers Speak

Honoring the spirits of the ancestors

By Spider

The spirit leads us to the cave of the Mother to rest . . .

In this time of Earth changes, the ancestor spirits are returning to help guide our paths. I hear them speaking in the rocks and trees and with gentle voices on the wind. If I open up my inner senses and listen carefully, these ancient ones, my grandmothers, will share their wisdom so that I may make the right choices. Especially during times of confusion and frustration, it is comforting to know that the wisdom of all the experiences of those gone before is available.

In the Caney Circle tradition, we know that all life comes from Guaturei, the universe. During life, the physical body and spirit body function together to manifest our unique realities. In this Central American tradition, our link with the universe is through the guardian spirit. It is this spirit entity, often manifested as an animal, that guides, protects, and brings us healing. The guardian spirit is a direct channel to the universe, Guaturei (gwa-too-ray). Everyone has a guardian spirit whether or not she is conscious of that connection. That spirit remains with us throughout life, and at death, leads us back to the cave of the Mother to rest, transform, and cycle around again in whatever form She chooses for us. Our spirits expand in the cave (womb) of the Mother to once again become Guaterei, and our life energy is manifested in the creation of new life forms – the fish, birds, trees and plants. The relationship between all life is cyclical and continually transforming.

When a person dies, they leave behind a spirit that we call the hupia. The hupia (hoo-pee-ah) is essentially a shadow of the person that remains with us in memory form. Some hupias are more powerful than others and influence a lot of people for a long time after the person is gone. Other hupias fade very quickly and leave little or no evidence of their lives. This is the spirit of the grandmothers that we can communicate with.

It is possible to contact the hupia of an ancestor and ask her to stay nearby. When a person dies or just when we want to re-connect with one of our grandmothers, we do a sacred ceremony. The song for releasing is sung, and the person is remembered for their special gifts. We honor the spirit and ask her to stay in our lives. In a small corn-husk hut floating on a bowl of water, we put a photograph of the grandmother and something of hers or something that reminds us of her. As the hut is set on fire, we watch the spirit transforming, and chant to send her power along her way, back to the cave. As the ashes cool, we feel our relationship transform and silently open the channel through which we will invite her wisdom to come through in the future. We chant, we pray on the smoke of the pipe to ask the spirits to help our grandmother, we cry the tears that bring our own cleansing. The sweet fruit of the guava (or apple) is passed around the circle, and, as we eat, we each know how she nourished our lives.

Next, an altar is made to be the home of this grandmother spirit. Usually, it is made out of a small piece of board with a small shelf and hangs on the wall, but it's the idea that's important, not the altar form itself. Another photograph of the person is pasted onto the board, and we write her name in fancy script. The ashes are put into two containers, a clay pot that will sit on the shelf, and a small hollowed-out gourd that will hang above the photograph. Both of these containers are capped with a small piece of cotton to keep the essence of the spirit on the altar. "When I die, let the ashes of my body be buried in an earthenware pit and watch the spirit of my giving soar on the four winds back to Guaturei . . ." The words from the funeral song tell of the symbolism of the clay pot and hanging gourd.

Once this ceremony has been done, the hupia

resides in the altar. Putting it in a conspicuous place and visiting it often will deepen the connection with that ancestor. One altar must be built for each ancestor, but they do not need to be large. It is to my altars that I go when I need help or healing from my grandmothers. I offer them gifts and fresh flowers, and burn sage and candles. I sing to them and share my accomplishments and disappointments. It is through my dreams that the grandmothers speak back with their wisdom and advice. Sometimes, I hear them talking or singing back to me as I am busy throughout the day. Never have I asked for help from my grandmothers that I have not received an answer. Although sometimes hard to understand at the time, the wisdom of the grandmothers has always been exactly the right thing for me to do. Trust and patience are necessary when honoring their wisdom.

During this very important time of the Earth, the ancestor spirits have come back to share their wisdom and help us through the trial of transformation. On a personal as well as planetary level, their wisdom is necessary for survival of our species. The ancestors speak of honoring the Earth and all our sisters and brothers, they speak of living gently and peacefully, they tell us how we can heal our bodies and call our spirit guardians. We need not be afraid of not knowing answers or feeling strong, for these are their gifts to us, the grandchildren. Lessons are learned through experience and it is by calling on the experience of the ancestors that we can find answers to the hard lessons of present times. All we have to do is ask.

I hear the voices of the ancestors, awake with the sounds of water and wind. I feel their presence in the sweat lodge and see their spirits in my dreams. They are calling their grandchildren to awaken to their voices and honor their hupias, for they have many gifts and much healing to share. ○

It is through my dreams that the grandmothers speak . . .

For All Those Who Died

A rite of remembrance for the Burning Times

By Gretchen Faulk

We honor the anger, the will to resist.

The following call-and-response style reading was developed for a "Burning Times" ritual. It is appropriate for ancestor-honoring, healing, reclaiming and remembering. While immersed in historic material preparing for this ritual, I often felt immense sadness, the huge load of pain surrounding the Burning Times. It was worth doing. Even this tremendous dark must be embraced. We must know the past in order to shape our future. The phrase, "Never again the Burning," has taken on fresh meaning for me. I hear it now, not as a call to legislation or even militancy, but as a personal commitment. *I* must never allow it to happen again.

For all those who died, stripped naked, raped and bound:
   We honor dignity, the right of all.

For all those who screamed in vain for mercy:
   We honor speech, we will listen to each other.

For all those who were crushed, racked, broken on the wheel:
   We honor spirits unbound by handicap, free in mind and soul.

For all those whose beauty was destroyed by torture, and for those whose plainness died as well:
   We honor our bodies, we will not be divided by form or color.

For all those who midwifed birth and death, Then were burnt for their compassion:
   We honor you who guard the doors of life.

For all executed not for harming, but for healing:
   We honor the green way, the skills that bring wholeness.

For the aged in poverty and helplessness, for the aged with life secure,

but helpless yet, still being women:
   We honor independence and wisdom, the lesson of years.

For all those able to think independently, uppity women, real humans, dying as slaves:
   We honor clarity and courage, the strength of the soul.

For all those who died in shame, tortured into naming other innocents:
   We understand, we forgive you.

For the very few who protested or aided the accused:
   We honor bravery and integrity, the ability to know truth.

For all those who died outspoken, cursing and raging, Womanhood unrepentant:
   We honor the anger, the will to resist.

For all those whose names are lost forever, Who vanished unrecorded, unmourned:
   We honor the conscious life, memory and our dreams.

For those counselors who advised in matters of this world or the next:
   We will remember.
For the singular, for the ordinary:
   We will remember.
For the children, starved, damaged, executed:
   We will remember.
For myself, this past reclaimed, our future sought:
   We will remember.
For those who burned, were hung, drowned, or simply disappeared:
   We will remember.

(In unison) We remember! We honor!
It will never happen again!
Blessed be. ○

Ritual

for Mary R.

When my mother dies,
I will wear a dress
I have nor yet worn
long and black
to attract white
light for this journey.

I will strip
to the barest of my skins
I will bathe
in waters softened by soaps,
stand naked before the mirror
and smile

My damp hair is apricot clean and
my dusted body, prepared, awaits
the threads woven by the Three,
the black silk
I will wear
when I hear the news –

I must be her ship of death,
hear and decipher the incantations
close the pine lid on her powdered
body
plunge with her into the depths
swimming, swimming hard
to emerge on the other side

Because there are no coins, no boat is
provided
I take wine and bread from silver cups
to strengthen us
for the crossing,

For the celebration
When my mother dies.

Wendy Ann Ryden

We honor
independence
and wisdom,
the lesson
of years.

Illustration: "Crone of Winter," by Wahaba Nuit-Cat Heartsun

The Power of the Queen

A fourth aspect of the Goddess

By Zsuzsanna Budapest

The Queen is not poor. The Queen thinks she owns the world.

Is there a fourth aspect to the Goddess? The Queen – nobody ever talks about the Queen. The Queen of Heaven, the Queen of Life, the Queen of this, the Queen of that. We're not talking about Elizabeth, Queen of England. But just power. Women with power, that's a Queen.

The Queen owns her body. The Queen rules her life. The Queen rules her environment. The Queen loves power. The Queen enjoys her power. The Queen is not *guilty* about having power. The Queen doesn't take shit from other people about having power. The Queen says, "Why don't you take some power, too? Then we'll be equal. I didn't get my power from you, how come you think I took it from you?"

Power is an "is" – somebody is going to have it – and you know, power happens by having permission to have power. Power is not a finite amount, you don't pass it out like food and consume it. Power is what you find within yourself. And that's how you get to be powerful. Then, the self-image heightens, and you get kinder to other people, because you don't feel threatened by them anymore. You don't see some people one-up from you, and making you angry. You don't see people attacking you, and making you insecure. You are a Queen.

Queens are not flustered by other powerful Queens. Queens enjoy peers. Queens would love to be included with other powerful groups. Many Queens putting their power together, making bigger power. Queens like to pull things together into communities. Queens like to create countries. Queens like to create osmosis and spread power. Queens take care of business. Queens are competent people. Queens are not weaklings. Queens are not victims. Queens have pride, but not excessive pride. Queens know moderation.

We talk about how powerful we are, but for what? The true power that we have as women is trans-formational power – we can transform the world. If we can transform ourselves, we can transform our children. Men will have to transform themselves. They are already doing it, because when the ladies are getting ahead of them, they feel a little weird about that, and try to catch up. I have seen this again and again – men will change because they finally got it in their heads that women have changed. It is not our responsibility, however, to nurture them into transformation. Our Queenly duties are to keep ourselves in good shape, to show a role model, to be kind to our children and teach them all we know. Extend ourselves to men, showing a role model, but not telling men to take strength from us. Let them work their way through, like we did . . .

Power and survival must include money. Women are afraid of money. We never talk about money. Things have to be always cheap because we have this self-image of being poor. We are not poor. We are poor if we believe that. The Queen is not poor. The Queen thinks she owns the world. The Queen thinks she is not merely a guest here, but that the wealth of the world is at her disposal. When you're a Queen, you take responsibility. You say, I've got resources, I'm going to organize, I'm going to pay people, I'm going to pay myself, and I'm going to put it out that this is how we get to be Queens and powerful. Then the Queen will be the fourth aspect of the Goddess, in Her fullness. ○

Dissolving a Coven

Every ending is a beginning

By De-Anna Alba

When a coven is functioning well, it becomes a set of interpersonal relationships of the highest order. In a coven of several years' duration or longer, the bonds of commitment and trust shared among its members become quite strong. The level of caring for individual members and the coven as a whole equates with that shared by a loving family.

Like a family, a coven is a dynamic, growing unit that proceeds through a variety of transformations. New members are added with the consent of the entire group. Pair bonding within the group may form. Coven responsibilities rotate and/or evolve as the various members progress in their training and their skill level increases. New covens may be generated out of the mother coven. Members leave due to relocation, thealogical or philosophical differences may arise, or due to the break-up of a pair bond within the group or the establishment of a pair bond with a member of another group. Occasionally, the coven as a whole is disbanded. Each of these rites of passage deserves ritual recognition within the coven sisterhood.

The breaking up of an entire coven deserves serious attention as well as careful and loving planning. The group needs to discuss the ritual dissolution of the coven. If there is a shared set of coven tools or altar pieces, how will they be disposed of? Will they be burned, buried, or given to a daughter coven? If an astral temple has been created by the group, it will have to be destroyed. If the group has established a magickal link with a piece of land or natural features, that link will have to be dissolved. Any group mind that has been established will have to be dissipated and its energies returned to the individuals who created it, with any excess given to the Goddess or the Earth. Magickal bonds linking each to the other within the group will have to be broken and replaced with a celebration of the

Goddess energies inherent within each woman as each now goes her separate way.

Here is an example of the type of ritual you might like to use. It utilizes a Facilitating Priestess (FP) to keep the energies of the ritual moving along and to provide the transitional bridges between parts of the ritual. It presupposes a group mind and its symbol to be dissolved, coven tools to be burned as well as buried, a magickal linking of each to the other to be broken with an ensuing recognition of individuality.

Ideally the ritual will take place outside and there will be some kind of archway large enough for each to walk through at the point of ingress and egress from the circle. A rounded depression should be dug in the earth and a small fire should be laid and lit within it. This is the Cauldron of Transformation. (Remember to have buckets of water on hand for dousing it.) Each woman should bring to the circle a black candle and a candle of a color that represents her energies. The FP will assemble all shared altar tools and shared symbols/altar pieces. She'll need to bring her own athame and her own chalice or goblet filled with a red fluid. She might do well to bring matches and a box of kleenex as well.

If there are tools to be neutralized and buried (i.e., they won't burn), a pit for them needs to be dug. Preferably, this pit will be at the base of a tree associated with death or endings and new beginnings. Have a shovel nearby.

The Ritual

In order for this ritual to be most effective, each woman must arrive and leave alone. As women arrive, they help the FP make the Cauldron of Transformation, set up the altar, dig the burial pit, mark out the perimeter of the circle and set up the arch. When all is ready, the FP invites the women to the circle. All share a chant as a method of

These rites of passage deserve ritual recognition within the coven sisterhood.

grounding and centering, preparing the Self for shared ritual. Each woman has both her candles in hand and places them on the ground before her. When the chant has ended, the circle is cast and consecrated, the quarters are invoked, and the presence of Goddess is sought in the coven's usual manner. All are asked to sit, either on the ground or on chairs they've brought for themselves. FP says something to the effect of:

When all tools to be buried have been around the circle, the FP asks the woman nearest the arch to cut an opening in the circle. FP and those closest to them pick up the tools to be buried. FP leads the women from the circle to the burial pit, moving in a widdershins (counter-clockwise, the way of death) direction. The last woman out of the circle reseals it. The tools are placed in the hole. FP says words like:

What was born in love will now be laid to rest.

"From the elements you once arose. Unto them now return. You've served us well. We thank you now for all we have learned. Rest ye well in sacred ground. May peace within you now abound."

FP picks up the shovel and throws the first mound of dirt into the hole.

"We gather tonight to honor and bear witness to what once was and what now will be. What was born in love will now be laid to rest. What helped us form and shape our lives will now itself be transformed."

FP removes from the altar any tools or altar pieces to be buried. She hands them around the circle one by one, and says for each one something like, "I am the coven (name of tool). Take back your power and remember me."

Each woman spends a few moments remembering how the tool was used in the circle, and then removes her personal energy from the tool. She then hands it to the woman on her left. When the tool returns to the FP, she lays in next to the Cauldron of Transformation and starts the next tool to be buried on its way around the circle by repeating the above statement.

The shovel is handed around the circle and each woman does likewise, speaking her own words of farewell, silently or aloud, as she does so. Finish with the "We all come from the Goddess" song if you wish. FP now leads a deosil (sunwise/way of life) return to the circle. She opens the circle and all enter. The last woman in reseals the circle.

FP removes from the altar the tools and altar pieces to be burned. She hands them around the circle with the same words used with the items to be buried. Again, each woman takes back her energy. This time, however, each item is consigned to the flames of the Cauldron of Transformation as it is returned to the FP, so be sure the fire is stoked. The FP may throw them in herself, or ask someone else to do so. As they tossed in, these words or words like them are spoken.

"Cauldron fire, burn away these symbols of our bygone days. With thanks return in smoke and flame to the Mighty Mother from which you came."

Illustration by Katlyn Miller

Pause to let each item get a good start on burning and to allow each woman to give thanks in her own way before moving on to the next piece. If the coven has a burnable symbol of their group mind, it too must be transformed in the same manner. If it is an image you visualize instead, it must be taken apart and dissolved mentally. In either case, each woman must re-absorb the energy she originally gave to its formation. Any excess should be magically channeled into the earth to ground it out. What is said by the FP or others here regarding its dissolution will depend on what it consisted of and how it was used by the group. Do include references to the fact that the coven will no longer be working magick as a group and that the group mind need no longer exist to serve that aim.

Once the group mind has been dissolved, it's time to break the bonds that link the group on the physical plane. Each now picks up her black candle. The FP calls each woman to the altar in the order by which they joined the coven. At the altar, each lights her black candle from the Goddess candle burning there. FP speaks a remembrance about each woman's initiation and/or group bonding ceremony as she approaches the altar, lights her candle and returns to her place in the circle. After all have finished, the FP lights her own candle and rejoins the circle. FP says something to he effect of:

"Take a moment now to look around this circle, at your sisters of the (coven name). Remember the joys and sorrows we've shared, the magick and the mystery, the bonds of friendship and of love and trust that have grown and flourished under the watchful care of the Goddess."

If women feel like speaking or linking arms, now is the time. When that feels complete, the FP continues, "Our coven has now come full circle. As (coven name) dies, so too is each member born to a new magickal life on her own under the loving care of the Goddess."

FP picks up the Goddess candle from the altar. She continues, "Our Lady of the Silvery Moon, (coven Goddess name if you have one). We thank you for your presence within the (coven name). Often have we felt your hand on our hearts as we worshiped and worked magick together. From this night forward, we are together no more. We return unto you our thanks for all that has been."

FP blows out the Goddess candle and throws it into the Cauldron of Transformation. She continues with something such as, "Sisters of (coven name), keep alive the flame of our memory within each of your hearts, for our coven flame has now gone out."

Each woman now blows out her black candle. The FP continues, "Remember the bonds of love we shared, for those bonds have now been broken, and not a word is to be spoken."

Each breaks her candle in half and throws the pieces into the fire. Each simultaneously picks up her personal candle. FP says, "Where once we were one, now we are none, except the one we each have always been."

Each now lights her personal candle from the fire in the Cauldron of Transformation. All remain in silence while the FP goes to the altar, leaves her personal candle there in a holder, and picks up her chalice of red liquid and her athame. She goes to the arch and cuts a gate in the circle where it stands. She puts the athame down. Standing at one side of the arch, she says something like:

"As we were each once born into the coven, so are we each reborn into the world – a solitary Witch, a powerful woman and beloved of the Goddess."

Each woman now leaves the circle one at a time through the archway. The FP marks the forehead of each woman with the red fluid, symbolizing the blood of birth, and gently pushes her through the archway in imitation of the final push of labor and delivery. Each woman proceeds to her car in silence, candle in hand, without looking back, and leaves immediately. The FP remains behind to close the circle, put out the fire and clean up. The rite is ended and the coven disbanded. ○

Remember the joys and sorrows shared, the magick and the mystery, the bonds of friendship and of love.

A Parting of the Ways

Marking the end of a relationship

By Nanette MacLellan

With the candlelight behind you, meet and speak with your Shadow Self.

I walk a spiritual path, and I'm so encouraged to know there are many awake and awakening to the personal power that's available using magic and taking action. I'm going to be explaining a ritual loosening the powerful connection of a committed relationship that has been and is no more. The multi-layered emotions that have built over time take deliberate action on your part to re-focus on yourself as one not connected to another one. A broken relationship can be compared to a broken bone, and the therapy and length of recovery is measured by the extent of the injury.

The first and very important point is that I ask you to do this ritual within three days of reading the process. If that won't work now in your schedule, or if you're wanting to do it with a particular moon phase, then stop, set it aside, and come back to read it through later.

The preparation:
• Decide on your time frame. I suggest one hour.

• Declare your purpose and write it down – something like: I want to feel whole and take back my power. I want to not feel stupid for being in a relationship with _____. I don't want to feel dumped. You get the idea – put it into your own words.

• Gather three or five candles, giving some thought to the colors you select and why.

• Have on hand a raw egg, a crayon or marker, along with whatever personal tools you use to create the pageantry that equals your style.

• Wash your hair and your body.

And we begin. Seat yourself. Concentrate on your breath. Take nine deliberate breaths while imagining roots descending deep into Mother Earth, sending the roots deeper with the exhale, drawing up energy with every inhale. Declare sacred space, light the candles, saving one that will be lit later, near the end. As you sit before the flickering flames, draw in a deep breath and tense your whole body, starting at the feet, up the legs, torso, arms, clench your fists, even tighten your jaw – hold as long as you can, then with breath that can be heard force it out while relaxing. Let it go. Return to normal breathing. Read your statements out loud (you can wing it if that's good for you) with expression and deep-felt feeling.

Turn away from your working space to face a blank wall or curtain, and with candlelight behind you, meet and speak with your Shadow Self. Allow yourself to be led, make contact – listen for response. Write things down, and if it's not exactly clear right now, don't worry, don't resist. Very important questions to ask: Is this relationship really over? Listen from the depths of your soul – Am I free of this relationship? Don't argue or bargain, just listen. When you feel finished, thank your Shadow Self, to return at another time.

Turn back to your working space, pick up the raw egg and begin writing words on it or drawing symbols, maybe a combination of both. The egg represents the things you hope for. Light the unlit candle, and while holding the egg, speak of your plans to call in a new love relationship, develop a talent further with classes or more time spent, discover a new talent or interest, join a group – you've got the idea. When the time feels right, close your sacred space, clean things up. Make a hole in the ground, crack open the egg into the hole, drop in the shells, cover it up . . . and it is done. ○

For the Goddess of the Desert

A women's seder for Passover

By Lunaea Weatherstone

Editor's note: While everything else in this book is as it originally appeared in SageWoman, *I took editor's (and author's!) prerogative to make some changes in this article, using material from seders I've facilitated since the original article appeared in issue #5 in 1988. Enjoy!*

Passover – or Pesach (PAY-sahk) – is a celebration of freedom. Traditionally performed in the home, the Passover seder (ritual) is a beautiful way to honor and celebrate our growing freedom as women. The haggadah (script of the ritual) that follows is a modified, eclectic, feminist version, with a Goddess-focus. It has been designed to take place before a potluck meal, rather than incorporating the meal into the seder itself (in case not everyone can stay that long).

Gather your women friends and family together after sunset on one of the seven nights of Passover, and have the following items ready:
- Two altar candles and one candle for each woman
- Wine, enough for 4 glasses for each person (they can be small glasses!)
- Matzoh crackers
- Charosis, a mixture of chopped apples, honey, wine and spices
- Parsley
- Horseradish
- One hard-boiled egg for each person (it's fun to decorate these beforehand, incorporating the fertility rites of Eostara as well)
- A small dish of salt water
- A shank bone (this can be real or a toy, as it is just used visually in this ritual)
- A copy of the haggadah (this ritual script) for each person

Take turns reading around the circle, each woman taking a paragraph. The entire ceremony is traditional read aloud. Feel free to add songs, prayers, etc., to make the ceremony your own. Set one extra place at the table. And be sure to have a feast following the ritual!

(Begin reading) For lo, the winter is past,
The rain is over and gone,
The flowers are seen in the land,
The time of the nightingale is come,
and the voice of the turtle is heard.
The fig tree perfumeth its green figs
And the vines with young grapes are fragrant . . .

Joseph Campbell writes that a ritual is an enactment of a myth, the mythological telling of metaphors for experiences that change the human consciousness. "Haggadah" means "telling." We are about to tell the story of Pesach or Passover, the Festival of Freedom, using the metaphors and symbols of the Jewish myth of the Exodus from Egypt. The story of escape from bondage and the longing for a home of the spirit are universal. In the Goddess tradition, we think of Persephone emerging from the underworld and rejoining her mother Demeter in the earthly home. As is traditional at this time of year, we give thanks for the preservation of our spirit in the face of challenge. We give thanks for the flame within us that inspires us to come together each year to kindle the lights of Pesach.

To begin, the candles are lit and the blessing over them is traditionally performed by the mother. In doing this, she asks for the spirit of the Skekhinah, the feminine aspect of the divine, to come to her Sabbath table.

(Lighting the two altar candles)
Blessed are thou, Eternal Sustainer of the Universe,
Who makes us holy with your sacred words
and inspires us to kindle your Sabbath and festival lights.

For thousands of years, Passover has been a time to reflect upon the quest for freedom, and the promise that freedom will be won. "Pharoah" is not merely one tyrant, but all tyrants in all times. This year, we will also be talking about peace, the freedom from struggle, and adding our prayers to the prayers for a peaceful world that are being raised around the world tonight at many Passover tables.

Pharoah is not merely one tyrant, but all tyrants in all times.

The word "seder" means "order" in Hebrew. It is the sequence in which the parts of the ceremony take place. Some of the references may seem warlike to us in this modern age. We choose to take each reference as a metaphor for the work we do to attain inner strength and a personal homeland of the spirit. Let us begin our "telling" with a traditional Aramaic prayer that begins an orthodox seder:

(Show matzoh)
This is the bread of affliction
that our mothers ate in the land of Egypt.
All who are hungry, let them come and eat.
All who need comforting,
let them come and celebrate with us.
Tonight we are here;
next year, may we be in Israel!
May those enslaved
next year be daughters of freedom!

Let us raise our first glass of wine to Ishtar, Queen of Heaven.

Tradition has it that we drink four glasses of wine tonight because four different expressions were used in the Talmud to describe the liberation from slavery. We drink our four glasses of wine tonight to cast the circle, one glass each to four ancient Goddesses of the Middle East. Let us raise our first glass of wine to Ishtar, Queen of Heaven, Morning Star, Goddess of the East, place of beginnings, of air, of speech and song. We also drink to the beauty of continuing oral tradition, to the beginning of our seder, and to our gathering here together tonight. Blessed be!

The seder table contains symbolic objects which are important to the ceremony. Pesach is a holiday of Spring. Parsley, a symbol of Spring's new growth, represents our love of nature and the Earth Mother. The tradition of dipping the parsley twice in salt water has several interpretations. One is that the water reminds us of the tears of all women who have lost their children. Another is that the salt water represents the oceans and the greens represent the land. Together they symbolize the Earth in all Her beauty and abundance. Tonight, as we dip and eat the greenery, we are shedding tears in acknowledgement of our abuse of the Earth.

With this blessing, we renew our commitment to the natural world, in the hope that with this act will come responsibility. *(dip parsley and eat)*

Praised be Thou, Great Mother, who has kept us in life, and has sustained us, and has permitted us to enjoy this festival day.

The egg looks very simple. It is smooth, white, rounded, easy to hold in the hand. But consider its complexity, a symbol of both life and death, of the eternal cycles of existence. Which came first, the chicken or the egg? There is no beginning and there is no end. We eat this egg as a symbol of the Triple Goddess, and to remind us of our own eternal growth and change. *(eat the eggs)*

Blessed be Thou, spirit of life, Goddess of renewal, who created the fruits of the Earth.

The bone symbolizes the Passover lamb, sacrificed so that the Hebrews could mark their doorposts with its blood. This was a sign for the Angel of Death to pass over their houses and strike only Egyptians, to cause them to set their slaves free. We know now that there are more peaceful ways to settle differences, and our bone is a symbol of the old ways of blood, war and violence. May they pass from the world forever! So mote it be!

The bitter herbs remind us of the bitterness of oppression. We cannot fully imagine what it must have been like for the Jews to be slaves in Egypt or to be imprisoned in concentration camps. There is suffering all over the world today so great that we, in our privileged lives, cannot even comprehend it. But each of us has struggles in her own life, and each battle seems great to she who must fight it. We eat the bitter herbs to remind us that, although our blessings are great, there is still much to be done. *(eat a pinch of the horseradish)*

Praised be thou, Great Goddess, Mother of the Universe, who created the fruits of the Earth.

From this hour I ordain myself loosed of limits and imaginary lines,
Going where I choose, my own master total and absolute,
Listening to others, considering well what they say,
Pausing, searching, receiving, contemplating,
Gently, but with undeniable will, divesting myself of the holds that would hold me.

I inhale great draughts of space.
The east and west are mine, and the north and south are mine.
I am larger, better than I thought.
I did not know I held so much goodness.
All seems beautiful to me.
I can repeat over to men and women, You have done such good to me
I would do the same for you,
I will recruit for myself and for you as I go,
I will scatter myself among men and women as I go,
I will toss a new goodness and roughness among them,

Whoever denies me, it shall not trouble me. Whoever accepts me, he or she shall be blessed and shall bless me . . .
From The Open Road, by Walt Whitman

Blessed be the matzoh, symbol of the unleavened bread that the mothers of Israel baked as they prepared to flee from Egypt. They had no time to wait for the bread to rise, so they took it with them and baked it on flat rocks. We eat it in honor of those women who, even in their fear and haste, took care to prepare food for their loved ones.
(*eat a small piece of matzoh*)

Praised be thou, Great Goddess, Mother of the Universe, who created the fruits of the Earth.

The charosis symbolizes the mortar used to build the great cities and temples of the Pharoahs. We eat it in the hope that all nations will learn to work together to build a world of peace and plenty for all. We give thanks for the growing signs that this is coming to be. (*eat a pinch of charosis*)

Blessed be Thou, spirit of life, Goddess of renewal, who created the fruits of the Earth.

We raise our second glass of wine to Inanna, Mother Serpent, Great Lioness of the Desert, Goddess of the South, the direction of fire, of action and creativity, and we drink a blessing to the endless work and spirit of the Mothers of the world! Blessed be!

Traditionally, the oldest child asks the four questions of Passover, and is instructed by her elders in the meanings of the seder. As daughters of the Great Mother, we direct our questions to our foremothers who are gathered here in spirit. Let us go around the circle and introduce ourselves as daughters and grand-daughters: [I am Lunaea, daughter of Delores, grand-daughter of Laura and Elizabeth, etc.]

We speak now of three Jewish women, in honor of the culture that has brought us together tonight, and we direct the traditional seder questions to them. The first question is asked: Mother, why is this night different from all other nights?

Deborah, judge and prophetess, considers this question carefully. The only woman judge in the ancient nation of the Israelites, Deborah held court under a palm tree outside her home, since no decent woman could be alone with men in her own home without her husband present.

"In Israel, they called me a judge. They called me a woman of great and rare distinction, a mother of my nation. And yet, when they came to draw on my wisdom, for advice and for the compassion of

We raise our second glass of wine to Inanna, Mother Serpent.

which they were in such awe, they made me leave my home and sit outside. For in their eyes, women were weak and wanton, not to be trusted alone with men.

"Tonight, we celebrate a festival of freedom, in the company of our sisters and free to be ourselves, not afraid that our actions will be judged or misinterpreted, considered bold or unwomanly. This night is the night when we celebrate our freedom as women of power, who will not be confined or controlled. Women of wisdom, who rule their own lives. Blessed be!"

Beruriah was the daughter and wife of rabbis, respected scholars who supported her study of sacred writings and laws. So highly respected was Beruriah's scholarship that her opinions were sought out during rabbinical arguments, an extraordinary occurrence in that time, and not common in Jewish culture even today. The second

Illustration by Wahaba Nuit-Cat Heartsun

question is asked of Beruriah: Mother, why do we eat the bitter herbs?

"My life was both bitter and sweet. The sweetness flows from the teachings of the Mysteries of the Universe, the study of which was a blessing in my life. The bitterness is equally evident. The scholars considered my degree of wisdom to be astonishing in a woman. They never realized that any woman, given the same opportunities, might have become my equal . . . or theirs! Be reminded by the bitter herbs that freedom must be won again by every generation. Do not let complacency blind you. Never submit to oppression of mind, body or spirit. You, too, must make your exodus from Egypt."

Hannah Senesh was born in Hungary in 1921, and through a series of humiliating anti-Semitic experiences, she became an ardent Zionist, and dreamed of the day when she would live in Israel. She arrived in Palestine when she was seventeen and fell in love with the land and its people. Hannah felt a sense of destiny, that she had a mission to fulfill for her people. This inner calling to service led her to enlist with a special military unit that was to warn Jews in Hungary of Hitler's lethal plans. Members of this unit parachuted into Yugoslavia and made their way by foot to Hungary. Hannah was caught, tortured and put to death – but not before she managed to smuggle out a note, assuring her comrades that she would never betray them. She was twenty-one when she died. She wrote:

Blessed is the match
consumed in kindling flame.
Blessed is the flame
that burns in the secret
fastness of the heart.
Blessed is the heart
with strength to stop
its beating for honor's sake.
Blessed is the match
consumed in kindling flame.

And now we ask of Hannah: Mother, why do we taste both the salt of tears and the sweetness of charosis?

"I shed many tears in my short life: tears of frustration and anger at the opportunities denied me, tears of terror during my secret missions, tears of pain at the hands of my tormentors, and at the end, tears of grief, for I loved life and did not want it to end. Yet, though all these salty tears, the sweetness of my love for my home sustained me. As long as my homeland exists, I will be there,

basking in its sweetness."

The fourth question we ask is: Mother, on all other nights, we sit upright at a table to eat. Why, on this night, do we recline and relax?

This question is answered by all of our own mothers. It is the women in each society who sustain and create life, who nurture, heal and comfort. Women are truly never at rest, as long as there is need for them somewhere in the world. As we, our mothers, and our mothers' mothers have all worked hard for others all our lives, tonight we relax and give thanks for our blessings, taking strength for our continuing work from each other's presence.

We raise our third glass of wine to Tiamat, Lady of the Waters, Goddess of the West, the place of emotions, of tears and of rejoicing. We ask the Goddess of Healing Waters to bless our lives with peace.

Joy shall come, even to the wilderness
And the parched lands shall know great gladness
Like a rose, like a rose shall the deserts blossom
Deserts like a garden blossom
Four living springs shall give cool water
In the desert, streams shall flow.

We have set a place at the table for the Goddess, and invite Her to join all those who gather together in celebration tonight. It is traditional at this point in the seder to open the door as a symbol of the belief that the coming of the new age is not an impossible dream. Tonight we open the door as a sign of our openness to new visions and our hope that the fresh air of women's spirituality will be allowed to enter all religions.

It is written that "whoever enlarges on the telling of the exodus from Egypt, those persons are praiseworthy." Therefore, we now tell our version of The Tale of Liberation.

Miriam, the older sister of Moses, foretold his coming as the liberator of her people. Unfortunately, the Pharoah of Egypt also heard her prophecy and commanded that all Jewish baby boys be killed at birth. The midwives, both Jewish and Egyptian, quietly rebelled against this by reporting to Pharoah that the Jewish women were "too lively" and gave birth quickly, hiding the babies before the midwives arrived. Thus do women help and support each other in the patriarchal world.

When Moses was born, Miriam hid him for three

We raise our third glass of wine to Tiamat, Lady of the Waters.

months in a basket that floated in the Nile. One day, Pharoah's daughter, Batiah, found Moses floating there and took him home. Miriam saw this and slipped in among Batiah's handmaidens, saying that she knew of a slave who had recently given birth, who could be the child's wet-nurse. Thus Moses was safely nursed by his own mother in the house of Pharoah, thanks to the cleverness of Miriam.

When Moses asked Pharoah again and again to let the children of Israel go free, Pharoah refused again and again. Moses called down ten plagues upon Egypt, to convince Pharoah that it would be a good idea to let the Hebrews leave. While we rejoice in the liberation of an oppressed people, we also mourn the suffering of the Egyptian people, brought on by the pride of their leader.

When reciting the list of plagues, it is traditional to put away a drop of our wine, in compassion for the suffering of our enemies. For as the Jews were singing and rejoicing in their apparent victory, the angels joined in. Seeing this, the Great Mother Goddess stopped them, saying, "How can you rejoice when my Egyptian children are suffering?"

The ten plagues were *(flick a drop of wine on your plate for each plague):*

(ALL:)
Blood – frogs – vermin – flies – cattle disease – boils – hail – locusts – darkness – the slaying of the firstborn.

When the wailing and mourning of the mothers of Egypt over the loss of their sons reached the ears of the Pharoah, even his

proud heart could not bear it. He told the Hebrews to leave Egypt. They were pursued by armies of Egyptians, armed and determined to wipe them out. Upon reaching the Red Sea, Moses found that the waters would not part, though he had prophesied that they would. The children of Israel stood fearfully on the shore of the wide sea, watching the Egyptians come closer and closer. Finally, in desperation, someone plunged into the water, and only then did the waters part and the Israelites pass

Peace must be draped around the shoulders of the world like a festival garment.

Illustration by Renée Christine Yates

through. By this, we see that we must help ourselves, as well as ask for divine help. We must always work for our own deliverance.

Women today have not yet gained our full freedom. As we recite some of the "plagues" brought upon women in this patriarchal age, we again spill some of our wine, in compassion for those whose pain and fear makes it hard for them to change. The plagues whose powers we resist are:

(ALL:)
The persistently male image of deity.
Lack of recognition for women's accomplishments.
Disrespect in the media.
Sexist language.
Rape and molestation.
Devaluation of aging women.
Fear for the future of our children.
(Improvise more, silently or aloud)

Having thought with compassion of the suffering of those who have caused us pain, and having recognized the struggles still to come in our own lives, we remind ourselves again that this is a time of beginnings, a celebration of all we have accomplished so far. We give thanks for our blessings, for there is always hope, beauty is everywhere in the world, and our gifts are many. Anne Frank wrote, from her hiding place:

"In spite of everything, I still believe that people are really good at heart. I simply can't build up my hopes on a foundation consisting of confusion, misery and death. I see the world gradually being turned into a wilderness, I hear the ever-approaching thunder, which will destroy us, too. I can feel the suffering of millions, and yet, if I look up into the heavens, I think that it will all come right, that this cruelty will end, and that peace and tranquility will return again. In the meantime, I must uphold my ideals, for perhaps the time will come when I shall be able to carry them out."

Our fourth glass of wine is raised to Asherah, She Who Builds, Mother of all Wisdom, Goddess of the North, in thanks for the blessings that have manifested in our lives. We ask the blessing of the Great Mother on all the work we still have to accomplish in our lives. Blessed be!

Great Goddess, we have enlarged upon the telling of the exodus from Egypt. Our seder is a festival not only of freedom from oppression, but of world peace. Peace must be draped around the shoulders of the world like a festival garment. We have cast the circle of peace around this seder table, and we

Our fourth glass of wine is raised to Asherah, She who Builds.

now ask your blessing presence for this, our final prayer:

Great Mother of the Desert, Ishtar, Inanna, Ashtoreth, Tiamat, Asherah, Lilith, Kokhma, Inanna, Erishkegal, Al Uzza, we ask for peace to come to the peoples of the tribes. Fill with love and trust the hearts of the children of Israel, Saudi Arabia, Jordan, Palestine, Iran, Egypt, Lebanon, Syria, Kuwait and Iraq. Guide their leaders on the path of wisdom, and heal the battered lands, which have held war and misery for too many for too long. Let all the children of the desert be set free from the bondage of the most evil Pharoah of all: hatred. We now light our candles for peace and healing for the Middle East, and add our own blessing and prayers.

(Candle-lighting and blessings – spell-binding)

"So we saunter toward the Holy Land, till one day the sun shall shine more brightly than ever it has done, shall perchance shine into our minds and hearts, and light up our whole lives with a great awakening light, as warm and serene and golden as on a bank-side in autumn. . ." *Thoreau*

This is the end of our seder. Once again, we have told the story of the sacred struggle for freedom. We have dedicated ourselves to continue this struggle, and we have asked for the guidance and blessings of the Mother.

(ALL:)
To a world of peace and freedom in our lifetime!
So mote it be! Blessed be!
Shalom. ○

The author thanks all those whose hagaddim have provided inspiration.

From Harmlessness to Right Livelihood

A Pagan perspective on work

By Diane Darling

"Firstly, do no harm." Hippocrates
"Harm no living thing." The Buddha
"An it harm none, do what ye will." Wiccan Rede

Existing in muddy waters with purity, like the lotus, this present era of widespread spiritual exploration unfolds. The lifelong walker is delighted and gratified to find her Path converging with others, comprising great confluences, rivers of conscious effort. A person beginning practice now experiences a richness, diversity and moderation of dogma not easily found in the past. This expansion of our definition of spiritual practice gives rise to a breakdown of borders, a dissolution of limits to what we think of as holy or mundane. We work towards creating our daily lives as seamless with our spiritual practice.

For some few, a monastic existence is the choice, submerging the mundane into the holy:

I lived for a couple of years on The Farm, a spiritual community, under the erratic guidance of Stephen Gaskin and the iron hand of one of his wives, Ina May. (But that's a whole story in itself.) On The Farm I learned some fascinating lessons in group reality, sexism, juggernaut dynamics, denial and social stratification. I also learned basic industrial microbiology (I developed the early phases of their now extensive fermented foods industry), field labor, foraging, meditation, truth-speaking, vegetarian nutrition, cooking for hundreds, and living fathoms below poverty level in comfort and even bliss.

But those of us who choose to live in the world move through a knitting together of work, pleasure, childrearing, human relations, maintenance of the physical body and material plane, and creative, political and spiritual efforts.

Thus we contemplate our livelihood with the same eye with which we track our magical and meditational practice. We hold livelihood up to the same standards of excellence, ethics, balance and non-attachment that we apply to work done in circle or in the meditation hall because we understand that in the seamless life there is no difference.

Leaving The Farm for Minneapolis to study Zen Buddhism, I was able to live very simply without much transition except for the improved plumbing. I took up blue collar and then office temporary work and learned that I would definitely rather serve people than push papers, load hides, stuff gaskets into boxes, or add up columns of numbers. I found that by conjuring my Southern accent I could give great phone, but then I took a full time job making huge salads for caterers and restaurants. There I got a good look at the truckside of town: the little local Mafia, the drunks and other deadenders, hard workers and achingly honest people with nothing to look forward to.

For example, for the Mahayana Gaian, the all-encompassing effort to save the world can be made at every moment. Every action, every interaction is a seed planted, to sprout in soil however barren, to root and reach to bridge Earth and Sky – or to die, fall back and enrich the ground in preparation for the next seed, or the next. No effort is ever wasted, no action is without effect. This is the law of karma.

I got a job in the lab of a giant nut-packing plant in St. Paul. I walked all over the plant all day, lab coat pockets full of cashews and pecans, sampling, analyzing and measuring things. I talked and joked with everyone and had an affair with a dashing young mechanic which, along with an innate inability to kiss ass, resulted in an early retirement. Even pregnant, I completed training as an Emergency Medical Technician.

No effort is ever wasted, no action is without effect.

I immediately accessed the vast pre-Reagan social welfare system, became a welfare mother and plunged into a time of deepening Zen practice. I sat zazen every day, sometimes for whole weekends, sewed meditation cushions and pants for the center and community. Later I also made tofu, twenty and thirty pounds at a time, for it was not widely available in those days. I was unconditionally supported by the Zen center folk, especially the other young mothers and Katagiri Roshi.

Since the increasing complexity of Western society dictates that a significant portion of our waking hours be spent securing the necessities and amenities of life, the spiritual woman deeply considers the impact of her livelihood on the body and consciousness of the entire biosphere. For an honest and compassionate person the basic standard of appropriateness of any action, including the act of earning a living, is Harmlessness.

To the Zen wizard, the World manifests as an organic synchronicity of sliding probabilities. No change occurs without touching each probability to greater and lesser degrees. Change itself occurs as a direct result of shifting probabilities. Cause and effect are the alternating current of the universe, cascading in fractal patterns from macro to micro and back again simultaneously. The intuitive surfer of probability waves knows that it is the sensuous response to changing currents that gives rise to life in balance.

When Zack was born I became fascinated with him and with my inner process of expansion to include him in my life. I had no thought of going out of the home to work. But when he was almost one, I was offered a wonderful job in a federally funded, sliding-scale basic primary care medical clinic, which needed a welfare mother with office skills and some medical training. There I learned pegboard, chart quality control, medical terminology and some back office, payroll, office politics, the federal funding dance and the inside of the doctor drama.

I left the clinic when all the interesting stuff I was doing was taken over by a CETA teenager. I went back to food service and helped develop a fast cuisine restaurant concept, One Potato, Two, complete meals based on the giant baked potato. There I developed new potato ideas, made all the

sauces, salads, soups and dressings, prepared the toppings and assembled potatoes as they were ordered. We were located in a proto-Yuppie part of town, so meals were fast and had to be excellent. During this time I also worked occasionally assembling PR exhibits for a large downtown bank. Twenty or so of us ex-Farmies would converge, sweep down upon the midnight lobby and construct a wonderland of whatever for the amazement of the employees and patrons who arrived in the morning. Here I learned to use power tools, scaffolding, wood glue and to get along famously with gay artists.

So it is with Harmlessness.

There is a sect of Jains whose practices center around Harmlessness. They wear gauze over their mouths so they won't harm a flying insect by inhaling it. They sweep the ground before them so as to not step on any living thing. They seem extreme, and so they are, but they do not even approach true Harmlessness.

Life eats life. Buddha serves Buddha to Buddha. Bird eats worm, bobcat eats bird, worm eats bobcat. In the same way that it is not possible to live without taking life, it is not possible to act without creating karma. Though in Buddhism it is taught that there are certain theoretical conditions of Mind which make possible karma-free action on the part of enlightened beings, that ain't me and the probability is astronomical that it ain't you either. So how do we approach Harmlessness and Right Livelihood in a realistic manner?

Zack and I moved to California so I could apply to Stanford's physician's assistant program, and we lived on a remote communal Zen farm of Kobun Chino's students. I decided to Serve The Poor, so I got a job as a nursing assistant at the county hospital. I also signed on with the local ambulance service and trained as an rural paramedic, EMT II/ACLS (advanced cardiac life support). I learned to get along with all parts, ages, products, failings and triumphs of the human body. I learned to detect schizophrenics by the way they smell, to stand by as death transpired, to talk with and enjoy the insane, deal with law enforcement, MDieties, morticians and county politics, as well as to perform the innumerable kindnesses and humiliations of acute caregiving.

No change occurs without touching each probability.

Leaving the hospital but not the ambulance, I worked for two years on a program for the county health department. This consisted of driving my orange Opel, with Maria and myself inside, into the deep green parts of the Emerald Triangle, finding pregnant women and helping them access the obstetrical support system. It was also a slush fund to support some other health services which were being gutted by the Reagan administration. In this capacity I learned discretion, some wisdom ("Don't take responsibility where you don't have any power"), and more than I cared to know about entrenched office politics and the effects of defoliants on children being born to back-to-the-land hippies.

During this same period I participated in a long and excruciating effort to bring advanced life support services to local rescue teams and ambulance services. I witnessed a vicious war between the hospitals over emergency rooms, OB services, ambulance services and county contracts, wherein I learned that the patient is the last person taken into account in such a debate. In working intensive care transfers and first line response, I also learned that it is alcohol and tobacco abuse upon which the vast majority of chronic and emergency medical crises can be blamed.

Let us proceed through an internal process of evaluation and action with regard to livelihood in which we will assess, minimize, balance and then think about putting something extra into the pot.

First an excruciatingly honest assessment of the effects of your livelihood upon several important

Take your power, observe with clear eyes, and act.

people: you, your co-workers and those whom you serve, and the biosphere, our Mother Gaia.

Look deeply inside yourself and bravely confront what you know of how your work affects you: are there physical hazards such as noxious fumes or chemicals, high noise levels, substandard safety precautions? Is your body harmed by the physical

Illustration: "The Ethics of Payment," by Renée Christine Yates

stresses of your work, such as sitting in an uncomfortable chair or standing on concrete all day, or by heavy lifting? Do your co-workers and managers treat each other with respect and integrity? How do you feel about spending half your waking hours with them? Do you feel like you're on another planet when you're at work? How high is your emotional stress level? Are you accomplishing personal goals by the work you do? Is the gratification vs. frustration ratio acceptable?

that dried L.A. sewage sludge was an organic soil amendment. Undaunted, I went on a bicycle tour of Europe and the British Isles with my son and lover. Upon our return I did several months as a rural housewife (loved it) until my heart was smashed into a million pieces and Zack and I moved to town.

Next, how does your line of work affect other people: your co-workers, those you serve or who ultimately consume what you make? Serving greasy

How does your line of work affect other people?

hamburgers, designing electronic components that are used in missile guidance systems, saving a drunk driver or a premature baby, selling overpriced solar energy systems, publishing a magazine, doing data entry for an insurance company: all these have positive and negative effects on the humans involved. Deeply consider whether, in the balance, you are helping or harming your fellow human beings by your work.

About this time (1973) I met Otter and Morning Glory, who were wrapping up the deal that sent the Unicorns to the Circus (but that's another story . . .). We began a triadic relationship that has weathered numerous

Is your day divided into work and personal time in reasonable proportions? Sit with these questions until you have a clear feeling of how, in the balance, your work affects you.

When I found myself developing a real shitty attitude towards drunken drivers and slow cigarette suicides, not to mention county and hospital politics, I got a job at the two local counter-culture dry goods stores selling ecoutrements of back-to-the-land: woodstoves, paraphernalia, solar technology, doo-dads, clothing, kitchen and growers' gear. I got fired for refusing to pretend

crises, ebbing and flowing like any living thing, and continuing into this day.

While designing and sewing with a small cotton clothing collective, I began a carrot juice business, based on my Champion juicer, and soon found myself working for a merry caterer. We worked hard and had fun, made a little money, but in 1985 I folded up my apron to go as the medical officer on the Ecosophical Research Association's mermaid hunt to the South Pacific (yet another amazing tale). Afterwards I hung around in Australia, basking, playing in pubs and folk clubs, doing a

Illustration by Wahaba Nuit-Cat Heartsun

little catering, living on black bread and tropical fruit. I discovered that I really hate performing for strangers and really love playing music with friends.

Returning home, I was immediately struck down by a series of maladies which included prostrating malaise, breathlessness and palpitations, and a feeling as if I were living in twice normal gravity. There were weeks when I did not rise from my pallet except to attend to the needs of my body. Fortunately, for me, my pallet was on a deck in front of Suntop yurt, deep in the woods on Pagan land. When we all left the land and moved back to civilization, I was also having waves of crippling arthritis. I stayed home and worked in my own French intensive garden for half a year before taking a job as a back office nurse for a family practice doctor.

My boss cured me of the Lyme disease and I guess I'm still grateful because I still work for him, nearly six years later. When I was a little girl, this was what I wanted to do when I grew up: be a nurse in a doctor's office. My job is to make it smooth and cheerful for and among the doctor, the nurse practitioner, the patients and our outside contacts. I do this by maintaining the physical plane of the back office in good working order, by being positive and well-informed, professionally impeccable, excruciatingly honest and making people smile. Our office is comprised of three children of the Sixties, a former Vietnam combat nurse, a Roman Catholic (whose husband is the chief forester for the major local timber pillager), and an ex-Mormon who bootstrapped herself up from terrible disability to office manager. We get on famously, have deep respect for each others' professional integrity and cultural differences. Our patients find our office comfortably down-home, the medical care excellent and generous, and many have a deep loyalty to us, as we to them.

Further contemplate the ripple effects of what you do: How does your work feel to the Earth? Do you walk lightly, in service to the elderly, poor or homeless? Do you drive the trucks or work in the accounting office of a multinational company which plunders and wastes? Do you drive to work alone in your car and home again, ten times a week? Do you teach truth and environmental consciousness? What dream of reality does your art reflect? What about waste levels: disposable plastics, wasted paper, overpackaging, worthless products? Most of us have a pretty clear idea of the environmental impact of our work, but it is daunting to squarely face and assume our share of the responsibility and karma.

Otter started getting into the Macintosh and he found he had a knack for the damn things. When he got a Mac Plus at his house, right next door, he taught me how to use it and I began writing for a local green publication. With Morning Glory and a little help from our friends, in 1988 we incubated and hatched Green Egg: The Next Generation.

Green Egg *and the Church of All Worlds are central to our shared goal in life, which is to save the world, awaken Gaia, and have a wonderful time doing it. Our partnership has given rise to a remarkable synergy, especially between Otter and me, the most obvious product of which is together we conceptualize, choose the material, synergize and generate* Green Egg *four times a year. We also raise miniature Unicorns, travel, do workshops, interact with some of the world's most interesting people, share our mother, lovers, children, selves, animals and Water. Also our frustrations, fears, money problems, CAW burdens and so on.*

Having considered these things, we are bound to minimize the harm done in our working. Even benign jobs like mothering, community service, teaching, healing, can be examined and finely tuned. What do you need to make your work good for you? Of this, what can you begin changing today or tomorrow? How can you modify your work and environment so that your work is better for others? What can you do to minimize the harmful impact of your work on the earth?

Both Green Egg *and Zack and Josh's* How About Magiic? *are printed on recycled paper. Otter conserves by composing a maximum amount of information on every page, while I tighten up the text of the articles and edit for length. Our printer is experimenting with soy-based inks and getting us recycled cover stock, perhaps for the next issue. We are planning to remodel OZ's office to admit sunlight and fresh air and shopping for an orthopedically correct computer chair for him. We are also looking to buy a laserwriter, thus saving innumerable trips to town (15 miles one way). We*

We are bound to minimize the harm done in our working.

even wear funny yellow glasses when we're working on our computers.

What if the answer to one or more of these questions is nothing at all? Then may I suggest that you are in error: whereas there may be no absolute resolution to an unhealthy aspect of work, there are doubtless ways to minimize. Take your power, observe with clear eyes and act.

Give a bit

more,

take a bit

less.

Perhaps you can research recycled computer paper and make a good case for it to your boss, or set up recycling bins in your office. Develop a flexible work schedule that allows you more important time with your family and yourself. Check into public transportation, and catch up on your reading or listen to teaching cassettes during the ride. Ride your bike, get a very small car, walk. Read one of the very accessible modern psychology books, or have a chat with a therapist, to understand your relationships with your coworkers. Decline to partake of office politics and gossip. If you feel like an outsider in the workplace, look at it like an anthropologist! (Wow! Strange local customs, dominance rituals, colorful native attire!) Scan the classifieds for a better job, even if you feel you can't really make a radical change, and put yourself in the hands of the Gods. Make prayers and dedicate previously wasted time to Making Things Better. Bravely walk though the portal of change whenever you see a light shining through. Be open to surprises, boldhearted towards growth, and cheerful about the fact that Mom Loves You.

We are buying more and more recycled paper products for the offices I work in. In addition, I have instituted recycling at my medical office and everyone, even the commercial forester's wife, is cooperating beautifully. This year I got another week's vacation as part of my raise. My coworkers can and are usually willing to work for me whenever I want some time off, and when Green Egg *and CAW grow to the point of needing and being able to afford me full time, the person who will take my place is already prepared, so it won't be real stressful for my coworkers. They all know and accept that this day will come.*

As you are working out the details at work, plan to counterbalance the residual ill effects with Good Works. What can you give yourself to revive your joy of living, to make it all worthwhile? Can you

pursue your true life's work in the evenings? Satisfy your curiosity by taking a class at the community college, or be an artist or learn computers or go to the meditation center one night a week? Have some folks over for music or dinner, start a discussion group, take up ballroom dancing or join the health club and actually go there regularly? Write letters and articles for magazines like this one?

We pay ourselves small but growing monthly salaries and allow the Green Egg *to take the staff out for pizza and to festivals occasionally. We also get to disseminate important ideas and information, promote dialog among Pagans, offer up beauty and humor and, hopefully, save the world. Since we live far away (not exactly nowhere, but you can see it from here), in a shadow where we get no television transmissions, we rely on our readers, phone callers and publishers to keep us in contact with the outside world, which they do admirably by sending us articles, video and audio tapes, and books, letters and art. A three way symbiosis occurs, among GE writers, artists and editorial staff; the readers and thus the Pagan community at large; and the Gods whom we all serve.*

Bring flowers from your garden, chocolate chip cookies to share, say yes much more often, show interest in your co-workers' feelings and lives. Dress cheerfully, smell good, smile, say thank you, tell funny stories. Look out your eyeholes at them, feel compassion for their suffering, forgive them their instinctive defenses, plant seeds.

And for the Earth, give a little bit more, take a little bit less. Pack your lunch and recycle your containers. Eat low on the food chain, donate time, materials and money to groups on the front lines of environmental and political actions. Get your dog or cat spayed. Recycle at home, teach your children the truth about the world they will have to spend their lifetimes healing. Vote green. Sacrifice harmful actions, such as abusing food, tobacco or alcohol, to the good of the planet. Discover and discard obsolete baggage that is bogging you down: possessions, dead-end relationships, extra pounds, grudges, petty preferences and harmful indulgences.

Then, when you've done what you can to compensate for the resources you use just existing in this time, put a little bit more into the pot. Turn off the TV and talk with your kids (teach them, praise them, ask them questions and listen to them), your spouse, your parents, even if you have to call them on the phone or write a letter. Forgive someone. Adopt your next kid. Give the gift of yourself, rather than some trinket or redundant gadget. Look around for ways to take up some slack: shop secondhand, buy organic, support local public radio, pick up litter and write your congressfolk. Be alert to ways to maximize your positive impact by being a living example of a Mother-loving daughter. Be grateful for this wonderful life and show it.

I have achieved Right Livelihood in my work as a nurse and as a writer and editor. We plan to keep on as long as we can diddle a keyboard and people want to read what we publish, invite us to their events and work together to save the world. In our future we see books, anthologies, plays, workshops, lectures and ritual presentations. We work steadily for the sake of our Mother, by publishing, networking, teaching, learning, doing the work of the CAW and supporting each other. Although we have comparatively low monetary incomes, our lives are rich and satisfying, expansive, hopeful and challenging.

So by these and many other means we set before us the impossible goal of Harmlessness in Everyday Life, and the very attainable goal of Right Livelihood. To trek upon this long and winding road is the effort of the Bodhisattva travelling in company with the EcoWarrior. On the quest for a vast and shining future for Gaia and all who comprise Her, we are in good company. ○

Rose Blessing to Venus

On a Friday, a day sacred to Venus, the Witch shall bring to her altar a chalice of red wine, a red candle, rose or jasmine incense, and a handful of rose petals. She shall light the candle, and burn the incense. After a moment of reflection upon all the gifts of Venus, the Witch shall then put into the offertory bowl the rose petals. Sprinkling them with the red wine, she shall say:

An armful of roses before you
in your verdant grotto, Venus.
Resting against a perfumed bed of cyclamen
Laughing and luxuriant
Radiant, garlanded with lilies
Smiling from the corners
of your impudent eyes.

I rejoice in you . . .

in your birthing
magnificent, fertile, powerful
First Mother of the Race
in your abandon
untamed, raucous, drunk with moonlight
Aphrodite Urania
in your strength
fierce, courageous, unparalleled
She Who Battles
in your love
empathic, forgiving, caressing
Dove of the Heavens
in your sensuality
lush, sumptuous, healing
Star of the Sea
in your passion
musky, voluptuous, erotic
Golden Crowned
The thoughts of your Daughters may travel
centuries . . .
but we return to rest in Your embrace.
I call upon you as Lady Rosamond,
for surely,
You are the Rose of the World.

Anne Coffey

What can you give yourself to revive your joy of living?

From the Heart of the Goddess

A group blessing ritual

By Ondine Webb DeMer

Our combined energy, warmth and power which come from the same source, the Goddess.

This is a ritual I designed for the final meeting of "Cakes for the Queen of Heaven," a seminar on feminist thealogy created by the Unitarian Universalist Church. As a dedicated follower of the Goddess, I was pleased to see this course being offered in our small, conservative midwestern town. We were a group of eight very diverse women. Each was open, but a bit unsure and afraid of the material which was, of course, already a part of me. So, in creating this ritual, I wanted to make it as inclusive and non-threatening as possible for the more conservative members of the group. The main purpose was to provide a visual and emotional symbol of our bonding and a memento to take home as a reminder of our experience together.

We had a potluck meal, and before eating I created the centerpiece. This consisted of a pan of fresh potting soil, in the center of which I placed a large white candle with a ceramic Goddess face attached. She looks down into the candle, the flames illuminating Her serene face. In front of the candle is a red ceramic heart held in the palm of a white hand like a gift or offering. The red heart is a box, and inside I placed many small treasures, representing the four elements of the universe plus Spirit: seashells, stones, and crystals, bells, candles, and dried whole rosebuds.

As I put this centerpiece together, I explained how the candle with the Goddess face is a symbol of the Goddess, Spirit, Higher Power, Source of Love, or whatever concepts appeal to you. She is grounded in the Earth, our Mother. I lit the candle.

Each woman was given one Celebration candle, lit it from the Goddess Source Candle, and placed it in the earth. This act showed our combined energy, warmth and power which come from the same source, the Goddess. And it also represented the energy and wisdom generated from our study and support in the group. Each woman told what she had given the group.

Then I asked each woman in turn to choose as many treasures or gifts from the Heart of the Goddess as she would like and to take whatever she needs. I explained the meaning of each treasure. The stones or crystals represent the Earth and being grounded, centered, secure and earthy. The seashells are for Water, emotions, fluidity, receptivity and introspection. The candles represent Fire and energy, passion, warmth and creativity. The bells are symbolic of Air and thought, decisions, communication and intellect. And the rosebuds represent Spirit, the sweet scent of the Goddess. Each woman told what she was taking from the group.

To end, I asked each one to take home the symbol she had chosen, meditate on it, sleep with it under her pillow, and let it help her to develop the qualities she needs and desires. "Remember, all qualities are a gift from the Goddess and all your unique talents are treasures to cherish and nurture. Let your chosen gift be a reminder of the unity and bond we have developed in our group."

Blessed Be! ◯

Part 3

Deepening

As a babe in blood I am born
As a maid with blood I flow
As woman in blood I birth
And from blood the milk doth go
With age comes the ending of blood
And the shadow of death I know

By Shekhinah Mountainwater

Inanna

Dark journey to the center

By MaryScarlett Moon & Deep River

I am the daughter of the Ancient Mother,
I am the child of the Mother of the World.
Inanna!
It is you who teaches us
to die, be reborn and rise again.
Die, be reborn and rise!

Queen of Heaven and Earth

The Goddess Inanna ruled the people of Sumer, and under her rule the people and their communities prospered and thrived. The urban culture, though agriculturally dependent, centered upon the reverence of the Goddess – a *cella*, or shrine in her honor, was the centerpiece of the cities. Inanna was the Queen of seven temples throughout Sumer. Probably the most important Sumerian contribution to civilization was the invention and creation of a standard writing and literature; the Sumerians even had libraries. These literary works reveal religious beliefs, ethical ideas, and the spiritual aspirations of the Sumerians. Among these works are the hymns and stories of Inanna – important here because these were recorded at a time when the patriarchy was beginning to take hold, and the position of the Goddess, although strong, was changing.

My Lady looks in sweet wonder from heaven.
The people of Sumer parade before the holy
Inanna.
Inanna, the Lady of the Morning, is radiant.
I sing your praises, Holy Inanna.
The Lady of the Morning is radiant on the horizon.

Inanna's Descent

The hymns to Inanna are beautiful, poetic, and a testament to both her power and to her humanity. She outwitted Enki, the God of Wisdom and her grandfather, and she endowed the people of Sumer with the seven *me* – wisdoms and gifts that inspired and insured their growth as a people and culture.

She is also depicted as a passionate, sensuous lover in *The Courtship of Inanna and Damuzi*. Indeed, Inanna is herself the Goddess of Love, and it is this aspect and power – creativity, procreativity, and raw sexual energy and passion – that generates the energy of the universe. In the *Courtship*, Inanna is both the shy virgin and the sensuous mistress. Her coupling with Damuzi is one of the most erotic and passionate passages in literature. The marriage is one of body and spirit, and Inanna's passion and expectations link her to women all over the world. After their lovemaking, when Damuzi asks for his freedom, Inanna's poignant lament is "How sweet was your allure . . . " *The Descent of Inanna* plays a key role in the Sumerian literature.

My Lady looks in sweet wonder from heaven.
The people of Sumer parade before the holy
Inanna.
Inanna, the Lady of the Evening, is radiant.
I sing your praises, Holy Inanna.
The Lady of the Evening is radiant on the horizon.

The Goddess Inanna descended twice – first from Heaven to Earth to rule her people; second, to the realm of the underworld, the domain of her sister Ereshkigal. It is the second descent of Inanna that is the focus here. Inanna was Queen of Heaven and Earth, but she knew nothing of the underworld. Her quest for clarity and knowledge, as well as her sense of duty as Queen and Goddess, led her to the Earthly realm in the first place. She was a powerful ruler, and yet she felt the strong desire to challenge herself further. "My daughter craved the great below," was the response of her fathers upon learning of her descent and death in the other realm.

In her naivete, she wrapped herself in the *me,* transformed into garments and jewels, and began her descent. Her sister Ereshkigal, upon hearing Inanna at the gates of the underworld, demands that

Her names are manifold. Let us look at the names she wears and the powers she teaches.

Inanna must give up all of her earthly trappings before she can complete her journey. There are seven stations through which Inanna must pass through before she meets Ereshkigal, her sister and rival.

What Inanna discovers about herself and about life itself as she makes her descent is not implicit in the texts. However, by the time she relinquishes her final garment, she is no longer the commanding Queen. She is open, exposed, vulnerable. This knowledge, and acceptance of her vulnerability, as well as her first-hand discovery of the necessity of sacrifice and death for the cycles of life to continue, increased her power, her understanding, her beauty.

Her sister learns a lesson as well. She has her heart opened to compassion. When Enki sent two creatures, *galla,* below to rescue Inanna, Ereshkigal was struggling to give birth, even though she was barren. The creatures moaned in sympathy with her – for the first time in her life, Ereshkigal felt a connection to another. As a reward for their compassion, the creatures were permitted to take the corpse of the Goddess Inanna away with them, where they revived her. But Inanna was not free to leave unless she insured that there would be someone to take her place. When she returned to Earth, she found that her husband Damuzi did not mourn her, in fact he had taken on even more power in her absence. She allowed the *galla* to take Damuzi to rule in her place. Damuzi's sister Geshtinanna volunteered to take his place half of each year. This six-month cycle insured that the lands would maintain their abundance and fertility, and also served to humble the imprudent King.

Inanna Today

In the Inanna cycle, she is maiden, mother and crone. Her encounter with Ereshkigal can be seen as a meeting of the creator and the destroyer – the light and dark aspects of the Goddess. For modern women, Inanna is a powerful role model – she indeed has it all: she is Goddess, protectress, sensuous, a politician *par excellence*, intelligent, beautiful, powerful. She is aware of Her position in the world, of Her great responsibility. We, like Inanna, challenge ourselves, often taking ourselves to task to know more, learn more, be more. This is not necessarily good or bad. But in the doing, in living this life, we too must know the power of the underworld and its mysteries, as well as know the

For modern women, Inanna is a powerful role model.

power of compassion. Our personal growth, suffering and pain can be likened to physical death – our psyche's journey to the underworld again and again. Old ideas, old visions, identities die; myths are shattered, and are created anew. We rise up, like Inanna, aware of our vulnerabilities and the strength created from them.

Dark Moon Ritual – Inanna's Journey

Things you may need: black candles, a candle in your favorite color, bowl of water, mirror, thurible and incense (your choice of flavor), and tarot cards. The altar can be directional or devoted to Inanna, whatever is your preference. All altars are perfect in their beauty. Each participant needs a necklace, a shawl, and one tarot card (from the aforementioned deck).

Preparation for the Journey:
Like the Goddess Inanna, you are choosing to travel to the underworld. Before you go, you clothe yourself, like Inanna did with the *me,* protecting, wrapping yourself in your Earthly powers and attributes. In this case, the seven *me* are symbolized by the necklace, the shawl and the tarot card. The tarot cards are shuffled; as this is done, you ask the spirits to bring you a shield, a symbol of protection. Choose one – study it, hear your inner voice telling you what it symbolizes to you. As you put on necklace and shawl, take time with each item, endowing them with the power that you think you will need in the underworld.

Creation of Sacred Space:
- Athame delineates the circle/invocation of the East
- Wand stirs up and charges the circle's energy/ invocation of the South
- Water purifies the space/invocation of the West
- Pentagram is drawn for protection/invocation of the North
- Casting of the Circle, the calling forth of the directions. The powers of Inanna include those of the dark moon, the High Priestess, Regulator of Divine Order, Judgement, the planet Venus, the control of the law of Heaven and Earth, the Lioness.

Invocation to Inanna:
Inanna, Ishtar, Astarte – Goddess powerful, wise. From the Great Above She opened Her ear to the Great Below. Inanna abandoned heaven and earth

to descend to the underworld.
O Great Queen, wrapped in wisdom and beauty;
she who fixes destinies at the time of the each new moon!
Guide our journey, strengthen us, as we open our ear to the Great Below.
Praise to Inanna! Queen of Heaven and Earth!
Blessed be. The circle is cast.

The participants are seated in a circle around the altar. Each is dressed for her journey, the shield/talisman that is her tarot card is before her, in her hand. The black candles have been lit, and are glowing softly; the power of their energy fills the circle. It is time to begin. The participants can act as co-priestesses here, or a High Priestess can guide the journey. But like Inanna, each shall travel alone.

The Ritual Begins:
(spoken) The Goddess Inanna, powerful Priestess, beloved Queen of her people descended two times; she descended from Heaven to Earth to rule Her people, where she made the sacred marriage to insure the fertility of the lands so that Her people would not know hunger; and she made another descent, this time into the underworld, a journey of great danger and fear – a personal journey for spiritual growth.

As Priestess and witch, we too must be willing to learn, to descend into the underworld, not as a place of no return or dread, but as a place of magic and mystery – a vital force in life and in our training. All we need do is be open, to feel the power of the dark moon within us. To listen. The Goddess Inanna gained her insight in the underworld as a corpse hanging on a peg – if she can gain wisdom

in that fashion, think of what we can do!

Priestess, do you seek to journey, to explore the inner womb of the Earth, your innermost self? Why do you decide to travel, to journey deep within? Is there an answer you seek? A mystery you must explore? A desire you must fulfill? Ask for the power of the dark moon, and for the wisdom of

O Great Queen, wrapped in wisdom and beauty; she who fixes destinies.

Inanna to guide you on your journey.
(Each Priestess gives her answer. She may elaborate aloud, or silently align herself and decide her path.)

The journey begins. (*During the meditation, music can underscore the journey, or perhaps a drumbeat. In solitary work, you can pre-record the meditation.*) Travelling afoot, toward the setting sun. You feel the gravel road beneath your feet, the warmth of the sun, the breeze in your hair, you

Illustration: "Inanna, Treasure of the Underworld," by Katlyn Miller

drink in the surroundings. Yes, this is the path. There is nothing discernible in the distance, yet you are drawn forward, onward toward the unknown that is the Underworld. You have chosen to make this journey.

As you walk, you are aware of the boundaries of your physical body – experience it in its earthly incarnation. You become aware of the garments about you – necklace, shawl, tarot card – that which you have endowed, empowered with protection, identity, magic; earth gifts and trappings that you have taken with you.

Standing on the path, facing the gate, you call the Goddess.

The sun disappears just as your path begins to curve to the left – your descent has begun. Darkness surrounds you – there is no moonlight, the dark canopy overhead is like soft black velvet. You are frightened, but all the same you know that you must continue. No sooner do you restate your resolve than you reach an obstacle – it is a gate that impedes your progress. There is no key. You try to force it open, but it is no use. The iron bars are too close together for you to squeeze through. They are too high to climb over. Standing on the path, facing the gate, you call the Goddess. What should you do? Her message becomes clear to you: you are no longer in the earthly realm, and you must make an offering if you are to continue your journey. But an offering of what?

You are wrapped in your glamours – your talismans and shields. Remove one if you are to travel further. This offering is not an easy one to make. You are aware as you relinquish it what powers this item possesses, what it means to you, what it says about you. But the offering must be made. Once the token is removed and you have laid it at the foot of the gateway, the gate opens wide. You may go forward on your journey . . .

The surroundings are vastly different on this leg of the journey. Be mindful of the sights, sounds and smells you encounter. Listen to Inanna as she guides your way. You feel the weight of your offering lifted from you – you travel with greater ease – you are different, changed. Feel what that is like. Remember the sensations.

The spiral path pulls you along. Your initial fears have been replaced by anxious curiosity. Your pace quickens, as does your breathing and heartbeat.

Your eyes are opened wide in the darkness as you strain to memorize all that you are experiencing. Just ahead you see a light-colored object. As you draw closer you see that it is a huge stone – so large that it blocks the entire path.

Again, you are thwarted—the path to the underworld is indeed an arduous one. Again you listen to the voice of the Goddess – the stone is too large and smooth to climb over, there are no tools or sticks to pry it loose from this spot – if you are to continue your journey, you must make a sacrifice, an offering of one of your earthly garments. This offering is more difficult to make than the first one, for this protection is more important to you. You look behind you at the path you have walked thus far – and you know that there is no question about continuing this journey.

The second offering is made, and as you remove it from you, you are reminded again of what this token means to you, says about you – how you need it to protect, define you. The stone crumbles to dust right before your very eyes. Your journey continues.

As you walk, as the spiral path beckons you, you feel the lightness of your being without the lost token. Your step is easier, your load is lighter – that which you have needed on the earthly plane becomes expendable here. Again, the surroundings have changed. The decline of the path has steepened, your feet can not walk fast enough, your physical body can barely keep up with your racing, curious spirit. Be mindful of all that you see in this part of the journey – what you are learning, seeing, experiencing.

Mesmerized by a soft glow in the distance, your feet and body guide you toward it. You come upon its source – a wall of flames. Inanna is in you, you know now what you must do – you must make a third and final offering. The last vestige of earthly power, safety, identity must be given up. Hold the object in your hands – remember what it means to you, what it signifies. Throw it into the fire, release it – you do not need it here.

There is again a lightness, a freedom that rains down upon you as the fire slowly subsides. Feel the weight of the glamours three as they are lifted from you. How are you changed?

When Inanna descended into the Underworld, she removed all of her garments, eschewed the *me* that enshrouded and protected her. And you have done the same. Remember, in leaving these belongings behind, you cast off not your power – for that is deep within and always with you.

You are deep within the Underworld now, and you are conscious of all that is around you – that the Underworld is not a place of dread, but a place of mystery, magic and transformation. It has no one destination, but is infinite.

As is the wisdom of the Goddess Inanna. Once Inanna shed and discarded her garments, She was no longer the commanding Queen – she could accept her own vulnerability. In this acceptance, she can also own her sorrow, her suffering, her pain.

(Each participant is handed a small mirror) Look deep within, look into Inanna's mirror – and see yourself, unadorned, and feel your vulnerability. See it in your face, in your eyes; feel it in your body – your pain, how and where you have suffered. The dark moon rains down the darkness that is within you. Feel it now.

In your vulnerability is power. The power of the Goddess, of Inanna. You are Inanna. Listen to the voice of the Goddess – mysteries will be revealed, desires fulfilled. See these things manifesting now. Your destiny is yours to change.

(To celebrate this change, light your candle here. Tend the flame well to bring these things to pass.)

It is time to return to the circle, to leave the underworld now. *(Take as much time as you need – some take the elevator, some need to retrace their steps.)* As you reach the gate, you find your glamours, garments and talismans. *(Each may end up with a different card or shawl, indicating the changes wrought by their journey. Or you may choose to draw a new card.)* Rededicate them and yourself, swear allegiance to your inner and higher powers, to the path that you have chosen.
A necklace was presented as a gift to remind Inanna's people of the powers of the cycle – of life, death, and life again. *(Necklaces are returned here. Each should receive her own)* Rededicate your necklace now – remembering the wisdom and vulnerability of Inanna, and the message that she has made manifest to you this night.

(Pass about a bowl of water) It is said that Inanna sent forth healing after the great flood, and indeed that the cleansing waters themselves refreshed the entire Earth. Refresh yourselves now with Inanna's clear waters. Be born anew, the dark moon waxing to fullness now – your new destiny fixed.
(Thurible is set alight here, a symbol of the power of change)

The Wisdom of the *Me*:
The Gifts of Inanna to Her People:
(say or chant together)
The rights, privileges and duties of Priestess,
The arts of warfare and statesmanship,
The arts of lovemaking, creation, family,
The arts of prostitution – sacred and profane, of the temple and the tavern,
The arts of music and the artisan,
The power of judgement and wisdom.
(Add to these the powers of Inanna that are yours – the power to change, etc.)

Inanna, Ishtar, Astarte
Goddess powerful, wise,
To my Queen, wrapped in wisdom and beauty;
she who fixes destinies
at the time of each new moon!
Our vulnerabilities are our power!
Praise to Inanna! Blessed be!
Sing the praises of Inanna in Her song!
Close the circle.
Blessed be. ○

The Underworld is not a place of dread, but a place of mystery, magic and transformation.

Confessions of a Scry Baby

Learning new magical skills

By Annie Goodwitch

It's not easy being connected to every living thing.

"Eeeny Meeny, Chili Beany! The spirits are about to speak!"
"Are they friendly spirits?"
"Friendly? Just listen!"

While the Tao of Bullwinkle may raise some womanist dander (he *is* a bull, you know), the oft-unwitting moose does expound many a pearl of wisdom. The spirits do talk to us, and often. Magic is always afoot. All we need do is listen.

Listening is difficult, however, when our Magical self is inundated with the demands placed upon our Earth-bound self. When we first find the Goddess, reclaim the mysteries, learn to make magic, we are less distractable – some might say obsessed. Rituals every day. Brimming-over Books of Shadows. Spells galore. But as we settle in to our ability, our power . . . it's not that we really get lazy. And we certainly do not lose interest. No. It's not even a case of boredom. We just get more and more bogged down in the day-to-day. It happens. It is not always easy to integrate the Magical and the Earthical. As women, alive, concerned, responsible, we find that there are simply too many things to do, too many tasks to accomplish. We may block out 20 minutes of our hard-pressed time to meditate, but while we are in the crystal cave cavorting with the wise women, we are also aware that the milk expires today, the recycling center closes at six, and we have to get to bed a little early tonight to be at the pro-choice rally by daybreak. It's not easy being connected to every living thing.

While Wiccan Time Management is a cottage industry waiting to happen, we are making strides in that direction on our own, and in other areas of our lives as well. We can make meals in minutes, do a five-minute workout, heck, we're even learning to will a decrease in absolute refractory time to increase the frequency of orgasm. What a world. We've learned to say no, set limits, be co-dependent no more, be our own best friend. But self-help does not necessarily ensure spiritual and magical living day-to-day. This must be why I can't scry. I don't get enough daily spiritual exercise.

I must say right here that this fear of scrying is hard for me to admit. It makes me feel inferior. Less of a witch. Scrying is as witchy, as traditional, as the pentagram. But I just can't do it! Help!

In *The Spiral Dance,* Starhawk defines scrying and crystal-gazing as "ancient techniques of trance [that] always involved restricting sensory awareness." Perhaps this is the source of my trouble. I am somewhat a sensory slut, in the most sacred sense. My mind, never empty, is filled with sights, sounds, images – things to do, projects upcoming. To keep on one track, to gaze in one bowl, is difficult for me.

Maybe it is the "one on one" aspect of scrying that scares me. When you look in that bowl, you are basically saying, "All right, Spirits! Talk to me!" There is an assumption, a kind of "I'm worth it" mindset here. I'm uncomfortable about expressing my needs, shy about asking for help, for guidance. I get embarrassed if anyone knows that I can't do it on my own, that I actually need assistance. Which does not fit into the basic Wiccan tenet about life's interconnectedness, I realize. This is old baggage that I'm trying to ditch, but often comes back on that damned baggage carousel like a boomerang. And what if I do it wrong?

What I find interesting about being such a scry baby is that I am kind of a spell-baby, too. If one of my Sisters is in need of some magical care and asks for assistance, I'm at the cauldron in a New York minute. No questions, no fears. If my circle calls upon me to create a ritual or meditation for personal growth, or to cast a spell to cleanse the Earth, I find the time, make the time. Yet when it comes to doing something for myself, it is often the last item on the list. Time and again, I will find myself in a money crisis or in the midst of a hurt that really needs healing, and finally, after more worry or suffering than is necessary, I'll have the V-8 experience, "Wow, I coulda done some magic!" All too often, I depend on the benefits of the threefold law to see to it that my magical needs are met – if I do magic to heal others, that magic will also heal me. Again, an ungainly magical confession; again, my own insecurities running counter to the spirit and application of Wicca.

But I am not powerless! I am a magician, one of the Mother's own! I am a Goodwitch, after all. I must not forget who I am. At least, not completely. What will be my plan for conquering my magical fears, to spell and scry for my very own benefit, harming none?

I am a magician, one of the Mother's own!

will honor my feelings and needs." To ask for what I want!

Get ready, Spirits! I'm fillin' up that old bowl. This time for sure – *presto!*

Annie Goodwitch's Pre-Scrying Luxury Bath
Bathtub magic is a great way to integrate the Magical and the Earthical. You bathe each day – why not do a spell at the same time?

I think I shall begin by looking at life as one big spell, every day a ritual. The wheel turns each moment, and in drawing breath, I transform energy that helps to perpetuate the turning. When I smile or sing or whisper, I change the world. I tend a hearth-fire that warms and purifies; the blood flowing in my veins both reflects and ignites the will of the life. My powerful womb is as delicate as the chalice, yet as deep as the ocean, and as mysterious. As an Earth Goddess, everything I touch can change. Including myself. I hereby challenge myself (and all of you!) to take better care of myself, to bless my food as I prepare it. To keep that journal. To say three times, "I am Goddess, and

You will need:
One 6" muslin square; purple thread; mugwort, rosemary, rue, clove, star anise; red rose petals, dried and charged; Marge Simpson (or any other Wise Woman) bubble bath; purple candles; one seashell (the larger the better); one glass of champagne, sparkling cider or mineral water; loose, comfy kimono or robe for *apres le bain*.

Cast a circle, call for protection. Invoke the intuition of the West. Place herbs in the muslin square, call to their powers Bind and charge the charm three times with the purple thread.
Set candles and shell altar-style in the tub area;

Illustration by Renée Christine Yates

make sure that you can reach the shell from the tub; light the candles.

Draw your bath, tending the water carefully. The bathtub is your cauldron, the water your magic potion. Place the herb charm under the running water, wringing it out occasionally to release the herbal essence. As the tub fills, be aware of your intuition, your psychic energy. Thank the Goddess for Her gift of water and herbs.

With your hand, stir the brew in a clockwise spiral.

Add bubble bath to your liking, a little or a tub full. Your psychic energy was at its height when you were a child; invoke the inner child now. She trusted her instincts and can help you to trust yours.

When the bath is at desired temperature and bubble content, sprinkle the rose petals on top. Admire the beauty of this cauldron, brimming with power and mystery. With your hand, stir the brew in a clockwise spiral. Invoke the spirits of your ancestors to help you raise psychic energy.

Once you are in the tub, you may sip the bubbly of your choosing, and just listen. Hear the bubbles popping, the candles flickering, the water dripping. Take in the delightful smells of the herbs and roses. Open your mind and awareness. Chant the names of the Goddess.

Relax. Breathe. Pick up the shell and put it to your ear. Listen. Patiently listen to the message of the Goddess or to your own inner voice. Often they are one. Know that you can hear it. Watch the reflection of the candlelight in the water, the way the light plays on the bubbles. What do you see? By doing this you are exercising your eyes, including your third eye, to see not only what is without, but within.

When you are relaxed (or just too wrinkly!), you may leave the tub. Take the herb charm and wring it out, drain the water and thank the elements for their blessing, presence and power (or you can use this water for scrying, after the bubbles pop). Dry off and wrap yourself in your robe of beauty and magic. The bath candles can also serve as your scrying candles. If you are not intending to scry right away, release the circle; if you are, expand it to your magical altar. Take the seashell with you as a reminder of your ability to hear Her voice. Scry away! Blessed be. O

Circle Casting

By Gretchen Faulk

This is a group circle casting done by guided visualization.

High Priestess leads when all are ready. Feel free to adapt these words. I've kept them brief so they can be memorized. Take it slowly, don't move on to the next step until you can feel the results.

Let us cast a circle, our meeting place
between the worlds.
A place separate from all that is without,
but accessible to all that is within.
We have the power to do this.
Join hands, close your eyes and center.
Feel the Earth beneath us,
the source of all.
Feel the power that rises from the Earth,
into us . . . part of us . . .
The power extends and begins to move
around the circle . . .
Flowing around . . .
Becoming stronger each time
it passes through us. . .
Focus on the power . . .
Visualize it as a wall that rises
above us and below us.
Feel the energy arching above us . . .
then traveling down to curve below.
The energy encloses us completely,
a glowing sphere
Turning . . . Reaching . . . Flowing . . .
Protecting . . .
Expand the sphere.
Push it back to the walls, up to the ceiling
Further around us.
Still turning, flowing, around,
over, under.
This is sacred space,
we are sacred women.
So mote it be!

Living the Dream

Finding myth and meaning in every day

By Andrea Lyman

I am going backpacking in a well-known national park and fill my pack with the food I need for several days. Because I am going to return and load up again for a second hike, I leave some of the food in the car. Upon my return, I discover a bear has broken into the car through a back passenger window. The bear has eaten all the food and made a total mess of the car with the broken glass, food containers everywhere and claw marks.

• I have recently completed a recording of some original music and am putting together the information for the sleeve jacket. I had planned to include my spirit name, but then went back and forth about it. I have a pair of shield earrings with the symbol of that spirit name on the left earring. The day I need to make the choice about the name being used, I wear those earrings. Throughout the day, my left ear becomes more and more sore and I eventually have to take off the earring.

• Over a period of several weeks, I receive in the mail a series of anonymous mailings, advertisements about some fantastic weight loss product. I think this is odd since I don't consider myself overweight, and yet the mailings are addressed by hand as if they were personally sent to me by someone who knows me well.

All three of these vignettes could easily have been night dreams, but, in fact, are true stories. However, when looked at as if they *were* dreams, they can be interpreted as such. In a dream, each thing would have meaning: the bear, the car, the food or the earring, the name, music tape, or the "fat" mail and the handwritten address. We are eager to interpret our dreams because we know they have significance and have come to us to tell us something important. Why not then do the same with the events and characters in our waking reality? If we begin to interpret all signs as if they

were a part of a dream, we will attune to their message or lesson for us.

There are many forms of reality: our three-dimensional waking state, night dreams, altered states such as meditation, visualization and dream work, shamanic journeying, spiritually receptive states such as a vision quest or sweat lodge ceremony. However, most of us tend to listen and give credence to only our waking reality. The only time we take the other states seriously is when something happens that is so obvious it hits us on the head – sometimes even literally. If we can perceive and receive inclusively all of our realities, we could enhance our quest for wholeness, recognizing that the oneness of all things begins with us and the facets of our own being.

To me, the bear/car experience was symbolic of the need for introspection, going within to get spiritual "food," nourishment gained from looking inward as I go along the "trails" of my life. Between experiences, I need to go within to reflect on their gifts to me. The earring/cassette tape lesson was clear that I was not to use that name. The earring represented the hearing of the music or messages in the music, and the fact that it was in my left ear (left being the receptive, female, yin side of the body) meant the "secret" spirit name given to me in vision was not to be shared at this time, in this way. The mailings were a way of telling me to get rid of excesses in my life, things that I had surrounded myself with which keep me from expressing my true self and claiming my power. The excesses had become a part of me and I needed to take drastic measures to let go of them. The handwritten address was symbolic of the intent solely focused toward me so that I would take notice. My dream life has only reinforced the power and dynamic of my waking state and helped me to see meaning in all things.

The oneness of all things begins with us.

One snowy morning I drove along the country roads to town from my little cabin in the woods, on my way to a workshop that I was giving, mentally creating anticipated dialogues that would occur during the course of the workshop. I imagined a probable question posed to me and then planned a "perfect" response, conjuring up a lengthy and profound answer. At precisely that moment, all the snow fell off a telephone wire – the entire length from pole to pole, and I said, "Hmmm . . . that line was too heavy." Hearing myself say those words, I laughed as I suddenly realized that my imaginary response was the "line" that was too "heavy." I was in awe of the fact that even small, mundane things can be powerful lesson-givers and have such significant meaning.

Some would call this coincidence. I personally do not believe in coincidence, which suggests random happenings that are totally unrelated. Another way to look at it is from a wholistic and cosmic viewpoint which would explain the incident as something agreed upon on some level by all energies involved to provide a lesson or insight. In other words, I may have "called" the appropriate Universal forces to provide an event for me that would illicit the response, "That line was too heavy."

My dream life has reinforced the power of my waking state.

My understanding of Universal Law, oneness, cause/effect and cosmic timing is growing, and I am learning to see and trust in the magic of life around me. I know all things are connected. Why couldn't I have drawn that event to me at that very moment? All things are sacred, therefore everything has a potential meaning, lesson or relevance, even if it's not a sensational, world-shattering event. When we tune in to the "medicine" or gifts of all things, we become aware of the sacredness in all things as well. We do not take anything for granted anymore. We are thankful for each and every moment and all that occurs in that moment.

There are many examples of this in our everyday lives. One evening I was on my way to a full-moon celebration of the Goddess, and was to stop and pick up my sister in the way. It was "spring break-up" as the locals call it, when the mud is so deep it swallows cars and they are never seen again, so I left plenty of time. We had looked forward to this wonderful evening for several weeks and were determined that nothing would stop us. About a

mile from my house, I came upon a mother moose and her youngster trotting along the road in front of me. As I hadn't seen any moose all winter, I was truly happy to see my four-footed friends again. Most of the time you can pass them or they just go off the road into the woods. But because this was a mom and her baby, they stayed close together, and the snow piled high on the roadsides made it extremely difficult for Junior to dash off the road. They'd go to one side, I'd try to pass, they'd go back to the center, I'd honk, they'd run, get tired and stop. Five miles and thirty-five minutes later, another car approached and we both stopped with the moose in between us. The moose were tired and nervous, I was very late and starting to ask, "Why is this happening?" Finally, I inched ahead and when there was no more room for them to dawdle, they lunged up the snowbank. As I passed the other car, I saw the driver was also a woman, and proceeded to my sister's house, thinking about how women helping other women, done in a peaceful way with patience and love, can accomplish the seemingly impossible.

An hour later than we had planned, we arrived at the celebration only to find that they had started quite late and we hadn't missed a thing. We enjoyed a powerful evening with beautiful women who had gathered to remember the Goddess in our lives and ourselves. On the way home, after dropping off my sister, I was inwardly chuckling at the situation and its lessons of woman power, expectations, living in the moment – all the while being thankful to the moose for the insights. Suddenly, the *same two moose* jumped out onto the road in front of me! This time, I didn't just think it, I said out loud, "Why is this happening to me?" In a flash of insight, I remembered that the "medicine" of moose is self-esteem. I realized that I had been going through some self-worth issues and the Goddess celebration had facilitated in bringing me back my self-awareness – who I am and the strength and beauty of the Goddess moving through me. Now, instead of asking, "Why is this happening to me?" I remember to ask, "What can I learn from this?" That one simple question change has made all the difference.

I was on my way to Montana for a personal retreat with one of my dear teachers, which was to include a vision quest for which I had been preparing physically, mentally and spiritually. I had been fasting for eight days and planned to come off the fast that evening. I began fantasizing about all the foods I could eat again – some not so honorable or healthy, especially coming off a fast. When I stopped to get gas, standing there holding the nozzle, I thought of how a car is like the body, needing the proper kind of fuel to keep it running smoothly, and how detrimental it is to put a poor quality fuel into the car. I looked up and immediately saw some signs that lined the bank of a nearby creek. Every other sign read "NO DUMPING," interspersed with signs stating the amount of the fine for such a crime. I laughed out loud – this was a blatant message for me to watch what I put into my pure, clean body, or else there would be some heavy consequences!

These insights come more easily when we are receptive and ready to go within, to look deeply at life and our involvement in it. I had readied myself to look for signs, meanings, messages, omens, and when they came so abundantly, I was able to fully take them into my being and gain the insights they offered. Inner dreamwork, altered states, night dreaming, etc., all apply the use of symbols, archetypes, traditional and cultural meanings, numerology, astrology and other "decoding" systems. To interpret and integrate experiences or situations in this waking reality, it is helpful to be familiar with those kinds of symbologies. More importantly, however, is to always ask, "What does this mean for me here and now?" Similar events touch our lives every day, but because we are too busy or preoccupied with so many other thoughts and worries, we miss the great lessons they can provide. We pass them off as common experience without meaning. When we begin to look at all life as sacred, nothing is ever meaningless – not the phone call from the neighbor, the ant crawling across the grass, the color of the clothes you chose to wear today. When we put ourselves in a constant state of receptivity to all life, then glorious awakenings come flooding in.

For someone embarking on this "new" perspective, there are two potential challenges. One is becoming overwhelmed by the idea that anything and everything has meaning, resulting in over-scrutinizing. One might begin asking questions like, "Why did I just move my right foot?" or "Why did the cat yawn just now?" The other danger is intellectualization, instead of trusting that whatever you need will come in its own perfect way, and that when you need to understand, you will. If we ask to learn the lessons of our daily lives, they will come – in every shape and size imaginable. But we need to be open to our connection with all life and be receptive to all movement within that life, no matter how small, simple or seemingly mundane. If we think only eagles and ravens can bring us omens, then we will never receive the message of joy and freedom that the hummingbird brings us. If we think only the giant redwoods have something important to say, we will never hear the blades of grass sing their sweet song of simply letting go, allowing themselves to be moved by the wind, surrendering to spirit . . .

At one point during my first vision quest, I was lying on the ground with my eyes closed. When I opened my eyes, I actually saw the heaving motion of Mother Earth below me as She breathed in and out. It was a slow regular movement, and I felt like a baby lying with my face on my mother's bountiful breasts. Then I heard a deep, sensuous female voice say, "Where Earth and Sky meet, there you are – and when the moon and stars are in the very stones themselves, you know you are one with all things."

On my way back to camp, I looked down on the path in front of me and saw a red rock, flat on one side, with a perfect circle of white stone imbedded in it – resembling the full moon. A few steps away was a dark stone, flecked with thousands of mica sparkles – the night sky. I picked them up and held them to my heart, crying in joy and thankfulness. My Mother had given me these signs to help me remember who I truly am. ○

These insights come more easily when we are receptive.

Ix Chel

A Mayan Moon Goddess

By Tracey Hoover

Ix Chel is an inspiration for women trying to break free.

Pre-Columbian, Central American, Mayan deity. When I first became aware of Her, I stumbled over Her name ("¿Iks Shell?"). My daughter, then a toddler, promptly dubbed Her "Eggshell." So in our private rituals, we honored this snake/eagle/vulture/dragonfly/spider/crab Goddess of rebirth, healing, water, resurrection, weaving and the Moon in Her pregnant, egg-shaped form. Thinking back on this, I realize that we were reclaiming and re-mythologizing Ix Chel in an image of our own understanding.

Lady of Cozumel. I doubt She would recognize Her white-washed Club Med island today. In the time of Her worship, a shrine on the island was visited by pregnant women or those desiring to become pregnant. Rather than cursing women with pains in childbirth, Ix Chel eased their labor. Her lunar cycles set the rhythm for their menstrual courses, so Her intercession in stopping the Moonblood flow was believed to be critical in inducing conception.

Merlin Stone, in *Ancient Mirrors of Womanhood,* gives a lovely paean to this Goddess and recounts a myth of Ix Chel that may have been that of another pre-Colombian Moon Goddess worshipped in the same region – Ix Actani. In this myth, the jealous sun is Her lover/husband who physically abused Her after accusing Her of infidelities with his brother (the planet Venus – Chac Noh Ek), the King of Vultures (who rescued Her after the sun hurled Her from the Heavens, and who became Her second bird-lover), and a god represented by the constellation of Scorpio (Zinaan Ek). The sun ultimately scarred her so badly that Her own anger finally flowered and She flew off into the night to reign over the night sky.

Stone points out that the mythic element of male/female sun/moon antagonism appears in other world myths, such as that of Japanese Ukemochi,

the abundant food Goddess murdered by the Moon god Tsumi-Yoki, who was then punished by the sun Goddess Ama-Terasu, and the Inuit Sun Sister, raped by her Moon brother, who was then condemned to flee from the sun. It is also significant that the antagonism is engendered by male violence.

This myth is also capsulized in Patricia Monaghan's *Book of Goddesses and Heroines.* Both mythographers point out the resolution of Ix Chel to break free from the abusive cycle and re-establish her own independence and divinity. Through her successful effort, Ix Chel can be an inspiration for women suffering, trying to break free or healing from physical, verbal and emotional abuse.

The violent patriarchal proclivities of pre-Columbian cultures taints most images of the Goddess in Central and South America. Ix Chel is no exception. Stone and Monaghan also recount another myth, in which Her lunar light was originally as bright as that of the sun, who became infatuated with Her. To trick her guardian/grandfather, the sun became a hummingbird and attracted Her attention. This part of the myth is similar to the transformation of the Greek Zeus into a cuckoo in order to effect the seduction of the Great Goddess Hera.

The guardian/grandfather wounded the hummingbird; in the process of nursing him, Ix Chel developed an affection for the disguised sun. He convinced Her to fly off into the heavens with him. The storm god Chac (whose attributes are akin to other patriarchal thunder gods such as Zeus, Yahweh, Jupiter and Odin) aligned with the guardian/grandfather and threw lightning bolts at the fleeing couple. As Ix Chel transformed into a crab, one bolt found its mark and she died in the river of heaven. Dragonflies performed a 13-day ritual involving thirteen hollow logs; out of twelve logs emerged the snakes of heaven and out of the last came Ix Chel in Her restored fullness. She and the sun married, ruling jointly in the heavens. The subsequent myth of Her abuse accounts for the diminished luster of the Moon.

Her sister-Goddess in the Aztec mythic tradition, Coyolxauqui, fares worse than Ix Chel. She is decapitated by her brother, the solar hero Huitzilo-pochtli, as his first "heroic" deed; Her head is flung into the heavens to become the Moon. Parallels with the abusive sun-husband of Ix Chel are found in Huitzilo-pochtli's solar character and his association with the hummingbird. Some versions of the myth justify this murder, claiming that Coyolxauqui led a revolt of Huitzilopochtli's siblings against their mother mother Coatlicue. Another version depicts Coyolxauqui running ahead of the rebellious clan to warn Huitzilopochtli and Coatlicue; she is killed by mistake before Coatlicue can inform Huitzilopochtli of Her loyalty. In this version, Coyolxauqui's head is placed in the heavens to honor her sacrifice.

Contemporary patriarchs take pains to diminish Ix Chel's light as well. Cotterell *(World Mythology)* paints her as an "angry old woman" who helped the sky serpent manifest a great deluge. The Mayans, like many ancient cultures, preserved a myth of primordial watery destruction and attributed it to the evil of the first human beings placed on the earth by the gods. Cotterell claims that Ix Chel, rather than Chac, was a storm deity; her malevolence manifested in floods and tropical storms, and she was propitiated with presumably human sacrifices. He pairs her with Itzamna, lord of the heavens, who is probably the same sun god

referred to by other mythographers. Cotterell describes Ix Chel in her most ancient form as a "clawed water Goddess, surrounded by the symbols of death and destruction, a writhing serpent on her head and crossbones embroidered on her skirt."

Neumann, in *The Great Mother,* reproduces the image described by Cotterell, which is taken from a

Mayan codex. The caption reads, "The old Goddess Ixchel destroying the world by water." Defining her as a negative elementary character (an aspect of the archetypal Terrible Mother), he claims that her water vessel was fatal, the "overturned vessel of doom . . ." In fact, most of her attributes are described grimly: "Devouring water, rending earth-womb, abyss of death, hostile snake of night and death . . . sea – all are aspects of the negative unconscious, the 'water of the depths,' which lives in the nocturnal darkness beneath the world of men and threatens to fill the world with water."

Stone's reclaiming of the Goddess describes the myth as "the time of the Haiyococab, the flooding

She is independent virgin, compassionate mother and death-dealing crone.

and remaking of the earth. . . " Either Ix Chel brought the waters of the ocean over the land or poured water from a huge jar. Stone described the time of the Haiyococab as required for the cleansing of the earth and renewed life, not as the cruel whim of a perverse deity.

Her myths hint at the all-encompassing triple nature of Ix Chel – like Greek/Amazon/Near Eastern Artemis, she is independent virgin, compassionate

Women spin tapestries of destiny like their divine counterparts.

mother and death-dealing crone. Like the Moon, she flows through these phases, disappearing but always returning; she reminds me of the image of Navajo Changing Woman walking through the cycles of the Moon, becoming older and younger as she spins through the night sky. Ix Chel's Great

Goddess character is also indicated by her parthenogenic birthing ability.

The transformations undertaken by the sun and Ix Chel resonate with several Celtic myths – most notably that of Cerridwen and Taliesin. As a child, Taliesin (originally named Gwion) was assigned by the Goddess to stir her cauldron of inspiration. A drop spilled on his finger. When he licked it off, he imbibed the wisdom of the Goddess. Enraged, Cerridwen pursued him through many guises; finally, as a hen, she swallowed him as a grain. Nine months later, Gwion was born from Cerridwen's womb as Taliesin, the legendary sixth-century Welsh bard.

Stone describes Ix Chel in Her lunar aspect as enthroned and crowned by an eagle feather motif. Eagles were believed to be her messengers from the moon. This is an interesting association of eagles with the feminine principle; they were a primary attribute of Quetzalcoatl, preeminent male deity of the ultra-violent Aztecs.

Stone and Monaghan both associate Ix Chel with the art of weaving. According to Stone, the Goddess observed a spider weaving its web and was inspired to weave the Goddess Ix Chebel Yax in her womb. Ix Chebel Yax later introduced women to the mysteries of weaving intuited by her mother Ix Chel, offering her own spider-inherited wisdom of the art of dyeing cloth.

Women and weaving are a universal combination (refer to Mary Daly's *Wickedary* and Marta Weigle's *Spiders and Spinsters* for insightful connections). A woman's womb weaves life-threads of being; thus, women spin tapestries of destiny like their divine counterparts – Norse Norns, Japanese Heavenly Weaver, Greek Moirae and Roman Parcae. And the spider's weaving as an archetypal image of the weaver is embedded in many mythologies, including those of the Pueblo Indian's Spider Woman, and Greek Athene and Arachne.

Ix Chel was also associated with healing. Her association with childbirth probably augmented her reputation as a healer and giver of the gift of

Illustration by Cyntia Smith

medicinals. Stone lists some of Ix Chel's remedies: incense of copal and tobacco; ground crab; turkey broth; guava tips and haaz papaya; rubber tree sap; and honeymead balche to dampen fevers. Her image as healer depicts her with a reed cradle in her arms.

Naming her Ix-Huyne, Durdin-Robertson, in *The Goddesses of India, Tibet, China and Japan* and *The Goddesses of Chaldea, Syria and Egypt*, commonly associates Ix Chel with other Moon Goddesses such as Levanah, Astarte, Tanit, Alilat, the Japanese Maiden from the Moon, Selene, Phoebe, Artemis, Hecate, Bendis, Cheng-O, Luna and Diana, Coatlicue, the Mother Moon of the Celebes, and the Moon card of the Tarot deck. Her watery attributes are similar to those of the Aztec Rain Goddess, Chalchihuitlicue, who visited a flood upon humanity. Her association with the snake aligns her with Aztec Coatlicue, the Cretan Snake Goddess, Medusa, Pythoness and Athene, Eve and the serpent, aboriginal Ayida and the Djanggul Sisters, Egyptian Uadjit and Phoenician Astarte.

On a personal level, I am drawn to Ix Chel because of my interest in the pre-Columbian culture from which she is evolved. My partner is Hispanic, and his rich cultural heritage is my daughter's inheritance as well. What will my daughter's response to that heritage be? How can images of Ix Chel, Bachue, Ix Chebel Yax, Tonantzin, Ix Actani, Coatlicue, Ilmatecuhtli, Mama Pacha, Chalchi-huitlicue, Xochiquetzal, Coyolxauqui and Itzpapalotl positively reinforce her identity as a woman? How can I extract the pre-patriarchal essence of these Goddesses to present her with positive images – especially when some have been so twisted by a woman-hating mindset that reclamation doesn't seem possible? Beginning with Ix Chel, I extract her symbols and attributes, dust off misconceptions, and bring her back into the Moontide flow of woman-being. I can tell my daughter a tale of Ix Chel that is truly a tale of wonder. ○

From "Shine On, Goddess Moon"

By Nancy Amaris

From the hard-learned lessons of Ix Chel, we embrace the notion of personal freedom. If, like Ix Chel, we are subject to physical or emotional pain, we say, "No More," and, like Ix Chel and the daughters of the Moon who loved her always, trust that the light will never be put out. From Ix Chel comes the lesson of deep appreciation for love that comes without jealousy, like the great love of sisters who inhabit the universe of women.

When we call upon the powers of the Moon, in ritual space or in the beauty of nature, our feet are planted firmly on the Mother, our foundation. Raising our hands to the heavens, we adore the spirit of the Queen of the Wise, and are overcome by the power of the connection between Mother, self and Moon.

Arms outstretched, you embrace Ix Chel, who shines there as a reminder to you that you too are Goddess, free to transform and become in endless cycles:

Great, glorious Ix Chel,
you who have withstood
adversity and betrayal
only to triumph in the heavens,
we call upon you.
We draw down your powers
to heal and to shine.
We honor the courage of those
who dare to be free.
We dare to be free!

We honor the courage of those who dare to be free.

A Moon Mirror

Making a magickal tool

By De-Anna Alba

Look within your Moon Mirror and see the face of the Goddess emerge in you.

To create this magickal tool, you will need: a round piece of glass (to represent the Full Moon and your full face); a frame of silver or white (lunar colors) that will hold the glass; some black enamel paint and some red paint that will stick on metal if your frame is metal; one or two paint brushes; powdered herbs – wormwood, valerian root and dittany of Crete – and a small bowl to blend them in; incense associated with the moon, such as jasmine; sea salt and a small bowl of water; some pomegranate juice or red wine; a black velvet cloth large enough to wrap the mirror in; and your usual altar set-up.

On the first night of your bleeding time, assemble all necessary items and go to your altar. Light your altar candles and your Moon incense. Put the pomegranate juice or wine in your chalice. Place the sea salt on your altar next to the bowl of water. Invoke the Goddess, either your matron deity or a Goddess associated with psychic work, and ask Her to aid you in your task.

Mix equal parts of the powdered herbs in the bowl you've provided. Stir a small amount of this mixture into the black paint. These are visionary and trance inducing herbs. Their presence in the composition of your Moon Mirror will help you achieve and maintain a trance and see visions in your mirror when you use it. Now paint one side of your glass with the paint and herb mixture. As you do this, meditate on the visionary qualities of the Moon and on Her connection to your subconscious mind, the realm of the psychic and women's wisdom. Set it on your altar to dry, thanking the Goddess for Her help.

On the second night of your Moon time, light your candles, incense, and invoke the Goddess again. Pick up the frame and dip a clean brush in the red paint. On the frame, paint symbols you associate with the Moon times of your body, such as fertility of mind, body and spirit; life, death and transformation; the ebb and flow of your emotions and energies; self-nurturance and care. Set this on your altar to dry as well, again thanking the Goddess for Her help.

On the third night of your flow, relight the altar candles and incense, invoke the Goddess's aid again, and assemble your Mirror. Now consecrate the Mirror with the four elements. To do this, dissolve the sea salt in your bowl of water and anoint the mirror and frame on both sides, blessing it by Earth and Water as you do so. Next, pass it through the incense smoke on both sides as often as feels right, and bless it by Air. Now pass both sides over a candle flame until it feels complete, blessing it by Fire. Finally, bless it by the spirit of the Goddess and all women by rubbing it all over with the pomegranate juice or wine. (You could use your own menstrual blood if you prefer.) Now purify the black velvet cloth and consecrate it by the four elements as well. Then wrap your mirror in the black cloth and lay it to rest under your altar until the night of the New Moon crescent.

To charge up your mirror, on the night of the New Moon crescent and each succeeding night through the night of the Full Moon, unwrap your Moon Mirror and place it where it will catch the light of the Moon on each of these nights. As you do so, visualize the Mirror drawing Moonbeams into itself and keeping them there. See the Mirror take on a soft, silver-white glow. Rewrap it each time and store it under your altar. Once it has been charged in this manner, it should be kept from the light of day. It is a Moon Mirror, after all. It should be used at night, or in a darkened room lit only by candlelight.

To use it, sit with the candlelight coming from

behind you. The candlelight itself should not be reflected in the Mirror. Sit comfortably, relax and gaze into the Mirror. Ground yourself and do whatever it is you do to induce a trance or walking reverie in yourself, and wait to see what happens. The Mirror may begin to mist over and colors or images begin to appear. Or the act of gazing may cause images to appear in your mind or voices to speak in your head. This is all fine. The reflection of your face in the Mirror may change in subtle or drastic ways as well. Don't be alarmed. This is normal, too. If it would make you feel better, do whatever it is you do to magickally protect yourself before you begin to gaze (called scrying in occult terminology). Stick to it. You may not be able to "see" for some time. This skill often takes awhile to develop. "Seeing" in your mind will probably come first.

Look within your Moon Mirror and see the face of the Goddess emerge in you. See visions of your strength, your future, your creativity and your Magickal self. Draw power to yourself by using it during your Moon time each month. Then reflect Her light out into the world. ○

Sounding Sphere
(what is heard beneath the surface of the dolphin's sea)

In a sphere of sounds
that are silent –
where innocents meet intellect,
in waters that surround
and try to still the chattering mind –
these ancient children
glide forth
to ponder my odd belief in self importance.
Saying in their way,
"Relax! we are all just here to see new games;
why do you struggle to know us now?
We have always been here –
your search for spirit concerns not our hearts,
for we need no enlightenment,
nor even light, clearly to see.
We need no excuses for unhappiness
nor reasons to be . . .
You chose to dwell with Earth and weight,
labor and learning –
leggedy being who forgets to breathe;
we have never forgotten, we just chose to leave.
We took the path of the Moon-tide,
to love on the wave ride
swallowing life whole and head-first."

In this sphere of sounding
they ask me,
"Can you love us the way we love each other?"
And I begin to wonder how . . .

Katlyn Miller

Visualize the Mirror drawing Moonbeams into itself and keeping them there.

In the Dolphin Dreamtime

Tales from the sea

By Katlyn Miller

All dolphins are not of a like mind, especially concerning company.

I have always loved dolphins from afar. Though living near the sea, I only watched them from the shore. I dreamed of them, drew them, and cherished their form as a symbol of joy and honesty. When the intensive research and preservation programs became prominent, I was elated, more than willing to aid the cause. Then the seminars and "New Age" dolphin mysticism were born on the tide of ecology and transformation. With some of these beliefs I had my doubts, but still felt that anything to bring awareness of the beauty and scope of the dolphins to the public was beneficial. I thought the more people knew and experienced the dolphins, the better off the dolphins would be. Yet now, after some first-hand encounters, I believe it is time to think again, and plan for their future welfare.

We went to the Florida Keys in November of '89, Kathleen McMaster and myself, for eight days to meet and swim with these magnificent merfolk. It was a journey long and carefully planned to include every way possible to experience the dolphins, both captive and free. Kathleen had been there twice before for dolphin swims, once alone (her joyous vision quest) and once with a seminar type group (a "learning experience"). So she quite capably arranged our trip and told me what to be ready for. She said each day, each encounter, would be very different; expecting and projecting too much would get in the way of the experience. She was so right! In the days to come were moments and meetings (with dolphins and humans) so amazing and so disappointing that one could not help but learn great lessons. Needless to say, I returned with a good tan and many lasting internal changes.

When you define magick as "the art of causing changes in consciousness," then the dolphins are quite magickal! But perhaps many today expect too much from them, and in desiring their joyous spirit so intensely, may unintentionally be acting selfishly and not in the dolphins' best interest.

My first meeting was with a solitary captive dolphin at our out-of-the-way resort hotel. At first I thought that this beautiful female, Shelly, must be very lonesome. I felt a wave of sadness and over-righteous anger as I watched her in the evening, pushing her constant companion, an old inner tube, around her private lagoon and breathing sighs through her blow hole. Her home was adequate, clean, open to the tide, and set in an idyllic tropical atmosphere. Yet, to me, the thought of a dolphin alone was a depressing one. I was to learn many lessons from Shelly – most important of which was that all dolphins are not of a like mind, especially concerning company.

Shelly performed short shows for the guests each day at feeding time – she obviously adored her trainer, with or without a bucket of fish. She had been there since she was three and had several dolphin companions along the way, none of whom worked out well. I was to hear many stories from residents about Shelly and these others. The other dolphins could not or would not adapt with the ease she did. One male brought to the lagoon from the navy base nearly killed her trying to mate when she was still too young. An older female was tried, but she dominated the food, the trainer and poor Shelly. Both of these dolphins died of supposedly natural causes a few years after being put into this environment. With dolphins, you never know. They are conscious breathers, and if they are unhappy enough in captivity they simply stop breathing and commit suicide. Yet through all this, Shelly remained healthy and I believe happy in her own little world with her human family. This should not, however, be viewed as a typical example, but as an exception to the rule. It is a rare and isolated case, but a way for me to learn first-hand how much like us the dolphins are. That each is unique in choosing its own lifestyle and companions. They are individuals.

It was a treat for us to be able to live so close to such a sociable being as Shelly. It didn't take a handful of frozen fish for her to want to play and perform. I was told by one of the owners of the retreat, after several heart to heart chats, that if I really wanted to meet Shelly in her own element, I should quietly swim around to the back of the lagoon. This I did, and to my surprise the fence blocking the lagoon to the opening of the channel had a door cut into it under the water. Not wanting to break the rules, at first I just dove down to the opening to find Shelly eagerly awaiting me and sending out her sounding waves to find out who I was. There was an immediate feeling of welcome

and a desire to play. She stayed exactly at the opening facing me underwater, nose to nose. We interacted like this for awhile, diving and waving and nodding to one another, until the temptation became too great, and I dove under and through the fence.

She circled me and rubbed up against my body, in a very strong but loving way, and then began to "taste" my leg. This can be a very unsettling experience the first time, for their teeth are sharp and dangerous-looking, but they mean no harm. This is their way of touching you, using their tongues, which are very sensitive. What a joy it was to stroke her soft smooth skin and to know that she was happy about the meeting, for she could have turned away at any moment, and I would not have been able to follow her. The next day, I tried the

What a joy to know she was happy about the meeting.

Illustration by Wahaba Nuit-Cat Heartsun

same thing, and she swam to meet me as before, but stopped short after sounding in my direction. I dove forward, but she just nodded at me, squeaked, and backed off a bit more. At first I didn't understand what was wrong, but as I turned to surface, directly behind me and about a foot from my face was a very large barracuda! I was out of that water faster than you can say "flying fish"! Shelly must have known that I'm not too fond of big old curious cudas. These times with her were very rewarding, and I'm thankful I was able to know her, even for a short while.

The magick of the sea and her children brings like souls together.

Our next type of encounter was with captured dolphins, in what they called a structured swim program. This means that a licensed operation with special trainers can offer anyone the chance to swim with and touch dolphins. There is first a lecture and period of instruction, after which people enter the dolphins' pool or tank with snorkel equipment. The experience here is rather empty, for the dolphins are rewarded with food every time they appropriately interact with a human. We found out that the owners of such operations make a fortune off their captives. However, I must admit, it is fun to get a dorsal fin tow ride, and the ability to actually touch a dolphin is guaranteed. It felt a bit

like a whorehouse!

Next, we visited "Dolphins Plus," a "research center" where, again, you can rent time in the water with several dolphins. Here, though, the dolphins are not rewarded for their actions, and you are told not to be aggressive or reach out to them. They will come to you if they feel like it. You become *their* toys. Kathleen has spent many days at this facility and can truly attest to the variety of moods, types of play, and reactions that can be experienced in this environment.

Sometimes they ignore you completely, and sometimes it's a human-dolphins orgy. My experience was nice, for I was able to swim very close to them, and they did approach and touch me, but not as much as I had hoped. The underlying feeling was that they were bored that day and thought that teasing me might be fun – coming up and stopping right next to me, offering their dorsal fins, giving one small touch and then darting away. I knew these were the same dolphins that Kathleen had practically had carnal knowledge of last year, but that day they wouldn't play with her either. It was a little frustrating for us. We had spent $300 for the two of us to spend about two hours with young females in a teasing mood. They were very unpredictable during these swims – while we were there, a girl was literally swept away by a large male dolphin. There was obviously some great attraction for him, but the girl was terrified! The males like to touch and push humans and each other around with their erect penises, which serve as sense organs, like a finger, as well as for recreational sex and reproduction. It was an interesting day.

The introductory lecture at "Dolphins Plus" is excellent and informative, giving the latest research findings and what seems to be a very loving and honest attitude toward the dolphins. But though they fight for dolphin rights, they are still making a ton of money off them. (And by the way, where did you guys acquire your dolphins?)

Now we come to the best part of our journey – sailing out to visit the wild dolphin pods. We signed up with "Dolphin Watch" for four wonderful days. Dolphin Watch is actually just one catamaran and two great people, Melinda and Ron. They take dedicated dolphin watchers out almost every day. You don't have to sail far to meet the pod and in

Illustration by Katlyn Miller

one day can have several encounters. There is no comparison to seeing the cetaceans in the open ocean and in captivity – the feeling is completely different. The first time you see them leaping toward the boat makes your heart sing, for they choose to meet you, they bid you welcome. Speeding through the blue waters, dancing and jumping with sheer delight, right up to the bow, they turn their thoughtful eyes to you and seem to size you up in a glance, then circle to show their approval. The pod knows Ron's boat well and he is always a welcome guest in their waters. We were privileged to be aboard. The dolphins did not come every day. When the wind whips up the waves and the waters are rough, they seem to have a secret hiding place, for on those days we did not see them. But when the weather was fair they came out to play, to our great delight.

The people we met on these outings were fascinating as well, and several friendships were made that I'm sure will endure. The magick of the sea and her children brings like souls together, and all can feel childlike again. We would sing, sound or chant, whatever felt right, every day – the dolphins seemed to be drawn to singing, for when they would begin to leave, a good vocal chorus would bring them back like a siren's song. When the time was right, Ron would pull out the little "aquaplane," really just a half-circle of board attached to the boat by a rope. We would take turns being towed behind the boat, and if we were lucky, the dolphins would approach and come close to sound behind us and dance in our wake.

I was particularly blessed the first time I tried this, for as soon as I entered the water, six dolphins surrounded me, three on the surface and three below – what an overwhelming experience that was! At first I felt a bit insecure, out in the middle of the ocean far from the boat, enclosed by these awesome creatures. I forgot to breathe, I was so excited and surprised! Sounds came from all directions, and I soon began to relax. I let go of the rope to bask in their presence and realized why I had come so far to visit these magnificent beings. This was the experience I had hoped for. I received no ancient wisdom nor miraculous healing, no messages from Sirius or directions to Atlantis – just a feeling of pure joy and heartfelt gratitude for their presence on the planet.

There are so many things to consider when addressing the dolphin issues. Of course the programs to save them must be supported. But new problems are going to arise because of our very love and interest in the dolphins. Many people will discover that much money can be made from them, and begin to capture the wild dolphins to train and sell in ever-increasing numbers. This would be a tragedy, yet how do we avoid it? Issues are coming up now that may be decided upon in the very near future. Should these dolphin swim programs be licensed in order to continue? And if they aren't, will the seas be filled with dolphins watches? Then no one will be able to share this experience to its fullest.

Dolphins are not a metaphysical product to be strip-mined like the crystals – they are sentient beings. When you tap into the consciousness of your personal power animal, it doesn't mean you have to physically touch that animal or keep it in captivity to connect with its essence. We wouldn't go off looking for a bear or an eagle to touch, for example. I know that I have decided to back off from the promotion of dolphin mysticism and help more with preservation and understanding. Regulations need to be set so the pods can roam free and not be put on "reservations," driven far out to sea or held captive for our amusement. If people are drawn to swim with the dolphins, let it be in the wild and with responsible, caring people. The dolphins' magick is in their freedom. Their gift to us is simply the joy of their existence. ○

The dolphins' magick is in their freedom.

Hestia

Bringing the Goddess back home

By Callista Lee

She dwells at the center of that elusive place we call "home."

Dorothy, in the Wizard of Oz, cries, "There's no place like home, there's no place like home." And we've all heard that "home is where the heart is." But what is "home"? And what makes a house a home?

Most dictionaries suggest that your home is your "fixed residence; the dwelling place in which you habitually live, or regard as your proper dwelling place." But if you read on in one of the more comprehensive dictionaries, you get closer to the "hearth" of the matter: "the place of one's dwelling and nurturing; a place to which one properly belongs, in which one's affections center, or where one finds rest, refuge, or satisfaction." In sports, home is "the place in which one is free from attack, the goal."

The idea that our home is just the address on our driver's license is a relatively new one, one that suggests that the larger, more personal concept of home as a source of nourishment and a place of sanctuary has somehow been diminished. Seventies feminism released us from the bondage of emptiness home had become and allowed us to participate in the "real" world outside of it. Homemakers/housewives were demeaned as not having real jobs by those of us who had escaped into the male realm of money and power. Today we are careful to catch ourselves before saying about a friend, "She doesn't work," and say instead, "She doesn't work outside the home." But the emphasis is still clear: home is less valuable in terms of what you can buy; there is often an emptiness where the hearth fire used to be. "What are you doing tonight?" "Oh, I'm just going to stay home." "Sounds boring; let's go out."

In ancient Greece, the central hearth of the house was the symbol of "home," for it provided not only physical warmth and a way to cook meals, but also

acted as a spiritual center and gathering place for the family. The hearth was sacred in every home and temple, for in the hearth burned the living flame of the Goddess Hestia. Hestia (later Vesta, among the Romans) is the flame that burns at the spiritual center in each of us; She dwells at the center of that elusive place we call "home," and She is the fire at the center of the Earth. She is the shapeless foundation upon which our lives are built, the original "home maker."

A house was not a home until Hestia was duly installed in the sacred hearth. In *Goddesses in Every Woman,* Jean Shinoda Bolen tells us that, "When a couple married, the bride's mother lit a torch at her own household fire and carried it before the newly married couple to their new house to light the first household fire. This act consecrated the new home." New babies in the family were promenaded around the hearth by the parents to symbolize their admission to the family. And among some peoples the hearth fire was extinguished for a time to honor the passing of a dead family member. Each community consecrated a central public hearth to Hestia as well. Hestia's most important temple was in the town of Delphi, which the ancient Greeks considered to be located at the exact center of both Greece and the Earth itself.

Hestia was often paired with Hermes (Mercury), the messenger God. He was represented by the pillars of the doorway into the home. He "posted" guard at the doorway, keeping evil out of Hestia's sanctuary. When family members ventured outside, he was there to guide and protect them on their travels until they returned home to Hestia again. Together, Hestia and Hermes represent the balance of female and male energies and ensure fertility within the home, although they were never actually paired romantically themselves. Hestia is a Virgin Goddess, whole unto herself. Despite Aphrodite's

In the hearth burns the sacred flame of the Goddess Hestia.

attempts to woo Her with the affections of both Poseidon (God of the Sea) and Apollo (God of the Sun), Hestia chose to remain unmarried and inward-focused.

Her reward for insisting on the importance of honoring Her own independence and integrity was to receive a place in all the temples of the other Gods and Goddesses, not represented (as they were) by painters and sculptors, but by the round hearth fire that burned eternally at each site. She received the best or first portion of each sacrifice offered to the God/desses in whose temples She burned.

The Romans were keenly aware of Her importance and installed young women as Vestal Virgins to maintain the eternal flames of Her temples. Anyone studying the Romans must realize that they had

more than a few problems leading to their eventual downfall, and one was that they seem to have put too much emphasis on the symbology of Vesta (Hestia) and too little working to embody Her spiritual message of personal knowledge and strength within one's self. Besides being flame keepers, the Vestals were to maintain strict sexual virginity and were made to shave off their hair, a symbol of female beauty. After one particularly devastating military loss by the Romans, several of the Vestals were put to death because it was assumed that the loss had been caused by their infidelities (gee, it couldn't have been because of poor military strategy, could it?). In *The Woman's Encyclopedia of Myths and Secrets,* Barbara Walker reports that the Vestals did have sex, but only in a secret ceremony in which they were married to the phallic deity of Palladium through

Illustration by Wahaba Nuit-Cat Heartsun

his priestess, the Pontifex Maximus, "great maker of the pons." Look up "pons" in a human sexuality textbook, then think about the Catholic Pope's title of "Pontiff." All of these circumstances sound like good reasons for the Goddess to want to leave home!

So we find ourselves today, feminists of the Nineties, heady from our successes in the world, but also feeling the tug of the old apron strings that call us back home. For women trying to have it all, there is often little joy in the work (and little appreciation and/or support from our families) of maintaining the home: shopping, preparing meals, cleaning, laundry, caring for young children, etc. These things are chores to be finished as quickly and painlessly as possible so that we can get on with "real" life. In Hestia, we can come to understand why it is that women have had to leave home in order to not be depressed by what it has become: a place of little value compared to other measures of worth in Western culture. When our homes are like airport terminals with family members flying in and out, staying just long enough to change clothes, sleep or eat a meal, or showplaces for the wealth we have accumulated from our "real" jobs, we find that the spiritual fire of the hearth may only be a faint flickering or even totally extinguished.

Is there not also a feminism that could bring us back home?

In *Pagan Meditations,* Ginette Paris asks, "Is there not also a feminism that would bring us back home, so that our homes would reflect ourselves and would once more have a soul?" This doesn't mean giving up our careers and financial independence; what it does mean is remembering the importance of having a solid inner foundation upon which to build our busy outer lives. Yes, it's about the dreaded "B" word: balance! In honoring Hestia the Virgin in our homes, we reclaim personal power and knowledge. We create a sense of strength that lets no stranger penetrate our spiritual interior. We create a home that is a place of nourishment, refreshment, sanctuary and peace. We also strengthen our relationships and workings in the outside world.

Nineties feminism is about androgyny; we are both Hestia and Hermes. We honor Hermes in the world of outside relationships, work and recreation. But without Hestia firmly placed in our homes, we are adrift in a "man's world." Hestia is our anchor and our rudder. She burns brightest within us in those moments when we remember who we are on the deepest level. The paradox of the circle is Hestia's lesson: you are best connected with all points of the circle's circumference when you are exactly at its center. Instead of seeking knowledge of the circle by tediously treading its outer ring, we can see all of it from a seat at its center. Hestia is the spider at the center of its web, the axis upon which the Earth turns, the sun at the center of our solar system.

In encountering problems with interpersonal relationships, we can turn inward and ask, "How am I contributing to this problem?" For each finger pointing out to blame another, there are three pointing back towards ourselves. Hestia calls on us to take responsibility for ourselves. And She offers a refreshing change of pace from the often tense energy we exert in the work world, the kind that leads to burn-out. Hers is a calm energy, the energy found in yoga movements and zenlike meditations. She is the one who whispers, "Physician, heal thyself" as She reminds us that we have little to offer others as mothers, lovers, friends and workers when we let our own inner fire die out from lack of fuel. We see the damage done by neglecting Hestia within ourselves as we increasingly fall victim to lifestyle-related illnesses connected to emotional stress, poor eating and exercise habits, and environmental pollutants.

Ginette Paris tells us that the Greeks had an expression, "One must sacrifice to Hestia," which meant that we must put our outer lives on hold from time to time, put ourselves first, refusing to share the resources that we need to maintain our own lives. These resources may include time to be alone with our thoughts, creating a comfortable home environment, proper nourishment, clean air and water, and permission to say no to the requests of others. This is the aspect of Hestia Tamia, guardian of food supplies who reminds us that "charity begins at home." She is honored by a full pantry, freezer, etc. (Yes, you can honor her by finally getting that earthquake/tornado/survival larder put together.) In this aspect, Hestia offers us a feeling of security and stability. These feelings of confidence and wholeness allow us to go into the outside world, take the risks and confront the challenges that will bring us so many of the riches that human existence has to offer.

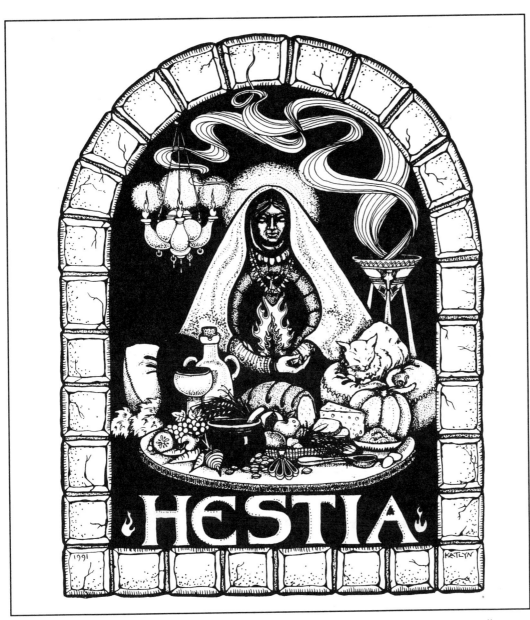

Hestia offers us a feeling of security and stability.

We also see the consequences of neglecting Hestia on a global level, our collective household. By acting as temporary tenants on this earth, we use up its resources while poisoning it with our waste. From this perspective, Hestia is not just a single circle, but a series of circles, each with the same center. We honor our spirits, our bodies, our homes, our relationships, our communities, our planet and our universe by beginning with the source that Hestia represents.

Where to begin? At home, of course! According to the '91 *SageWoman* reader survey, many women are reluctant to "come out" as Goddess worshippers or witches to family and friends by setting up permanent altars to the Goddess. (Actually, you'd be surprised at how many people come into my house and leave without a clue as to my "true identity.") Well, Hestia is the perfect Goddess for you to honor in very outward ways without anyone being the wiser. She is honored when you claim your own space and time in which to nest. She is found in the zen of housekeeping. Making quiet, unhurried time to enjoy some of the work of maintaining your home and making it a comfortable, nourishing place honors Her. If you have a fireplace, keep it relatively clean and arrange the furniture so that it becomes a gathering place. If you don't have a fireplace, set up a special candle for Her – people decorate with candles all the time, so no one will suspect what it's really there for. Take a stroll around your house and look for places that are already centers of your family's affections, needs and preoccupations. When you're alone,

Illustration by Katlyn Miller

invite Hestia to bless those places. Even if it's not appropriate to leave a candle there (like on top of the refrigerator upon which your children's artwork is displayed), burn one there during your own private time.

Make private time for yourself! Insist upon it, especially if you are the busy mother of young children. Send the family off to the movies so that you can take an uninterrupted bath, scented with fragrant oils or flower petals, candles and incense burning, and meditate on Her, on your own inner flame. Families with older children often find that the problem is having a quiet family meal without friends being invited over or family members being out, telephone calls and the like. You might consider holding a family meeting to make a decision to choose a special time each week to honor home and family. If all members of the family are included in this decision, you'll be much more likely to get their cooperation. Of course, to honor Hestia is also to let go of attachment to ego and the comings and goings of other people. If your family members are not interested in honoring Hestia in these ways, it would be very un-Hestian to try to force the issue. You will go on finding ways to honor Her yourself, learning to become a point of stillness and peace within the chaos.

Singles and young couples often find their social lives so full that they neglect to enjoy quiet time at home. Look for relaxing activities that you can do at home that leave you feeling peaceful and refreshed. This should be at least as high a priority as attending meetings, playing sports or going out with friends. The outer life is not given up for Hestia; rather, it is nourished and supported by Hestia. People who live alone are sometimes fearful of being lonely at home alone. Hestia can teach you the difference between painful loneliness and nurturing solitude.

After finishing the paragraph above, I turned off the computer, wondering how I was going to conclude this article, and headed out the door to school, where I was to give a final exam to my college students. The car started right up, but when I went to put it in gear, I discovered that I had no clutch. Great! Well, I can't let this stop me; my students have been studying their brains out and I can't just not show up. So I went back inside, changed into motorcycle-appropriate apparel, packed my papers

The outer life is nourished and supported by Hestia.

into my tank bag and headed out to the garage. I pulled the bike out, attached the tank bag, put on my helmet and gloves and attempted to start the bike. It wouldn't start. Fine! It looks like rain anyway. I don't even *want* to ride my bike! Grrrrr! I put the bike away and once again returned to the house. Now, I realize that sometimes things really do happen for a reason and other times shit just happens. The world is out there "worlding" and you get in the way. At that moment, I really didn't care why this was happening. What I cared about was getting to school on time, which was now quickly running out.

"Hestia! I really do want to honor you by staying home more, by finishing this article, by cleaning the fireplace, but right now I need to get to school!" I phoned the only taxicab company in town and got a message that the number was no longer in service. "Okay, Hestia, what do you want?"

Just then, my cat poked his head out from beneath my Solstice tree and beckoned me to come to him. I took a deep, cleansing breath and let my heart open to the love the two of us share, to the warmth of my kitchen on a cold winter's night, to the smell of the evergreen, my own creativity in decorating it, and the familiar sights of my home. I took a moment to honor Hestia's fire within my own soul, remembering who I am. I called the taxicab company again and got through. While waiting for the cab, I did some straightening up around the house. Rather than trying to get another cab after the exam, I walked the three or four miles home, enjoying every minute of solitude. Hestia's fire within me kept me warm until I got home. ○

Blessings of the Corn Dolly

The Goddess and the land

By Rose Buffalo

The land at Rose Farm – two and a half acres. This is my home; this is where I have planted myself, deep, with every fruit tree, rose bush, herb, and vegetable bed. This is where my roots are. Sometimes these roots make a bitter brew, and then there is the taste of honey, the bitter and the sweet.

When I left my husband nine years ago, I bravely said, "If I have to give up the farm, so be it; I want to be free." Oh, the Goddesses and the grand-mothers were watching out for me. He got his pension, and I – for twenty-one years as wife and mother – got the land, the sweetness, the worry, and a mortgage. This is my future, my work, my life, my dream. Most of what makes life rich and good is here on this magic piece of land. Healing soft earth, spirit-filling silence, trees and plants and grasses that move in the wind. Warm stars in summer skies, green willows, hawks and humming-birds, mellow old farmhouse, and wild overgrown gardens. Women are starved for what is natural, for what is here, as I am.

Country women are everywhere across this land, living much as I do. The Women's Movement contributed to this group, and some have always lived so. They are fierce and independent, self-reliant, and lovers of solitude and group living. I have met many out here on the other side of Watsonville (California), working very hard to nurture the priceless heritage of the land. Strength and self-sufficiency are learned along with the art of splitting wood, a very empowering task. The values of country living make a way of life, forming something more permanent. It takes seven years for a tree to bear fruit; that is the reason ancient Greeks chose the olive tree as a symbol of civilization. How different the symbols of American civilization are.

Of the women I know, most have found, as I have – just as so many farmers find – they need other work, because it is very difficult to make a living on the land in these tines. According to a bulletin from the University of California, Small Farm News, "10% of the main operators of California farms are women. Farm families now make 62% of their income from the farm. About 70% of employed farm women work at jobs in nearby cities and towns, compared with 30% of employed farm men. The outside income allows farmers to keep small-scale operations going."

Food Raised with Love and Her Own Hand
One of my neighbors is in her seventies; she has farmed all of her life. She is strong and healthy, and beauty shines from her face. Her five-acre farm, once much larger, is very ramshackle by most standards, but feeds my hungry eye every time I pass by. I receive strength and encouragement when I see what she has chopped for fuel, with her small hatchet, from a giant pine felled on her land. She has cooked and heated on a wood stove all her life. There are new fruit trees in her garden. She raises goats, chickens, geese for milk, eggs and meat. Her animals are tenderly cared for and lovingly conversed with every day in Russian. Her living is caretaking an elderly woman who is bedridden. Once it was dairy farming where I live. She harvests the grain for the goats with a scythe, working through the fields easily as any man. She attributes her good health to the food that she has raised with love and her own hand, and "no junk food."

Other country women I know are teaching school, one is a successful writer, a horse groomer, and so on. Several are raising food and flowers with partners in greenhouse operations. Statice and gourmet vegetables have been big recently, and now I suspect it has been overdone. Two women I

Healing soft earth, spirit-filling silence

know work in the high-tech world of Silicon Valley.

"The Earth is my sister"

I was born on the Rosebud Indian Reservation in 1933 to a family of farmers. Those were terrible years; they left the land and ended up in San Jose. I spent forty years of my life there. When I was a girl, it was a blossomed, perfumed countryside filled with small farms. Now, it is cemented over – the orchards torn from the earth, the air and water polluted, growth spreading like cancer out of control. It tears at my heart to remember how it was, and as I write this, tears run down my face.

Susan Griffin says, in *Woman and Nature, The Earth, What She is to Me*, "I am weeping openly. I have known her all my life, yet she reveals stories to me and these stories are revelations, and I am transformed. Each time I go to her I am born like this. Her renewal washes over me endlessly; her wounds scare me; I become aware of all that has come between us, of the noise between us, the blindness, of something sleeping between us. How my body reaches out to her. They speak effortlessly, and I learn in no instant does she fail me in her presence . . . I feel her pain . . . I know why she goes on . . . with this great great thirst, in drought, in starvation, with intelligence in every act does she survive disaster. The Earth is my sister . . ."

Yes, and she is our mother and our very great great-grandmother. She has nourished us for so long, and I hear her speaking to women of the fields and women of the valleys. "You must take care of me. Plant your gardens, if only on a windowsill. Start your seeds; this will feed your hungry spirit as well as your body. I love your offerings, your lighted candles, songs and prayers. Raise your children, make your art, grind your corn and weave your cloth. These are part of the holy sacrament between us."

These are the blessings of the corn dolly I want to share with you. When I first came here nine long years ago, I did an art piece called Blessings of the Corn Dolly. It was in celebration of my return to the land. The City of San Jose Fine Arts Commission had kiosks on South First Street, and there she stood – five feet tall – in all her shining glory. Today I am still celebrating, and making corn dollies and Goddesses. One was in a show in Berkeley recently, and a lovely woman bought her and took her home. A nice blessing for all of us. Closer to home, one of my pieces is in a local restaurant, dressed as a Squid Goddess.

Our English word "dolly" comes from the Greek root meaning "idol." Wheat and other grains are called corn in Europe. We owe this mix-up to Christopher Columbus and his men. So the corn dolly, in earlier times and even now, is really a Goddess woven of wheat, representing Mother Earth to ensure a good harvest. I have even seen them in import stores in the last couple of years, made in China.

Sometimes this life is hard, and I know it has aged me – that and trying to be an autonomous woman. Yet the corn dolly has called, and I have answered with joy in my heart. I wish you all sweet medicine and good harvest, a harvest of blessed food and wreaths and warmth and shelter and garlands of flowers and herbs for the healing, the celebration of the earth – the fire – the water – the air of our very lives. ○

A harvest of blessed food and wreaths and warmth and shelter

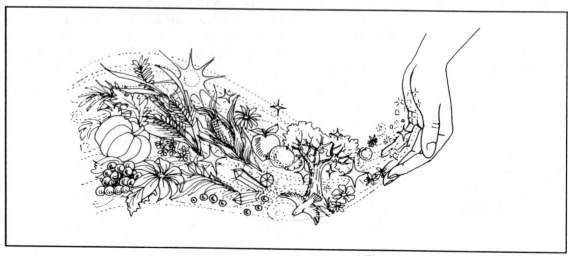

Illustration by Wahaba Nuit-Cat Heartsun

Talking to the Trees

Connecting to the Mother in Elvish lore

By Frodo Okulam

Tall they stand above me in the night
Great firs under the eternal stars
Their branches silver shadowed
Speaking in an old forgotten tongue
Of the starlight in a world beyond time.

I have always talked to trees. My mother tells a story of me, at about age 5. We were at Champoeg Park. When it was time to go, I wouldn't come, and burst into tears. My mother asked me what was wrong. "I don't want to leave this tree! It's my friend!" I cried, holding onto a young fir tree.

Living close to trees (we had eight fir trees and a cedar in our back yard), I grew up with their wisdom. As I grew older, I learned not to talk to other children about talking to trees, because they did not understand, and made fun of me. But I remember that when I was 12 I wanted to run away and just live with the trees, because they understood me and loved me just as I am. (I was beginning to realize I was gay.)

In recent years, I have begun carrying a small notebook with me when I walk in the woods and writing down what the trees tell me. Most often, they speak in words inside my mind. Other times I see visions, and sometimes they speak in an ancient tongue, Elvish, Quenya or Sindarin, which J.R.R. Tolkien chronicled in *The Lord of the Rings* and his other books. When trees tell me their names, they are always in Elvish, and I go home and look up the meanings in my Tolkien books.

Why Elvish? Has this language which means so much to me permeated my subconscious so that I hear the trees in that tongue? Possibly. Yet often the trees speak words I have not yet heard or leaned the meaning of. For instance, a tree spoke to me of Yavanna. Who or what was Yavanna? The only

place I had seen this word up to the time I heard it from the tree was a scant phrase in *The Lord of the Rings,* "The gardens of Yavanna." When the *Silmarillion* was published, I learned who Yavanna was: the Goddess of Trees, of course!

Tolkien spent a lot of time with trees and was known to talk to them. Can it be that he learned the language from the trees? Rootwords from many languages appear in the Elven-tongues. There are words from Old Norse, Old English, Irish, Welsh, Old Gothic, French, German, Spanish, Hebrew, Arabic and Sanskrit, to name a few. Did people originally learn to speak from trees? This is not as far-fetched as it sounds. The Celts named their letters after trees, and the word for trees in Hebrew also means advice! People first worshiped the Goddess in groves of trees, learning Her wisdom there. Maybe she taught both the trees and the people to speak.

Quessal (Feathered One) is an old tree who has been struck by lightning. She lives on the Wildwood Trail in Portland, Oregon. She sent this message through me to another tree who is her friend:

> *Na tindon Yavanna gorindon quiana*
> *Na caion barenda quiala cambor.*

I have translated this as "After sparkling Yavanna in days of dread fades/After lying at home fading further I reach out." Naia (Being), Quessal's friend, who lives on the Upper Macleay trail, sent this message back to Quessal:

> *Lilli lomeanor hwesta convindingo*
> *Taru bellumar Naia Quessal yavor.*

Which means, "Many sunsets and breezes renewing in our high mighty domes Naia and Quessal bore."

So here they are speaking to one another in the old tongue (and in poetry!). Quessal had been "fading":

Living close to trees, I grew up with their wisdom.

drawing into herself, forgetting the glory of the Tree-Goddess Yavanna in these days of dread, but chose to wake and reach out to Naia. Naia sends her back a message of hope, reminding Quessal that, though they have seen many sunsets, still the renewing breezes blow through their tall branches, and they are mighty still. More often, I get tree messages in English, but they are still powerful. The trees are prophets and teachers. They have taught me many things. Naia showed me the

When we connect with the trees, we connect with beings who are deeply in touch with the Goddess.

eruption of Mt. St. Helens five years before it happened!

When we connect with the trees, we connect with being far older than ourselves, who are deeply in touch with the Goddess. Yet they can speak only through us – those of us who are willing to take the time to listen to them. Listening is not hard. Touch a tree, really feel its bark, and imagine what it is to be that tree. In Naia's words:

Feel your roots going deep into the Earth,
Feel the waters coursing up through your trunk and out into your branches.
Feel the wind upon you, the silent gaze of the wheeling stars.
Feel the power within you.
Call on Elbereth (Queen of the Stars) to kindle in you the flame of Anor (the Sun).

When you are feeling one with the tree, take note of any thoughts that come into your mind. It does not matter if the thoughts are yours or the tree's. We are all one with the Goddess.

The trees want and need us to connect with them in this way. The old growth forests are being cut down. It is we who must act to prevent this. I spoke with an ancient redwood in California last year. Her name is Sulma (Wind Voice) and she is over 2,500 years old. This is part of what she said:

"Listen to those whose time here is long. You are our voice. I voice the wind, yet few hear my voice, fewer still understand it. I sing to you, do you hear me? Eternal life is found when our spirits cry out to one another. When we spark one on another and kindle souls. When we join with the one who is all souls, the Womb of Life."

At the Women's Spirituality Festival on Summer Solstice, I met a fir tree named Latana (High Valley) who spoke this blessing:
"May your songs leap from root to root until every tree has heard.
Let every knee of every being of Spirit touch the Earth, and all feet be planted,
until the hills cry out and the rocks report the Earth's reclaiming.
Let the seas join hands and the energy of all on earth be like lightning
shining from the east into the west.
Blessed be! Be it soon."

May the words and the songs of the trees touch your roots, too – and may you share them! ○

Illustration by Zelma of Halcyon Her Co.

The Stone Rosary

Quiet and deepen

By Cate DunCaoin

This is a simple ritual.
I have done it many times
For this you need a bowl,
a pouch or a basket
that you use only for the stone rosary.
The bowl, or pouch or basket
should not be too big –
a rosary is held
in the hands,
can be tucked away,
is portable.

Then you need stones.
How many? I don't know.
I don't know you, your needs,
your heart.
What you do is find a stone
that speaks to a pain,
an ache, a joy, a memory,
an image, a mystery.
You borrow the stone from its spot and
put it into your bowl or pouch or basket.
Gather the individual stones
as you find them
over time –
days, weeks, years.
You may start out with one stone. Or two.
Or seven. Or nine.
The number will change.
There may be times you put a stone back,
perhaps to the very spot you found it.
Perhaps you will replace that stone with another.
Perhaps not.

To celebrate the rosary,
go alone to a quiet place.
Become quiet yourself.
To do this, shut your eyes,
put your hand into the pouch
or bowl or basket and touch the stones.
Listen to the clicks and murmurs of the stones
with each other, the cool nudges against your skin.
Do this until you are quiet. Then
pick up a stone. Open your eyes.
Examine the stone in the palm of your hand
until you find the prayer within it.
Speak that prayer.

Some stones have the same prayer each time,
others bring a new prayer.
Speak each prayer afresh.

Sometimes you will want to touch the stones to
your body.
Or hold one lightly upward
so that the stone is silhouetted –
perhaps against the full moon,
caught between the tips of the crescent moon.

Whatever the stone says, speak only that.
All else is quietness.
When you have listened and spoken each prayer
and replaced each stone,
cup your filled bowl or pouch or basket
in uplifted hands.
Give thanks.
Depart immersed and shining. ○

Examine the stone until you find the prayer within it.

Your Magickal Name

A vision quest

By Ondine Webb DeMer

Enter the Cave of the Ancient Mother in search of your magickal name.

It is twilight and you are out in the cool evening air. The stars are brightly twinkling and a rising crescent moon shows her luminous face to you, lighting your way. You begin your Vision Quest on the shores of a secluded lake. Light three silver candles, one for each aspect of the Goddess. Leave the Maiden candle glowing on the shore to help guide you home. For though your voyage may seem long, it is only one small moment in time, the wink of the Goddess's eye throughout all eternity. Take the two remaining candles with you as you step into the canoe that is waiting for you. You begin to paddle your way across the Waters of Transformation to the Sacred Isle of Dreams, far in the misty distance. The rhythmic strokes of your paddling help you to center and prepare for your coming rite. You find an inner serenity as you become attuned to the gentle waves and become one with their flow. You feel as though you are floating in the wide expansive embrace of the Mother. You are safe and protected in Her loving arms.

When you arrive at the Sacred Isle of Dreams, you shore and secure your canoe, and step onto land that is luxuriant with singing grasses and a myriad of wildflowers. This land is sacred to the Goddess and is wreathed in the beauty of Her natural elements. You take a moment now to continue breathing slowly in and out, centering and calming your quickly beating heart. Soon your heartbeat is slowed and matches the natural pulse of the Earth. And now you are ready to enter the Cave of the Ancient Mother in search of your magickal name. The Crescent Moon watches over you and protects you in your journey toward new beginnings. You offer a silent prayer to the Goddess and place your Mother Candle at the entrance so you can find your way back again. You will carry your Crone candle with you for guidance and protection. Now you notice several paths leading in different directions as you enter Her depths, but one calls out especially

to you and you know this is the one to take.

You are winding slowly through a maze-like spiral into the very depths of the Mother. As you follow Her sacred labyrinth, holding your candle to light the way, you continue breathing deeply in and out. And soon you reach the deepest level of the cave, the womb of the Sacred Mother. Here you find the Cavern of Many Names. It is here that you will keep silent vigil awaiting the Name you seek. For it is here in the Womb of the Goddess that all names are formed and birthed. Perhaps you will be blessed by She Who Creates All Names with the message you seek. All possibilities are open to you.

Sit now, sit now and wait. Open your inner ear and listen to the sounds in the Ancient Mother's Womb. Hear their magickal song. In the darkness, lit only by your protective candle flame which you hold cupped in your hand, you hear a sound, the Song of the Ancient Mother. And as She sings Her name to you, the sound shapes mandalas, dancing, interweaving, creating all worlds into being. And as She sings your name, you know She is calling to you alone. And Her voice encompasses all elements, the entire universe.

Listen now to the Song of the Wind. She sighs and whispers words meant only for you. Listen to the Song of the Water. Her gentle, laughing music calms and soothes the weary heart. Listen to the Song of the Fire, roaring, humming, warming you soul. And listen to the Song of the Earth, a deep comforting lullaby of love.

Ah, and now you can hear names being whispered through the misty atmosphere of the cave. At first it sounds like wordless chant or humming. Soon you feel yourself being drawn closer to the Source of the names. You hear your name, your sisters' names, the multitude of names of the Goddess in an

*she sighs and
whispers words
meant only
for you.*

endless chant of devotion to Her. Mari, Aphrodite, Luna, Yemaya, Faithe, Lilith, Ondine, Cybele, Tara, Diana, Kali, Isis, Amaterasu, Kumari, Lucina, Arachne, Madrone, Antiga, Cerridwen, Shakti, Brigit, Shekhinah. If you listen closely, you may hear the Ancient Mother of All singing a name meant for you. Continue to journey through the names in your mind until the most perfect one calls to you and you know it is She. When you have found the Name, a personal message, or perhaps a nameless, wordless sense of the Goddess's love, you will feel ready to leave this place. Leave your Crone candle behind as an offering to the Goddess, knowing She will guide your way back to the Mother candle outside the entrance to Her depths.

And now, slowly, gently, you wind your way back, secure in your knowledge of the Goddess. If you have found a name, chant it in your inner voice, under your breath, and soon you will find yourself to be under the Crescent Moon on the Shores of the Sacred Isle. You will once again voyage across the Waters of Transformation back to the mainland of our everyday world. When you have reached land again, know you are home. Gently, slowly, open your eyes and be here now. Hold your sacred Goddess name deep within your heart. As you speak out your Name in ritual and in magick, She Who Creates All Names will surely remember you and answer your call. Blessed be. ○

Illustration by Renée Christine Yates

A Blessing of Wheat

Magical crafts

By Kris Fawcett

Invite the Goddess to dwell on your hearth all winter long.

Wheat weaving is a folk art as old as the cultivation of wheat itself. Every wheat-producing region has or had its own style of weaving (or "plaiting"). In non-patriarchal cultures, wheat figures were associated with the Goddess who is so important in the seasonal cycle of planting and harvesting. A few traditional wheat weaving designs have survived almost unchanged since the days when God was a woman. Mostly these are the figures made from the last harvest gleanings, which were kept safe through the winter and then plowed into the new-tilled earth in spring, to symbolize the continuity of life from season to season. Continuing this tradition, try making a house blessing of wheat for your own home, and thus invite the Goddess to dwell on your hearth all winter long.

The Welsh fan is one of the most ancient designs, handed down through generations of wheat weavers in the British Isles. The fan is an example of a Goddess-figure in the long, narrow Crone form (in contrast to the Maiden or Mother figures, which tend to be round or curved). The original name for this figure was the Long Burrow; note the similarity to "long barrow," which is a common type of Neolithic passage grave found in Britain and Ireland. As Christianity waxed, the shape lost its association with the Crone and came to be regarded simply as a "fan."

This variation is from the border region between England and Wales. Knowing its origins, we can see past the utilitarian fan shape to what it really is, what it's always been: the narrow womb of the winter Crone, who holds the dormant seeds of life safely within herself till spring comes again.

Of course, to be *really* authentic, you should grow your own wheat . . . but most city dwellers will have to be content with locating prepackaged wheat

in the larger craft supply stores. Avoid bleached or dyed cheat, as this processing weakens the straw considerably.

Materials needed:
- [a] Wheat, bearded or unbearded
- Buttonhole or carpet thread, matched to wheat color
- Needlecraft or other small scissors that won't be damaged by exposure to water
- Old towels for soaking and keeping wheat damp
- Clothespins (optional)

Wheat forms a natural protective wrapper around its base that is removed before weaving. This papery sheath slides away easily after you cut the straw just above the first joint ("knee"), closest to the head. The lower two or three segments contain "knees" that can't be woven, so these parts may be discarded or saved for use in other projects.

The cleaned wheat must be soaked to become pliable enough for weaving. Soak wheat in your bathtub or use one of the plastic wallpaper-soaking tubs sold at most paint stores. Wheat floats, so weight it down by wrapping it in your old towel while it is submerged. Most varieties require roughly 30 minutes soaking, but some kinds need as long as an hour.

If you're not sure how long to soak, try the "crunch test": gently pinch a straw at its large end between thumbnail and fingernail. If you feel or hear a soft crunch, let it soak awhile longer. When it can be pinched without crunching, it's flexible and ready for weaving. Warm water shortens soaking time.

1. Drain soaked wheat and select 25 straws, matching size of heads as closely as possible. Cover unused wheat with damp towel.

2. Tie three straws side by side below the heads (the small unformed nub at the base is considered part of the head.) Spread straws apart, two to the right and one to the left.

3. Add a new straw on the right, under the outside straw and over the inside straw. This new straw has now become the inside straw on the left.

In the same way, add a new straw on the left, passing it under the outside straw and over the inside straw. It now becomes the inside straw on the right, completing one round and leaving us with three straws on the right and two on the left. (Figure A)

Figure A

4. Before adding new straws, do a locking stroke to secure the weave. Move the outside straw on the right under the adjacent straw and over the next one, so that it becomes the inside straw on the left. Repeat the stroke on the left, moving the outermost straw under the one next to it and over the others, to become the inside straw on the right.

5. Repeat the steps in the first round, adding a new straw on the right, passing it under the outside straw and over the two inside straws (Figure B). Add a new straw on the left in the same manner (under outside straw, over two inside straws). Lock right, then left. There are now four straws to the right and three to the left.

Figure B

6. Continue rounds of adding straws to right and left, always positioning them under the outside straw and over all the others. Finish each round by locking right, then left.

Tips: Unsecured straws tend to come unwoven, so you may find it helpful to weight the side you're not weaving with small objects, or clip the ends together with clothespins. If it seems the heads are becoming too closely crowded together, try doing an extra locking stroke between each round.

7. When all 25 straws have been added, finish the fan by doing 14 locking strokes, seven on each side. then tie the ends on each side together about 2" beyond the last locking stroke. If you hold the straws flat as you tie each knot, they'll fan out nicely. Trim the ends into an inverted V or arrowhead.

8. Hangers can be plaited from three straws, using a simple hair-braid weave. Plait about seven inches, tie at each end, and use the same strings to attach the hanger to the back of the fan, at the points where each inverted V is tied off. Hangers can also be made of ribbon. If you want your home to be filled with a certain quality (love, peace, creativity, etc.), use a ribbon color that you associate with that attribute.

Now you have properly honored the Crone, and have a tangible reminder that no matter how bitter the winter, spring will come as the wheel of the year turns. Hang your Welsh fan above the doorway, and surely the Goddess will watch over your home all year long and fill it with your heart's desire. ○

The Crone holds the dormant seeds of life safely within herself.

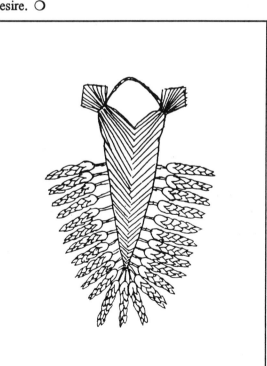

Working Alone

Simple daily spirituality

By Jeanie Geis Oliver

This is receiving, buying, finding and making tools mother-style.

Working alone, yes. Because I live in the country with my two daughters and husband. I have friends around here, and most of them are Christians.

At first I tried to make rituals, observe every holiday and cross-quarter days, but for me it seemed affected. And who has the time? Last February 2nd, I was folding laundry and Tim was cooking a late dinner. I threw some floating candles in a bowl of water when we had our meal and called it Candlemas.

Who says you have to pray or meditate daily a certain amount of time to get higher? Or that you need to spin with others of a like mind to raise power? They don't know what it's like for me to live in the country, raising children and running a home-based business.

My oldest daughter (6½) had an altar for awhile. She liked to put incense sticks and pictures of Krishna on it. She was sure that Krishna was a beautiful girl, and lost interest when she realized he's male. The altar was a box, and she used it to hide her drawings in after that.

My altar must be my kitchen sill. I go before it a lot to wash the dishes. There are plants, an infant oral syringe for medicine, a stained glass star from Jenni, a photo of my firstborn as a baby, a cat-shaped soapdish from Alice and an old jar that's a vase. This is receiving, buying, finding and making tools mother-style.

Working alone is wiping up the table and floor around the baby's seat after meals and sometimes thinking, "I love this. I really do." It's waking up before the baby whimpers in the night and yearning to hold her close and nurse her.

Working alone is a bowl of cantaloupe chunks in the garden seat. It's spotting a new bird or looking under a tile outside with the family to see what bugs are there. Working alone is pulling the kids up the long, hot, dusty road lined with woods and listening over the wagon wheels for the cow across the river gorge or the roadkeeper's guinea hens.

Working alone is recycling and hoping to find the time to try to get the town 23 miles away to stop spraying for mosquitoes. It's mailing orders and picking up the goods to make more.

Some women might work with others, but every woman also works alone. ○

Entering the Underworld
Journal writing for deepening

By Joann Powell Colbert

My winter journals always seem to be thicker than my spring and summer ones. As a January child, a Capricorn, I love to wrap the cold weather around me like a quilt and sit in front of a fireplace staring at the flames and writing down my thoughts.

Last year I spent the entire summer and fall in the hospital and at home, recovering from a serious illness. As winter approached, and my strength started to return to me, I began to make sense of my near-death experience by writing about it in my journal. I began to strongly identify with Inanna, who shed her ornaments and jewelry at each gate of the underworld. Like her, I descended further into my illness until even my moon-and-star necklace – which I *never* remove – was taken from me as I was wheeled into surgery. I felt as though my identity as Lover of the Moon was taken from me.

As my journal pages thickened with late-night scribblings, I began to see that I *had* confronted my dark sister, Erishkegal, *had* been slain by her, and then had emerged, bloody as a newborn babe, to return to the land of the living. Through meditations and trance visions, enhanced by the journal-writing, I saw myself making my ascent, and meeting different figures who greeted me at each of the seven gates.

First was Artemis, who gave me back my sense of wholeness and my sense of self. Then Brigit, who spoke to me of alternative healing methods and gave me back the spark of creativity. Demeter, who restored my identity as mother. Dionysus, who called me to frolic, dance and play. Aphrodite, who gave me back my sexuality. The Green Man, who brought Goddess-loving men into my life. And Isis, who anointed me as the Wounded Healer and as Priestess.

These figures began to make their way into my drawings – Brigit, drawn at Candlemas, was the first Goddess portrait I did in nearly a year.

My journal entry dated December 27, 1987 (which proved to be quite prophetic), reads:

I've gone underground.
I am in the womb, knitting together bones and blood,
weaving a new life for myself.
I've been to the brink of the abyss,
looked over it, been held there, hovering,
against my will;
I've returned, metamorphosed, changed.
I was immersed in despair; I've shed my despair.
I've screamed out in loneliness;
now my alone-ness makes me whole.
I'm in process;
I choose this color, that one,
shade this one, strengthen that one, outline these.
I shall emerge in the Spring like Persephone,
and be ready for the Beltane fires. ○

I've been to the brink of the abyss, looked over it.

Brigid

Spirituality at work

By Callista Lee

Brigid may well be the perfect Goddess of Work.

I found myself facing a crisis this year, feeling that I had to choose between spending more time on spirituality related activities and career related activities. There were cheerleaders on both sides, loving friends genuinely wanting "what was best for me." I belonged to a coven, a priestess study group and a pagan community service group that presented Goddess craft faires, workshops and public rituals, and in my "spare time" I created pottery images and tools to honor the Goddess. I was also teaching part-time at three different colleges (totalling about 50 hours a week). And yes, there was always home and family to make time for, too. Something had to give, before my energy and sanity gave out. But how could I choose? How could I drop any of these beloved tasks? How could I do the work of the Goddess that I felt called to and follow my very fulfilling and promising career path?

I was envious of the full-time priestesses whose books I read and whose workshops and rituals I was sometimes able to attend as they travelled to my city on their "Goddess Tours." I envied them because they were able to work for the Goddess full time. But I also thought about the struggles they must have endured to reach their national, even international, status, and how much time they had to spend away from home following their hectic schedules. I couldn't see myself dropping my teaching career and comfortable suburban life to follow that path, nor did I want to, and yet the more priestessing I did, the more I wanted to do. It became painfully clear that I just couldn't do everything I wanted (or others wanted) me to do. How to resolve this dilemma?

Just as I was allowing the despair of this crisis to wash over me, the answer began to show itself . . . as Brigid. I met Her while doing research for a public ritual celebrating and reclaiming pagan Celtica for St. Patrick's Day – we called it, "The Snakes Return to Ireland!" – that I was co-priestessing with two other women.

Brigid may well be the perfect Goddess of Work, as She has been called upon by workers of all kinds throughout many lands as their patroness. But be she called Brigid, Brigit, Bridget, Brid, Bride, Brighid, Brigantes, Brigantia or Brigeto, she, like any of the major Celtic Goddesses, is really the primordial Great Mother. She is the "Mother of Memory," having survived and thrived in the hearts and minds of people throughout the patriarchal movement of later pagandom and Christianity.

According to the Farrars in *The Witches' Goddess,* "Brigid is a glowing example of the Goddess who cannot be banished from the dreams of men and women; they turn to her in need, or for inspiration, whatever the religious forms of the time." Brigid is the Triple Goddess, sometimes seen as three sisters of the same name. She is most commonly known as the Goddess of poetry, smithcraft and healing. But she has also been associated with the martial arts, and it is said that her people, the Tuatha Dé Danaan, invented battle cries as she led them in raising their voices in outcry and barking against violence and pillage. Her soldiers have been known as Brigands (or as the Christians called them, outlaws). As the Mother of Memory, she is also revered for having fostered the creative and magical arts throughout generations of her followers and so is honored as a patroness of witches, as well. The symbol/element most commonly associated with her is fire.

The church of Rome could not hope to extinguish her flame, so they attempted to control and contain it by creating a new saint in her image: St. Brigid or St. Bride. Many church scholars admit that there never really was any human St. Brigid. Like Brigid the Goddess, St. Brigid is the triple patroness of

The Goddess who cannot be banished.

poets, crafters and healers, and is symbolized by the eternal flame. At her famous monastery in Kildare (presumed to have been built on the site already sacred to the Goddess), St. Brigid's perpetual fire was tended by 19 nuns – a twentieth being the immortal Brigid herself – in a garden where no man was allowed to enter. The convent was known for a long time for its "heathenish miracles" and evidences of fertility magic, making Brigid as patroness of midwives, too.

According to Barbara Walker in *The Woman's Encyclopedia of Myths and Secrets,* Brigid's priestesses at Kildare called on her as the "Three Blessed Ladies of Britain" or the "Three Mothers" and always identified her with the moon. Her feast day, February 1, is the first day of Spring in the pagan calendar, called by the Celts Oimelc, Imolg or Imbolc, a day of union of the God and Goddess.

In ancient Rome, the day was celebrated as Lupercalia, sacred to Venus and woman in general. The Christian church changed it to the Feast of the Purification of the Virgin, also known as Candlemas. This association with the Virgin Mary may be a reflection on the Irish writers who refused to reduce their Goddess to a mere saint and insisted on referring to her as "Queen of Heaven," which meant identifying her with Mary. And indeed, St. Brigid is said to have been Mary's midwife and/or the foster mother of the Christ child. (Fostering was a common theme in Celtic hero mythology, and the myth of Christ being fostered with Brigid may explain other stories of him receiving training in the Druidic tradition.) Typical of Brigid's fertility aspect, a favorite date for patroness rituals at her magical wells is August 1, the pagan holiday of first harvest, Lughnasadh or Lammas. As a saint, Brigid was and is second only to St. Patrick in popularity

Illustration: "Brigid," by Katlyn Miller

Invocation of Brigid for Candlemas

By Raven

Once again the Goddess arises from Her slumber to walk abroad on the face of the Earth. Close your eyes and see Her with me now.

Far away across the Irish sea, She stirs in Her sleep, wakens, stretching and yawning, and rises to begin Her journey. She walks through still-frozen woods, and as She passes, She brings the first stirrings of life to tender buds buried beneath the snow.

She passes . . . and as She passes, the small burrowing creatures rouse themselves, to behold Her with eyes still heavy with sleep.

She passes . . . and as She passes, the groundhog sense Her presence in his dreams. And he wakes, climbing from his burrow for one brief hour, and as She passes, the groundhog sees Her shadow.

She passes . . . and as She passes, buds and wondering creatures and groundhog all hear Her voice as wind in the barren branches of the trees. And She whispers a promise that Spring will come again. Not yet, not now, but soon, soon . . .

She passes . . . and as She passes, She walks over mountains and hills, through the land that is Her home. And Her steps lengthen and She walks over the waters of the ocean and through the deserts, and still She is home, for the Earth itself is Her home, the very planet is Her domain.

And She passes . . . and She rouses our slumbering hearts with Her passing, with Her voice murmuring in the wind. Soon . . . soon . . .

And now She is here with us, She passes by us now, nudging us from our winter dreams. Let's invite Her to linger awhile with us, to pause in Her journey and join our circle, by lighting a sacred fire. In Her homeland, in Kildare, Her priestesses kept a sacred fire burning at all times on the hearth of Her temple. Let us now relight that holy flame, rekindle the fires of Kildare. Let us gaze into the flames and see the face of Brigid!

Brigid's mantle brings spring to Ireland.

among the Irish people. Find a Catholic wearing a St. Patrick medallion around her neck and you're more than likely to find St. Brigid on the other side.

Caitlín Matthews (in *The Celtic Tradition*) shares a modern prayer to St. Bride that shows how the worship of the saint models the ancient reverence of the Goddess:

> *I take Brigid as my advocate*
> *Dear to me is Erin*
> *Dear to me each land*
> *Praise be to it!*
> *O white flame of Leinster*
> *Enlighten the whole land*
> *Chief of Erin's maidens*
> *Chief of finest women*
> *Dark the bitter winter*
> *Cutting its sharpness*
> *But Brigid's mantle*
> *Brings spring to Ireland*

For our Celtic ritual, we introduced Brigid as the Triple Goddess, patroness of poetry, healing and smithcraft. Then we bade the participants divide themselves into groups according to the work they did, explaining that all workers could be categorized into these three groups. Poets included all those who work with words, communication, music, and so forth. Healers included all types of mental, physical, emotional and spiritual healing, as well as parents and peacemakers. Crafters included all of those who create works of art, tools or other goods, and those who labor with tools. Once in their groups, the participants got to work creating gifts for the other two groups. The poets gave the gift of an uplifting song. The healers gave away herb-filled charms charged with their own life energy. And the crafters shared the paper and pipe cleaner snakes and other sacred symbols they'd created.

As each group shared their gifts, talents and work with the others, the others called on Brigid in thanks and asked her blessings for the group presenting its gift. The One Goddess blesses our own work and we thank her for blessing the work of others whose services enrich our lives, so that we may all serve one another and Her, each in our own way. Part of the beauty of Brigid is that she brings us together in this way, honoring our differences while showing us our interdependence. And many participants were able to finally acknowledge Her many blessings when they realized that they had so many talents that it was difficult to choose just one of the three groups to work with during the ritual. Like me, there were people who felt that need to choose, and the feeling of loss involved in choosing one activity over another.

But as I hinted earlier, Brigid has provided me with an answer for handling that awful choice between spirituality and work. As we call upon Brigid to bless our work, we have the opportunity to ask her to help us make our work a spiritual endeavor, an offering to her. We can see our work as "work of the Goddess" when we allow ourselves to see how our work serves others. Just as the poets in our ritual were able to serve the healers by giving them a new song to sing – giving back revitalizing energy to their healing hearts – so the mechanic who cares to do quality work for a fair price truly serves the public/other workers/children of the Goddess. A few years ago, when I competed on a TV game show, I promised the Goddess that I'd share my winnings with a local charity if she would lead me to success, and so went more confidently to my "work" and did indeed come out with some winnings worth sharing. We can also see our work as work of the Goddess when we treat our co-workers with kindness and respect, acting as agents of loving, healthy energy in the workplace.

We need to ask ourselves, "How can the work I do serve Her?" For myself, I realized that I get to do a lot of priestessing in my job as teacher. I don't get to lead pagan rituals in the classroom (darn!), but I do get to lead my students toward finding their own beauty, strengths, talents, skills and values. And isn't that the work of a priestess? I also get to lead them toward a better understanding and respect of others who are different from themselves, each special in her own way. And isn't that the work of a priestess? But perhaps the most important thing I get to do as a teacher is to encourage students to think for themselves, opening their minds to finding their own answers to some of life's questions. And isn't that the work of a priestess?

With this realization, it has become easier for me to give up a little of what I do in my "spirituality" groups, giving myself some breathing room. . . and hopefully some of my lost sanity! I'm still struggling with the concept that I don't have to do everything to be a good priestess. I don't have to

know everything, attend everything, lead everything, think of everything . . . none of us does. With each one of us doing her small part to serve Brigid, great works will be accomplished. I am reminded of the lesson in humility learned by Morgaine, in *The Mists of Avalon*, summarized in her prayer to the Goddess as she knelt before a statue of St. Brigid:

"Mother," she whispered, "forgive me. I thought I must do what I now see you can do for yourself. The Goddess is within us, yes, but now I know that you are in the world too, now and always, just as you are in Avalon and in the hearts of men and women. Be in me too now, and guide me, and tell me when I need only let you do your will . . ."

For if we ask Brigid to guide our work and fill it with meaning, we will find not only personal fulfillment, but do also the work of the Goddess on Earth. And none of us has to do all of the work ourselves, nor do we all have to do the work of the traveling author/high priestess to take our place as a beloved and important daughter of the Goddess. She blesses all our work.

For those wishing the protection and inspiration of Brigid, the daily recitation of this traditional prayer should draw Her near:

The Genealogy of Brigid

*Every day and every night
That I say the genealogy of Brigid,
I shall not be killed,
I shall not be harried,
I shall not be put into a cell,
I shall not be wounded.
No fire, no sun,
no moon shall burn me,
No lake, no water,
no sea shall drown me.
For I am the child of Poetry,
Poetry, child of Reflection,
Reflection, child of Meditation,
Meditation, child of Lore,
Lore, child of Research,
Research, child of Great Knowledge,
Great Knowledge, child of Intelligence,
Intelligence, child of Comprehension,
Comprehension, child of Wisdom,
Wisdom, child of Brigid.* ◯

Gaze into the flames and see the face of Brigid!

Resources

Goddess spirituality is blessed with many resources for further exploration of empowerment, community and deepening. We recommend (in alphabetical order):

The Beltane Papers
A journal of women's mysteries; aimed at the advanced practitioner, but with much wisdom for all. 1333 Lincoln St., #240, Bellingham, WA 98226.

Circle Network News
A newspaper for Pagans, containing Goddess information in every issue. A good all-around resource. P.O. Box 219, Mt. Horeb, WI 53572.

Circles of Exchange
Round-robin correspondence groups for women, with a Goddess focus. Great networking tool. 9594 1st Ave. NE, Seattle, WA 98115.

Green Egg
One of the oldest of the Pagan magazines, and still one of the best. Lots of Goddess lore. P.O. Box 1540, Ukiah, CA 95482.

Hecate's Cauldron Lunar Awareness Newsletter
Monthly moon cycles and astrological lore, with a Goddess focus. A must for every daughter of the Mother. P.O. Box 661673, Los Angeles, CA 90066.

Hestia: A Goddess Home Journal
Real-world Goddess magic and wisdom, with a loving, home-based touch. From Lunaea Weatherstone, former editor of *SageWoman*. P.O. Box 33-357, Long Beach, CA 90801.

Of A Like Mind
Newspaper of Dianic Wicca, Goddess wisdom, women's spirituality in general. Great resource. P.O. Box 6021, Madison, WI 53716.

Woman of Power
Magazine of women's political, cultural and spiritual concerns. Not every issue has Goddess material, but still important. P.O. Box 827, Cambridge, MA 02238.

To order *SageWoman*:
$18/one year, $32/two years
P.O. Box 641, Point Arena, CA 95468
707•882•2052

About the Editor

Lunaea Weatherstone is a writer, editor, Tarot counselor
and legally ordained Priestess of the Goddess.
Her interests include ritual, divination, world music,
obsessive and eclectic stuff-collecting
and, yes, Star Trek: The Next Generation.
She lives in Southern California (for the moment)
with about a zillion books on every conceivable subject,
her familiar, Muffy, and six other cats
belonging to housemate/artist Renée Christine Yates.